Dedicated to

My cherished parents, whose memories and
teachings continue to guide me
and
My beloved wife: **Khushboo**
and
My treasured children **Shaurya** *and* **Aarna***,*
who fill my life with love and purpose

About the Author

Rohit Ranjan is a seasoned IT professional with a deep passion for technology and over 16 years of experience in the field. Starting with a Bachelor's degree in Metallurgical and Materials Engineering from IIT Kharagpur, Rohit found his true calling in computer science and AI.

He has a strong foundation in data engineering and has developed a notable expertise in Hadoop, Spark, Kafka, Airflow, HBase, SOLR, and various databases. His skill set is not just limited to handling massive datasets but also extends to designing and implementing complex data pipeline architectures, making data flow seamlessly and efficiently from source to insight. This expertise is complemented by his deep knowledge of microservices architecture, where he excels in creating scalable, robust systems that integrate seamlessly with cloud platforms like AWS and Azure.

His expertise is not confined to data engineering or microservices, he has also ventured deeply into Machine Learning and deep learning. Through Python and Java, he has crafted intelligent models that learn from data to solve real-world problems, pushing the boundaries of what's possible with technology today.

Throughout his career, Rohit has been a beacon of knowledge and leadership, contributing to the tech community through research and sharing his insights with others. He has a knack for making complex topics accessible and engaging, which is evident in his work and his active presence on LinkedIn, where he connects with peers and industry leaders.

As the author of *Microservices for Machine Learning*, Rohit draws from his extensive background to guide readers through the intricacies of integrating AI with microservices architecture. His book is a reflection of his journey in technology - a path of continuous learning, adapting, and innovating. Through his writing, Rohit aims to inspire others to explore the vast potential of AI and Machine Learning, equipping them with the knowledge to create cutting-edge solutions.

Microservices for Machine Learning

Design, implement, and manage high-performance
ML systems with microservices

Rohit Ranjan

www.bpbonline.com

First Edition 2024

Copyright © BPB Publications, India

ISBN: 978-93-55516-886

To View Complete
BPB Publications Catalogue
Scan the QR Code:

About the Reviewers

❖ **Dmitry Vostokov** is an influential figure in the field of software diagnostics, debugging, memory dump, and trace and log analysis. Over the last 20 years, Vostokov has made significant interdisciplinary contributions to the development of new diagnostic methodologies, tools, and pattern languages, making it easier for professionals in the industry to understand and fix complex software problems. He is a prolific author, having written numerous books that cover a wide range of topics within his field of expertise. His work is characterized by a deep technical knowledge combined with a passion for teaching and simplifying complex concepts. Vostokov's contributions, educational efforts, and technical innovations have not only enriched the field of software diagnostics but have also provided valuable resources for IT professionals, developers, and analysts. His recent expertise includes Linux internals, cybersecurity, data engineering, cloud-native microservices, functional programming and languages, machine learning, and applied category theory. Currently, he works for one of the largest software companies as a Principal Cloud Security Engineer.

❖ **Shantanu Neema** is an accomplished data scientist recognized for delivering impactful insights in diverse industries through data-driven methodologies. With proficiency in managing and analyzing datasets to define precise business use cases, he excels in crafting solutions for intricate challenges spanning real estate, energy, transportation, environmental compliance, and manufacturing. Shantanu's extensive experience encompasses the entire data science process, culminating in model deployment using cloud infrastructure. His expertise extends to a robust foundation in CI/CD, ML pipelines, and testing methodologies, ensuring the efficiency and resilience of his solutions. Beyond his technical role, Shantanu actively engages as a researcher and serves as a technical reviewer for books centered around CI/CD, data science, and Python. This commitment underscores his dedication to advancing best practices and fostering innovation in these dynamic fields. Shantanu Neema invites readers to explore his insights and contributions, encapsulated within the pages of publications that reflect his ongoing pursuit of excellence in data science and technology.

Acknowledgement

This book is a testament to the unwavering support and boundless love that surrounds me, shaping my journey as an author and individual. First and foremost, I dedicate this work to the cherished memory of my parents, whose blessings continue to guide me from beyond, illuminating my path with their enduring wisdom and love.

To my beloved wife, Khushboo, my heart's companion and life's greatest supporter – your strength, patience, and faith in me are the cornerstones of my every endeavor. Your love is my constant inspiration.

To my precious children, Shaurya and Aarna, you are my joy and pride. Witnessing your growth and curiosity about the world fuels my passion and creativity, reminding me daily of the beauty and wonder life holds.

I extend my heartfelt gratitude to my family, whose encouragement and belief in my vision have been unwavering. Your support has been a source of comfort and motivation, reinforcing my commitment to this project.

A special thanks to the team at the BPB Publications for their expertise, dedication, and hard work in bringing this manuscript to life. Your guidance has been invaluable, and the collaborative journey we have embarked on has been incredibly rewarding.

To my colleagues and peers in the industry, your insights and feedback have been instrumental in refining my work, providing me with the perspective and knowledge that only a collective can offer.

And to the readers who embark on this journey with me through the pages of this book, your engagement, and enthusiasm make all the efforts worthwhile. Your support is not just the wind beneath the wings of this project but the very essence that makes writing profoundly rewarding.

Thank you, one and all, for being part of this journey and making this book possible. Your roles in this story are deeply appreciated and will always be remembered.

Preface

In the realm of software development, the confluence of microservices and **Machine Learning (ML)** represents a frontier of innovation, offering new paradigms for building dynamic, resilient, and intelligent applications. This book is a culmination of extensive research and practical insights aimed at unraveling the complexities and unleashing the potential of integrating microservices with ML.

Microservices architecture, with its promise of scalability, flexibility, and robustness, has revolutionized how we conceive and implement software solutions. When intertwined with the predictive power and adaptability of ML, it paves the way for creating systems that not only excel in functionality but also thrive on change and continuous improvement.

The journey through these pages is designed to be both enlightening and practical. We begin by setting a solid foundation, introducing you to the essential concepts and benefits of microservices and how they synergize with ML. As we navigate through the chapters, you will encounter a blend of theoretical discussions, practical examples, and insightful case studies, each chosen to illuminate different facets of building and deploying AI-enhanced microservices.

Our exploration is not just about understanding the individual components but also about appreciating how they come together to create systems that are more than the sum of their parts. From the architectural patterns that ensure robustness and flexibility to the deployment strategies that underpin continuous delivery and adaptability, this book aims to equip you with the knowledge and skills to innovate and excel in the ever-evolving landscape of software development.

Intended for developers, architects, and technology enthusiasts, this guide assumes a familiarity with basic programming concepts and a keen interest in leveraging cutting-edge technologies. Whether you are looking to enhance your existing skills or eager to step into the new era of cloud-native applications, this book promises a comprehensive and engaging journey into the world of microservices and machine learning.

Embark on this journey with us, and let us explore the transformative potential of these technologies, building applications that are not only technically advanced but also intelligent, adaptable, and ready to meet the challenges of tomorrow.

Chapter 1: Introducing Microservices and Machine Learning: We set the stage for the entire book by establishing a solid foundation in microservices and ML. This chapter explores the historical evolution of microservices, tracing their journey from traditional monolithic architectures to the modern, distributed, and modular approaches we see today. Simultaneously, we explore the dynamic realm of ML, unpacking its potential and how it is reshaping industries.

Chapter 2: Foundation of Microservices: The chapter explores the architectural intricacies of microservices, unravelling the principles that sculpt modern, scalable, and resilient software landscapes. This segment is a deep dive into the microservices blueprint, emphasizing modularity, decentralized governance, and agile scalability. It is crafted to equip you with the insights to architect robust microservices ecosystems, focusing on design patterns and best practices pivotal for engineering future-proof digital solutions. Through this exploration, readers gain the acumen to innovate within the ever-evolving microservices paradigm, laying a solid groundwork for the sophisticated integration of ML in subsequent chapters.

Chapter 3: Fundamentals of Machine Learning: This chapter unfolds the core principles of ML, laying down a comprehensive groundwork for understanding its profound capabilities. We navigate through the essentials of ML concepts, data preprocessing, and the pivotal algorithms that fuel AI advancements. This chapter is designed to transform theoretical knowledge into practical wisdom, enabling you to harness ML's full potential in crafting innovative solutions and pushing the boundaries of technology. Engage with this foundational guide to unlock a new horizon of possibilities in the AI-driven world.

Chapter 4: Designing Microservices for Machine Learning: The chapter covers the strategic design of microservices tailored for ML, specifically focusing on constructing a music recommendation system. Here, we transition from theory to practice, elucidating the architectural intricacies required to seamlessly integrate AI capabilities into microservices. This chapter explores creating scalable, flexible, and robust architectures, emphasizing hands-on examples and practical insights. It is structured to equip you with the knowledge to architect a system that not only meets the current technological demands but is also adaptable to future advancements, setting a benchmark in the fusion of microservices and ML innovation.

Chapter 5: Implementing Microservices for Machine Learning: The chapter is a deep dive into the practical aspects of implementing microservices tailored for a ML-powered music recommendation system. It meticulously guides you through developing ML microservices using Flask and FastAPI, orchestrating scalable and distributed ML pipelines with Kubeflow, and ensuring seamless inter-service communication. With a focus on real-world applicability, this chapter empowers you to craft scalable, efficient, and resilient microservices, paving the way for innovative, AI-driven applications. Embrace this journey to master the art of deploying sophisticated ML microservices that stand at the cutting edge of technology convergence.

Chapter 6: Data Management in Machine Learning Microservices: The chapter unravels the critical role of data management in ML microservices, spotlighting its significance in the robust music recommendation system explored in this book. Exploring essential facets like data ingestion, storage, versioning, and processing, the chapter equips you with the expertise to implement advanced data strategies effectively. It intricately details how to harness Apache Parquet, Hadoop, and cutting-edge real-time processing tools, ensuring your microservices are not only data-optimized but also primed for future scalability and efficiency. This chapter stands as your blueprint for mastering data orchestration in the AI-powered microservices realm, setting a new standard in innovative and data-driven application development.

Chapter 7: Scaling and Load Balancing Machine Learning Microservices: The chapter explores the critical realms of scaling and load balancing for ML microservices, focusing on optimizing the performance of a dynamic music recommendation engine. It navigates the complexities of handling escalating data volumes and unpredictable user demands while maintaining system responsiveness and cost-effectiveness. This chapter illuminates the art of seamlessly integrating horizontal and vertical scaling strategies, elucidating the transformative impact of stateless microservices, and demystifying the intricacies of advanced load balancing techniques. Embrace the journey through Kubernetes-driven auto-scaling insights and practical implementations, ensuring your ML microservices are scalable, robust, and efficient in the face of fluctuating workloads and evolving technological landscapes.

Chapter 8: Securing Machine Learning Microservices: The chapter ventures into security within ML microservices, focusing on safeguarding the intricate ecosystem of a music recommendation engine. It unravels the best practices for securing these advanced systems, emphasizing the critical balance between accessibility and protection. Through an in-depth exploration of encrypted communications, data anonymization techniques, and secure model deployment strategies, this chapter arms you with the knowledge to fortify your ML-driven applications against evolving cyber threats, ensuring the integrity, confidentiality, and reliability of your AI-powered solutions. Engage with this chapter to master the art of embedding robust security measures, which is pivotal for the sustainable operation and trustworthiness of ML innovations.

Chapter 9: Monitoring and Logging in Machine Learning Microservices: The chapter hones in on the pivotal role of monitoring and logging within ML microservices, using the music recommendation engine as a practical example. This chapter illuminates the critical techniques and strategies essential for maintaining system reliability, efficiency, and transparency. It explores sophisticated monitoring frameworks and logging practices that are indispensable for diagnosing, troubleshooting, and optimizing ML-driven applications. Engaging with this chapter will equip you with the knowledge to implement state-of-the-art monitoring and logging infrastructures, ensuring your ML microservices are robust, responsive, and resilient under real-world operating conditions.

Chapter 10: Deployment for Machine Learning Microservices: The chapter is an insightful exploration into the deployment intricacies of ML microservices, emphasizing the transformative impact of continuous integration and continuous deployment (CI/CD) practices. This chapter is a deep dive into automating the ML workflow, highlighting how to expedite the delivery of ML-driven services while ensuring precision, dependability, and adaptability in production environments. It elucidates advanced deployment strategies, automated testing, and the criticality of seamless model versioning and rollback mechanisms. Engage with this chapter to master the art of deploying robust, scalable ML microservices, ready to serve in today's fast-paced technological landscape, ensuring they remain at the pinnacle of innovation and operational excellence.

Chapter 11: Real World Use Cases: This chapter navigates the impactful implementation of ML microservices across various sectors, illustrating their transformative role from healthcare diagnostics to urban management in smart cities. This exploration showcases real-world applications and the strategic integration of AI, spotlighting a music recommendation system as a key example. By demonstrating success stories and practical insights, the chapter underscores the potent synergy between cutting-edge ML and microservices architecture, revealing their collective power to revolutionize industries, enhance decision-making, and elevate operational efficiency. Engage with this chapter to witness how ML microservices are shaping the future, driving innovation, and offering scalable solutions to contemporary challenges.

Chapter 12: Challenges and Future Trends: This chapter explores the evolving world of ML microservices, spotlighting the crucial challenges and emerging trends that are shaping this dynamic field. We explore the integration of groundbreaking technologies like sustainable AI, edge computing, and quantum computing, highlighting their pivotal role in enhancing the scalability, efficiency, and adaptability of ML-driven solutions. This chapter serves as a forward-looking guide, offering insights into how these advanced technologies are poised to overcome current limitations and redefine the future of microservices in an AI-centric world. Engage with this chapter to grasp the cutting-edge advancements that await on the horizon of ML microservices, ready to transform industries and innovate our approach to AI integration.

Code Bundle and Coloured Images

Please follow the link to download the
Code Bundle and the *Coloured Images* of the book:

https://rebrand.ly/a6052c

The code bundle for the book is also hosted on GitHub at
https://github.com/bpbpublications/Microservices-for-Machine-Learning.
In case there's an update to the code, it will be updated on the existing GitHub repository.

We have code bundles from our rich catalogue of books and videos available at
https://github.com/bpbpublications. Check them out!

Errata

We take immense pride in our work at BPB Publications and follow best practices to ensure the accuracy of our content to provide with an indulging reading experience to our subscribers. Our readers are our mirrors, and we use their inputs to reflect and improve upon human errors, if any, that may have occurred during the publishing processes involved. To let us maintain the quality and help us reach out to any readers who might be having difficulties due to any unforeseen errors, please write to us at :

errata@bpbonline.com

Your support, suggestions and feedbacks are highly appreciated by the BPB Publications' Family.

Did you know that BPB offers eBook versions of every book published, with PDF and ePub files available? You can upgrade to the eBook version at www.bpbonline. com and as a print book customer, you are entitled to a discount on the eBook copy. Get in touch with us at :

business@bpbonline.com for more details.

At **www.bpbonline.com**, you can also read a collection of free technical articles, sign up for a range of free newsletters, and receive exclusive discounts and offers on BPB books and eBooks.

Piracy

If you come across any illegal copies of our works in any form on the internet, we would be grateful if you would provide us with the location address or website name. Please contact us at **business@bpbonline.com** with a link to the material.

If you are interested in becoming an author

If there is a topic that you have expertise in, and you are interested in either writing or contributing to a book, please visit **www.bpbonline.com**. We have worked with thousands of developers and tech professionals, just like you, to help them share their insights with the global tech community. You can make a general application, apply for a specific hot topic that we are recruiting an author for, or submit your own idea.

Reviews

Please leave a review. Once you have read and used this book, why not leave a review on the site that you purchased it from? Potential readers can then see and use your unbiased opinion to make purchase decisions. We at BPB can understand what you think about our products, and our authors can see your feedback on their book. Thank you!

For more information about BPB, please visit **www.bpbonline.com**.

Join our book's Discord space

Join the book's Discord Workspace for Latest updates, Offers, Tech happenings around the world, New Release and Sessions with the Authors:

https://discord.bpbonline.com

Table of Contents

1. Introducing Microservices and Machine Learning..1

Introduction...1

Structure 1

Objectives..1

Understanding the evolution of microservices..2

Evolution of software architecture 2

Rise of microservices 3

Monolithic architecture 3

Microservices architecture..5

Exploring the world of Machine Learning 7

Machine Learning's data-driven revolution 7

Applications of Machine Learning 8

Need for microservices in Machine Learning 10

Conclusion...12

Points to remember 13

Multiple choice questions...13

Answer key 15

2. Foundation of Microservices...17

Introduction...17

Structure 17

Objectives 17

Understanding microservices principles 18

Single Responsibility Principle...18

Service independence 19

Decentralized data management...21

Resilient communication 23

Continuous integration and continuous deployment...25

Decentralized governance...26

Designing microservices for modularity and scalability....................................28

Different architecture styles in microservices...28

Gateway Aggregation architecture 28

Event-Driven Architecture *31*

Service mesh architecture *33*

Design patterns in microservices architecture *35*

API Gateway pattern *35*

Publish-Subscribe pattern *36*

Sidecar pattern *38*

Saga pattern *39*

Best practices for building microservices-based applications 41

Conclusion 43

Points to remember 44

Multiple choice questions 44

Answer key *46*

3. Fundamentals of Machine Learning **47**

Introduction 47

Structure 47

Objectives 48

Machine Learning concepts and algorithms 48

Types of Machine Learning *48*

Supervised learning *48*

Unsupervised learning *50*

Reinforcement Learning *51*

Key concepts of Machine Learning *52*

Features and labels *52*

Training and testing data *54*

Loss functions *55*

Data preprocessing and feature engineering 57

Handling missing data *57*

Deletion *58*

Mean/median/mode imputation *59*

Model-based imputation *60*

Data transformation *61*

Data encoding *62*

Feature extraction *63*

Feature selection *64*

Model training, evaluation, and deployment 65

Model training... 65
    Fitting models... 65
    Underfitting and overfitting 66
    Bias and variance 67
Model evaluation 69
    Confusion Matrix... 69
    Area Under the Receiver Operating Characteristic Curve 71
    Root Mean Squared Error 71
    Normalized Discounted Cumulative Gain 72
    Cross-validation 73
Model deployment... 74
Conclusion.. 76
Exercise 76
Key terms.. 80
Points to remember 81
Multiple choice questions... 82
    Answer key 84

4. Designing Microservices for Machine Learning 85
Introduction.. 85
Structure.. 85
Objectives.. 86
Domain-driven design for ML projects... 86
   Understanding the domain 86
   Bounded contexts... 87
   Understanding entities, aggregates and value objects 89
    Combining entities, aggregates and value objects........................ 90
Defining microservices boundaries 90
   Data and functionality 90
   Single Responsibility Principle... 92
   Cohesion and coupling... 93
    Cohesion 94
    Coupling 94
   API contracts 96
Data flow and communication patterns... 97
   Data pipelines 97

Synchronous versus asynchronous communication.. 100

    Synchronous communication... 100

    Asynchronous communication... 101

Message queues and event streams.. 102

    Message queues 102

    Event streams 103

API gateways... 105

Decomposing monolithic ML applications.. 107

    Identifying modules and components 107

Designing the ML microservice.. 108

    API gateway 110

        Benefits 110

    Inter-service communication 111

        Key interactions 111

    Event bus 111

    Data pipeline 113

    Data ingestion... 114

    Data processing... 114

    ML algorithm processing... 115

    Data serving 115

    Microservices API layers 116

Conclusion.. 119

Exercise 120

Points to remember 120

Multiple choice questions.. 121

    Answer key 123

5. Implementing Microservices for Machine Learning.. **125**

Introduction.. 125

Structure... 126

Objectives... 126

Developing ML microservices with essential technologies.................................. 126

    Flask for ML microservices 127

FastAPI for Machine Learning microservices 136

    FastAPI Catalog Service 136

    FastAPI User Service 137

FastAPI Playback Service 138

FastAPI Recommendation Service 139

FastAPI Analytics Service 139

Creating scalable and distributed ML pipelines 140

Scalable Machine Learning pipelines using Kubeflow 140

Kubeflow 140

Additional AWS features 142

Kubeflow pipeline outline 142

Inter-service communication 147

HTTP/REST 147

Message brokers 148

Event-driven architecture 148

Load balancing 149

Load balancing in microservices 149

Load balancing with Kubernetes 149

Load balancing with AWS API Gateway 150

Load balancing with Kong 151

Real-time vs. batch processing in microservices architecture 152

Real-time processing 152

Batch processing with Apache Spark and HDFS 153

Caching strategies in scalable ML pipelines 155

Caching methods 155

Cache invalidation 157

Orchestrating microservices with containerization 157

Dockerizing microservices 157

Kubernetes for orchestration 159

Setting up the environment on AWS 160

Conclusion 165

Assignment 166

Basic assignments 166

Intermediate assignments 166

Advanced assignments 167

Points to remember 167

Multiple choice questions 168

Answer key 170

6. Data Management in Machine Learning Microservices **171**

Introduction 171

Structure 171

Objectives 172

Handling data ingestion and storage 172

    Data sources 172

        Utilization of data sources 173

    Data ingestion 174

        Batch ingestion 174

        Real-time ingestion 176

    Data storage 177

        Relational databases 178

        NoSQL databases 178

        Distributed file systems 178

        Object storage 179

    Distributed storage: Hadoop 180

        Hadoop Distributed File System architecture 180

        Data formats supported by Hadoop 181

        Interacting with Hadoop Distributed File System 182

    Data format: Apache parquet 182

        Storing Parquet files 183

Data versioning and lineage tracking 184

    Data versioning 184

        Delta file format 186

        Delta and Hadoop 187

        Delta Lake 187

        Lineage tracking 191

Batch and real-time data processing for ML applications 194

    Batch processing 194

    Apache Spark 195

        Usage of Apache Spark in batch processing 197

        Real-time data processing 198

        Apache Kafka 199

        Usage of Apache Kafka and Apache Spark in real-time processing 200

Conclusion 203

Points to remember 203

Assignment 204

Multiple choice questions 204

    Answer key 206

7. Scaling and Load Balancing Machine Learning Microservices 207

Introduction 207

Structure 208

Objectives 208

Horizontal versus vertical scaling strategies 208

    Horizontal versus vertical scaling 209

    Deciding factors: Scaling strategy choices 210

    Hybrid approach: Combining horizontal and vertical scaling 211

    Use case: Scaling the music recommendation engine for a sudden influx of users 212

Stateless microservices for scalability 213

    Concept of stateless microservices 213

    Benefits of stateless ML microservices 214

    Implementation with TensorFlow and PyTorch 214

Load balancing techniques for ML workloads 217

    Common load balancing techniques 218

    Implementing load balancing for the music recommendation engine 219

Auto-scaling ML microservices 220

    The dynamic nature of ML tasks 220

    Need for auto-scaling 220

Kubernetes and its role in scaling 221

    Introduction to Kubernetes 221

    Kubernetes for ML microservices workloads 222

    Kubernetes auto-scaling: Standing out in scalability management 222

Challenges and considerations in scaling and load balancing 225

    Addressing these challenges in the MRE 226

Conclusion 228

Points to remember 228

Assignment 230

Multiple choice questions 230

    Answer key 232

8. **Securing Machine Learning Microservices** 233

    Introduction.. 233

    Structure... 233

    Objectives... 234

    Importance of securing ML microservices... 234

        Sensitivity and value of ML data and models 234

        Consequences of not securing ML services.. 235

    Best practices for secure communication 236

        Secure Socket Layer and Transport Layer Security...................................... 236

        API key authentication 237

        OAuth 2.0.. 238

    Privacy concerns in ML and data anonymization 239

        Risks of exposing personal information 239

        Data masking, pseudonymization, and differential privacy......................... 240

            Data masking and pseudonymization... 240

            Differential privacy 241

    Ensuring secure model deployment.. 241

        Secure containers 242

        Model encryption... 242

        Access control 243

    Use case: Music recommendation engine 243

        User service: OAuth 2.0 for secure user access 244

            Handling different grant types with OAuth 2.0.. 246

    Recommendation service: Ensuring data privacy 249

        Regulatory and legal repercussions 253

    Conclusion.. 253

    Points to remember 254

    Assignment... 254

    Multiple choice questions.. 255

        Answer key 257

9. **Monitoring and Logging in Machine Learning Microservices**................... 259

    Introduction.. 259

    Structure... 260

    Objectives... 260

    Importance of securing ML microservices... 260

The uniqueness of monitoring in ML contexts 260

Proactive error resolution and system optimization 261

Tool spotlight: Prometheus and Grafana 262

    Prometheus: The open-source monitoring solution 262

    Grafana: Visualizing your data 263

Implementing logging and metrics for ML services 263

    Key metrics to track in ML services 263

    Effective logging strategies and best practices 265

    Elasticsearch, Logstash, Kibana for centralized logging 266

    TensorFlow's TensorBoard for ML-specific visualizations 268

Troubleshooting and debugging ML microservices 269

    Common challenges and pitfalls in ML microservices 269

    Approaches to identify and resolve the challenges 271

    Tool spotlight: Effective debugging and tracing tools 272

        Python debugger for Python 273

        Jaeger 274

Use case: Recommendation engine diagnostics 275

Conclusion 278

Points to remember 278

Assignment 279

Multiple choice questions 280

    Answer key 281

10. Deployment for Machine Learning Microservices 283

Introduction 283

Structure 283

Objectives 284

Fundamentals of CI/CD for Machine Learning 284

    Differences between traditional CI/CD and ML CI/CD 284

    Key components and flow of ML CI/CD pipelines 285

Automation tools for ML CI/CD 286

    Introduction to Jenkins: Automating ML workflows 286

        GitLab CI/CD: A deep dive into ML pipelines with GitLab 288

        Leveraging MLflow for experiment tracking and model registry 291

    Kubeflow: Orchestrating ML workflows on Kubernetes 294

    Jenkins or GitLab CI/CD integration with Kubeflow 297

GitLab CI/CD integration with Kubeflow 297

Jenkins integration with Kubeflow 298

A/B testing in ML microservices 300

Continuous delivery and rollback capabilities 302

Continuous delivery for ML models 303

Case study and best practices 304

Case study: Music recommendation system 305

Conclusion 306

Points to remember 306

Assignment 307

Multiple choice questions 307

Answer key 309

11. Real World Use Cases 311

Introduction 311

Structure 311

Objectives 312

Implementing ML microservices in various industries 312

Success stories and lessons learned from real projects 313

Enhancing media and entertainment with AI 314

Personalization techniques in media 314

Personalization services architecture 315

Moderation methods overview 315

Moderation services and workflow integration 316

Challenges and considerations in personalization and moderation 317

Financial services: Fraud detection 318

Understanding banking fraud detection systems 318

ML microservices for real-time transaction analysis 319

Architecture of fraud detection ML microservices 320

Challenges and best practices 322

Healthcare: Diagnostics and personalized treatment 323

Predictive diagnostics in healthcare 323

Personalized treatment and patient data analytics 324

Architecture of ML services in healthcare 325

Challenges and future directions in healthcare ML 326

Smart cities: Urban management 327

Enhancing urban management with ML microservices..327

Tackling urban traffic challenges 327

Real-time traffic analysis with ML 328

Predictive modeling for smoother traffic 328

Case studies of success 328

Public safety and ML-driven insights 328

Predictive policing with ML 328

Optimizing emergency response 329

Integrating public surveillance with ML 329

Emergency services and ML insights 329

Challenges and future prospects in smart cities 329

Peering into the future 330

Agriculture: Advancements in precision farming 330

Machine Learning in yield prediction 331

Application of ML microservices for accurate yield forecasting 331

Case study: Yield prediction using ML 331

Case study: Implementing ML for enhanced farming practices 332

ML integration and solutions 332

Impact and results 332

Energy: Sustainable management and optimization 333

ML microservices in energy consumption prediction 334

ML solutions for energy consumption prediction 334

Real-world impact of ML in energy prediction 335

Case study: ML-driven sustainable energy 335

Recommendation engine...337

Conclusion..338

Points to remember 338

Assignment...339

Multiple choice questions..340

Answer key 342

12. Challenges and Future Trends..**343**

Introduction...343

Structure...343

Objectives...344

Core challenges in ML microservices 344

Scalability and efficiency...*344*

Interoperability and integration *345*

Security and privacy...*346*

Data management and quality *347*

Service orchestration..*348*

Monitoring and maintenance *349*

Emerging trends in ML microservices...349

Automation and AI-driven development..*350*

Edge computing and ML microservices *351*

Quantum computing and ML microservices *352*

Sustainable AI and green computing *353*

Generative AI in ML microservices...*354*

Conclusion..355

Points to remember 355

Assignment...356

Multiple choice questions...356

Answer key *358*

Index..**359-369**

CHAPTER 1
Introducing Microservices and Machine Learning

Introduction

In the ever-changing landscape of modern software development, microservices and **Machine Learning** (**ML**) have converged to become a powerful force for innovation and transformation across industries. This chapter marks the beginning of our exploration of microservices for ML, where we will delve into the foundational concepts and motivations behind this revolutionary integration.

Structure

The chapter covers the following topics:

- Understanding the evolution of microservices
- Exploring the world of Machine Learning
- Need for microservices in Machine Learning

Objectives

The primary objective of this chapter is to lay a solid foundation for the rest of the book by introducing the essential concepts of microservices and ML. This chapter aims to provide a comprehensive understanding of the context, significance, and inherent value that the convergence of these two transformative technologies brings to modern software development.

Understanding the evolution of microservices

Understanding the evolution of microservices involves tracing back the developments in software architecture that have led to the adoption of microservices as a popular architectural style.

Evolution of software architecture

To fully understand the significance of microservices and their relationship with ML, it is essential first to understand the evolution of software architecture. The historical shift from monolithic applications to distributed systems is the foundation of our exploration. The limitations of monolithic architectures, such as scalability, maintainability, and agility, were key factors in the rise of microservices.

The evolution of software architecture has traversed a convoluted path, with many trends and styles emerging over time. Here is a brief overview of some pivotal milestones in the annals of software architecture history:

- **Monolithic architecture:** For an extended period, monolithic architecture reigned supreme as the predominant software architecture style. Within this framework, all components of an application were intricately interwoven. While this integration facilitated facile development and deployment, it simultaneously posed challenges regarding scalability and maintenance.

- **Client-server architecture:** In the 1980s, the emergence of client-server architecture sought to enhance the scalability and maintainability of monolithic applications. This approach partitioned the application into two entities: the client, responsible for user interactions, and the server, entrusted with data processing and storage.

- **Three-tier architecture:** Building upon client-server architecture, the three-tier architecture evolved, further segmenting the application into three distinct strata: the presentation layer, the application layer, and the data layer. This division streamlined application development and upkeep, while augmenting scalability and bolstering security.

- **Service-oriented architecture (SOA):** This emerged as a paradigm where applications were conceived as an assemblage of loosely connected services. These services communicated via well-defined interfaces, simplifying development, deployment, and management.

- **Microservices architecture:** It marks a subsequent evolution of SOA by adopting a more streamlined approach. Microservices, characterized by their diminutive, self-contained nature, are autonomously developed and deployed. This design amplifies scalability, flexibility, and resilience even more than SOA services.

Software architecture's evolutionary journey remains ongoing, with the prospect of fresh trends and styles emerging in the forthcoming years. Despite this, the foundational principles of effective software architecture, such as modularity, scalability, flexibility, and resilience, remain steadfast. Adhering to these principles, software architects can engineer simple applications to develop, deploy, and maintain, effectively addressing user and business requirements for years to come.

Several key catalysts drive the evolution of software architecture, including:

- **Growing software complexity:** The escalating complexity of software necessitates solutions beyond traditional monolithic architectures.
- **Agility demand:** Agile business needs necessitate swift adaptability, rendering microservices architecture an apt choice for agile development.
- **Technological advancements:** Innovations such as containers and service meshes have simplified the implementation of microservices architecture.

The horizon of software architecture is promising. It aligns effectively with the demands of contemporary businesses and is likely to continue gaining traction in the foreseeable future.

Microservices have been influenced by security considerations as well and are beneficial when addressing the unique security challenges posed by ML applications:

- **Independent security layers:** Each microservice can implement its security protocols, tailored to its specific needs.
- **Reduced attack surface:** A breach in one service does not necessarily compromise the entire system.
- **Agile security updates:** Independent services mean that security updates can be deployed rapidly and specifically without overhauling the entire application.

Rise of microservices

The rise of microservices results from converging technological, organizational, and cultural trends that have highlighted the limitations of previous architectural approaches and offered new tools and practices for building scalable, resilient, and fast-evolving software systems.

Monolithic architecture

Monolithic architecture is a traditional approach to building software applications where all the components and modules of an application are tightly integrated into a single codebase and deployed as a single unit. In a monolithic architecture, the entire application, including the user interface, business logic, and data interface, is packaged together. This contrasts with modern architectural styles like microservices, where an application is broken down into smaller, independently deployable services. Refer to *Figure 1.1* given below:

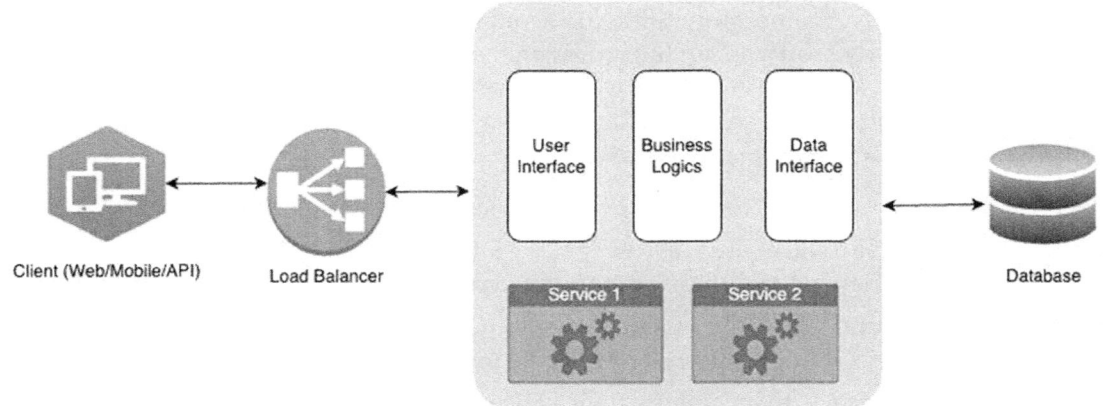

Web Server (Including all services with UI, Business layer and Data Interface in a single Application)

Figure 1.1: *Monolithic architecture*

The advantages of monolithic architecture are as follows:

- **Simplicity:** Monolithic architecture is relatively simpler to develop and manage, especially for smaller applications. All components are in one place, making it easier to debug and test.

- **Ease of development:** Since all parts of the application are in the same codebase, developers can work more efficiently and collaboratively. They have a unified view of the entire application.

- **Deployment:** Deploying a monolithic application is straightforward, as there is only one unit to deploy. This can be advantageous for smaller projects or when simplicity is a priority.

- **Performance:** Communication between components in a monolithic application is usually faster compared to distributed systems, as it does not involve network calls.

- **Shared resources:** Since components are tightly coupled, they can easily share data structures and libraries, leading to potentially optimized resource usage.

The disadvantages of monolithic architecture are as follows:

- **Scalability:** Monolithic applications can be challenging to scale horizontally. If one component needs more resources, the entire application might need to be scaled, even if other components do not require additional resources.

- **Flexibility:** As the application grows, it can become harder to add new features without affecting existing ones. Changes in one part of the application can have unintended consequences on other parts.

- **Maintenance:** As the application becomes larger and more complex, maintenance can become cumbersome. Updates and bug fixes might require the entire application to be redeployed.

- **Technology diversity:** Monolithic applications might limit the choice of technologies. All components need to use the same programming language and technology stack.

- **Development bottlenecks:** A monolithic codebase can lead to bottlenecks in development. As the team grows, conflicts might arise due to developers working on different parts of the application.

- **Resource utilization:** Since all components share the same resources, if one component consumes excessive resources, it can impact the performance of the entire application.

In summary, monolithic architecture offers simplicity and ease of development for smaller projects, but it can become challenging to manage and scale as applications grow. The tight coupling of components can limit flexibility and hinder the adoption of diverse technologies. As software development practices evolve, modern architectural styles like microservices are gaining popularity for addressing the limitations of monolithic architectures.

Microservices architecture

Microservices architecture is a modern approach to building software applications that emphasizes breaking down an application into small, loosely coupled, and independently deployable services. Each of these services is responsible for a specific business capability and can be developed, deployed, and scaled independently. Unlike monolithic architecture, where all components are tightly integrated, microservices promote modularization and distributed communication. Refer to the following figure:

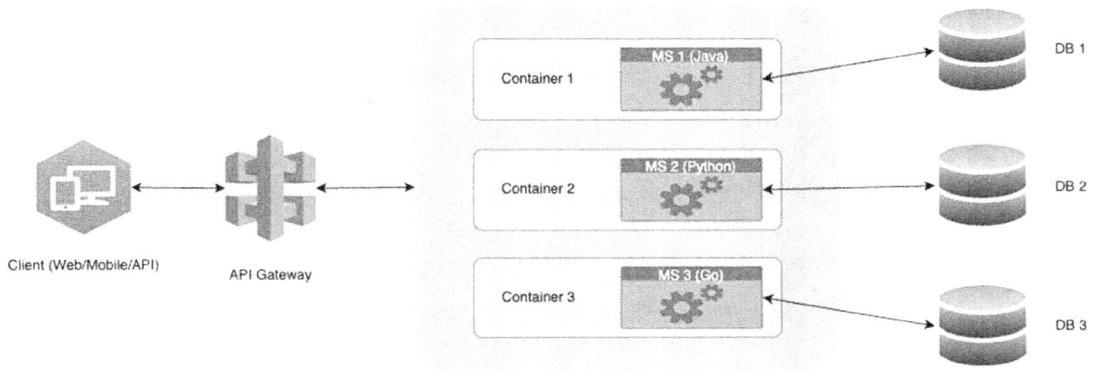

Figure 1.2: Microservice architecture

The principles and advantages of microservices architecture are as follows:

- **Scalability:** Microservices architecture enables granular scalability. Each service can be scaled independently based on demand, optimizing resource usage and improving performance.

- **Modularity:** Services are decoupled and focused on specific tasks, making them easier to develop, test, and maintain. New features can be added without affecting the entire application.

- **Decentralization:** Services in a microservices architecture are independent and autonomous. They communicate through well-defined APIs, allowing them to be developed, deployed, and scaled separately.

- **Loose coupling:** Microservices are loosely coupled, minimizing dependencies between services. This reduces the impact of changes in one service on others, enhancing overall system flexibility.

- **Independent deployment:** Services can be updated and deployed independently, leading to faster development cycles and reduced downtime.

- **Single responsibility:** Each microservice addresses a single business capability, promoting a clear and focused scope for development.

- **Polyglot programming:** Different services can employ diverse technologies and programming languages, enabling teams to leverage the best-suited tools for each service's requirements.

- **Flexibility and agility:** Microservices promote agile development. Small teams can work on different services concurrently, fostering quicker development and innovation.

- **Resilience:** Failures in one service do not impact the entire application, increasing overall system reliability and fault tolerance.

- **Continuous Integration and Deployment (CI/CD):** Each service can have its own CI/CD pipeline, enabling automated testing, integration, and deployment.

The disadvantages of microservices architecture are as follows:

- **Complexity in communication:** Microservices require well-defined communication mechanisms between services, which can add complexity. Distributed systems can be challenging to manage.

- **Operational complexity:** Managing multiple services, each with its own infrastructure and deployment, can increase operational complexity.

- **Latency:** Inter-service communication over networks can introduce latency compared to in-process communication in monolithic applications.

- **Data consistency:** Maintaining data consistency across services can be difficult, especially in scenarios involving transactions that span multiple services.

- **Testing challenges:** Comprehensive testing becomes vital due to the distributed nature of microservices. Ensuring end-to-end functionality requires careful testing strategies.

- **Overhead:** The overhead of managing multiple services can be higher than that of a monolithic application, especially for smaller projects.

- **Initial development effort:** Setting up microservices architecture requires initial investment in infrastructure, development practices, and communication protocols.

- **Deployment complexity:** Deploying multiple services and ensuring they work harmoniously can be complex, requiring robust orchestration tools.

In summary, microservices architecture offers benefits such as scalability, modularity, and agility, making it suitable for complex and rapidly changing applications. However, it introduces challenges related to communication, data consistency, and operational management. The choice between monolithic and microservices architecture depends on factors like the size of the application, development team, and scalability requirements.

Exploring the world of Machine Learning

Exploring the world of ML is an exciting journey. ML is a subset of **Artificial Intelligence** (**AI**) that enables computers to learn from data, identify patterns, and make decisions with minimal human intervention. Here is a structured guide to start your exploration.

Machine Learning's data-driven revolution

ML is revolutionizing the way we use data. By learning from data, ML algorithms can make predictions, identify patterns, and make decisions that were previously impossible. This is leading to a new era of data-driven decision-making, where businesses and organizations can make better decisions based on the vast amounts of data they collect.

This section explores the essence of this revolution, highlighting how ML leverages data to drive transformative changes across industries and domains:

- **Harnessing data for insights:** ML revolves around the concept of training algorithms on data to learn patterns and make predictions or decisions. This process is particularly potent in scenarios where human-designed rules or traditional programming fall short. By feeding large volumes of data into ML models, these algorithms can unearth intricate patterns, correlations, and insights that might remain hidden to the human eye.

- **Personalization and customer experience:** One of the most profound impacts of ML's data-driven revolution is its ability to customize and enhance customer experiences. Through data analysis, ML algorithms can discern individual preferences, behaviors, and tendencies. This knowledge empowers businesses to tailor offerings, services, and recommendations to each customer, fostering stronger engagement and loyalty.

- **Data-driven decision-making:** Traditional decision-making often relies on human intuition and experience. ML, fueled by data, introduces a data-driven approach to decision-making. By analyzing historical data and predicting outcomes, ML algorithms aid in making informed choices across various domains, from finance to healthcare.

- **Predictive analytics:** ML's predictive capabilities are integral to the data-driven revolution. These models can forecast future trends, behaviors, and events based on historical data. Industries such as finance and manufacturing leverage predictive analytics to optimize inventory, manage risk, and streamline operations.

- **Automation and efficiency:** The union of ML and data has enabled automation on an unprecedented scale. Repetitive tasks that previously demanded significant human intervention can now be automated through algorithms trained on relevant data. This not only enhances efficiency but also liberates human resources for more creative and strategic endeavors.

- **Healthcare and life sciences advancements:** The healthcare sector is at the forefront of ML's data-driven revolution. From diagnosing diseases through medical imaging to predicting patient outcomes, ML algorithms analyze vast medical datasets to enhance diagnostics, treatment, and patient care.

- **Challenges and ethical considerations:** While the data-driven revolution of ML holds immense potential, it also introduces challenges related to data privacy, bias in algorithms, and ethical implications. Ensuring that data is used responsibly and algorithms are transparent becomes paramount.

In conclusion, ML's data-driven revolution has transformed industries and redefined how decisions are made and processes are optimized. By leveraging the power of data, ML algorithms are shaping a future where insights, personalization, and efficiency are at the core of innovation. However, navigating the ethical dimensions of this revolution remains crucial to ensuring its benefits are harnessed responsibly and equitably.

Applications of Machine Learning

ML has permeated a myriad of industries, revolutionizing the way we approach challenges and uncover opportunities. This section explores the diverse applications of ML across various domains, highlighting its transformative impact:

- **Healthcare and medicine**
  - o **Disease diagnosis:** ML aids in diagnosing diseases from medical images like X-rays, MRIs, and CT scans.
  - o **Drug discovery:** ML accelerates drug discovery by analyzing complex chemical interactions and predicting potential drug candidates.

    o **Personalized treatment:** Algorithms analyze patient data to recommend personalized treatment plans based on genetic, medical, and lifestyle factors.

- **Finance**

    o **Fraud detection:** ML detects fraudulent transactions by analyzing patterns and anomalies in financial data.

    o **Algorithmic trading:** ML models predict stock market trends and optimize trading strategies.

    o **Credit scoring:** Algorithms analyze credit histories and other data to assess creditworthiness.

- **Retail and e-commerce**

    o **Recommendation systems:** ML powers product recommendations, improving customer engagement and sales.

    o **Demand forecasting:** Algorithms predict demand for products, optimizing inventory management.

    o **Price optimization:** ML models determine optimal pricing strategies based on market trends and competitor prices.

- **Manufacturing**

    o **Predictive maintenance:** ML forecasts equipment failures, reducing downtime and maintenance costs.

    o **Quality control:** Algorithms identify defects in products using image and sensor data.

    o **Supply chain optimization:** ML enhances supply chain efficiency by predicting demand and optimizing logistics.

- **Autonomous vehicles**

    o **Self-driving cars:** ML algorithms process real-time data from sensors to navigate and make driving decisions.

    o **Advanced driver assistance:** ML enables features like lane departure warnings and adaptive cruise control.

- **Natural Language Processing (NLP)**

    o **Sentiment analysis:** Algorithms gauge sentiment in social media and customer reviews to assess public opinion.

    o **Language translation:** NLP models translate languages in real time, bridging linguistic barriers.

o **Chatbots and virtual assistants:** AI-powered chatbots offer customer support and automate interactions.

- **Image and video analysis**

    o **Object detection:** ML identifies objects within images and videos, facilitating applications from security to self-driving cars.

    o **Facial recognition:** Algorithms recognize faces for authentication, security, and social media tagging.

    o **Medical imaging:** ML assists in detecting anomalies in medical images and diagnosing diseases.

- **Entertainment and content recommendation**

    o **Content curation:** ML tailors content recommendations on streaming platforms and social media.

    o **Music and movie recommendations:** Algorithms suggest music and movies based on user preferences.

- **Energy and utilities**

    o **Energy consumption prediction:** ML forecasts energy demand, aiding in efficient distribution and consumption.

    o **Grid management:** Algorithms optimize energy grid operations, balancing supply and demand.

- **Agriculture**

    o **Crop health monitoring:** ML analyzes drone and satellite imagery to monitor crop health and detect issues.

    o **Precision agriculture:** Algorithms optimize resource usage by providing insights for targeted interventions.

In essence, ML's applications span diverse sectors, reshaping industries by uncovering insights, automating processes, and enabling personalized experiences. Its adaptability and transformative potential continue to drive innovation across domains, propelling us into an era of data-driven decision-making and unprecedented possibilities.

Need for microservices in Machine Learning

The convergence of microservices architecture, carefully selected tech stacks, and powerful ML libraries constitutes a formidable solution to the complexities of constructing ML applications. This section delves into the compelling reasons behind the integration of microservices in the context of ML. It also outlines the essential technology components and key ML libraries necessary for successful implementation. Let us explore why microservices are beneficial in the context of ML:

- **Scalability of ML models:** ML models frequently demand substantial computational resources. Microservices provide the flexibility of scaling individual models independently, thereby optimizing resource allocation and overall application performance. As the load increases, resources are allocated dynamically to the specific microservices handling the workload, ensuring efficient resource utilization.

- **Model diversity and flexibility:** ML is characterized by diverse models, each tailored for specific tasks. Microservices architecture adeptly incorporates varied models, allowing developers to seamlessly integrate the most fitting model for each use case. This flexibility ensures that the right tool is employed for each unique problem, enhancing application performance and accuracy.

- **Efficient resource management:** Microservices architecture's modular nature facilitates fine-grained resource allocation. In contrast to traditional monolithic approaches, where uniform resource allocation is the norm, microservices ensure that computational resources are distributed optimally to each service, eliminating wastage and improving efficiency.

- **Rapid experimentation and deployment:** Microservices are designed for autonomy, allowing individual models to be developed, tested, and deployed independently. This facilitates rapid experimentation and innovation. Teams can work on specific microservices without affecting others, resulting in quicker development cycles and fostering a culture of innovation.

- **Real-time decision-making:** In real-time ML applications, quick decision-making is paramount. Microservices' low-latency architecture seamlessly aligns with the demand of these scenarios. Decisions can be made in real time as microservices process data swiftly, enabling applications like fraud detection, recommendation engines, and autonomous vehicles.

- **Specialization and collaboration:** Microservices support specialization by enabling individual teams to focus on specific models or components. Collaboration becomes seamless as experts can work on microservices independently. This approach accelerates development and ensures that each microservice is developed with precision.

- **Fault isolation and resilience:** The isolated nature of microservices architecture prevents failures from cascading one service into others. This fault isolation enhances the overall resilience of the application. A failure in a single microservice does not disrupt the entire system.

- **Modular extensibility:** Microservices' modular design accommodates the integration of new models, functionalities, and ML libraries. This extensibility ensures that applications can adapt to evolving requirements, incorporate cutting-edge algorithms, and leverage new libraries with ease.

The following is a list of essential technology stacks and ML libraries:

- **Hadoop and Spark:** For distributed data processing and analysis, handling large datasets efficiently.
- **Kafka:** For real-time data streaming and processing, supporting event-driven architectures.
- **Docker:** For containerization and consistent deployment, ensuring application consistency across environments.
- **Kubernetes:** For orchestrating and managing microservices at scale, automating deployment, scaling, and management.
- **Kubeflow:** For end-to-end ML workflows within Kubernetes, managing complex ML pipelines.
- **FastAPI:** For building efficient and scalable APIs, providing high performance and automatic API documentation.
- **Scikit-learn, TensorFlow, PyTorch:** For developing ML models, catering to various model complexities and use cases.
- **XGBoost, LightGBM, CatBoost:** For boosting algorithms, enhancing predictive accuracy.
- **Pandas, NumPy, Matplotlib:** For data manipulation, analysis, and visualization, facilitating data preprocessing and analysis.

By leveraging this comprehensive technology stack and integrating key ML libraries, organizations create a foundation for a successful microservices-based ML architecture. This approach effectively addresses challenges related to scalability, real-time processing, and efficient deployment. As a result, organizations are empowered to construct adaptable, scalable, and resilient applications that harness the full potential of ML. The strategic synergy between microservices, the chosen technology stack, and ML libraries propels industries toward intelligent applications that drive innovation and propel the future of ML forward.

Conclusion

As we close this chapter, we stand at the intersection of two transformative domains: microservices and ML. We have illuminated the evolution of architecture and the emergence of data-driven insights, setting the stage for the exploration ahead.

In the chapters to come, we will dive deeper into the intricacies of implementing microservices for ML, unraveling the methodologies, challenges, and opportunities that shape this revolutionary integration. With our foundation firmly laid, let us journey further to unlock the boundless potential of *Microservices for Machine Learning*.

Points to remember

- Microservices and ML are joining forces to revolutionize modern software development and industry transformation.
- Monolithic architecture's simplicity suits smaller projects, but it struggles with scalability and adaptability as applications grow.
- Microservices architecture addresses these limitations with benefits like scalability, modularity, and agility, tailored for complex and dynamic applications.
- Microservices' benefits include flexibility, resilience, and improved resource utilization.
- However, challenges arise in communication, data consistency, and operational management.
- ML leverages data to revolutionize industries, enabling insights, personalization, and efficiency-driven innovation.
- ML's applications span various sectors, reshaping industries by automating tasks, uncovering insights, and enhancing personal experiences.
- Its transformative potential continues to drive innovation across domains.
- Organizations can create a foundation for microservices-based ML architecture by leveraging a comprehensive technology stack.
- Integration of key ML libraries addresses challenges related to scalability, real-time processing, and efficient deployment.

Multiple choice questions

1. **What was a significant limitation of monolithic architecture?**
   a. Scalability
   b. High maintainability
   c. Low agility
   d. Simple complexity

2. **What is a distinguishing characteristic of microservices architecture when compared to SOA?**
   a. Larger, intertwined components
   b. Less scalability
   c. Autonomously developed and deployed components
   d. Centralized communication

3. **Which is an advantage of monolithic architecture?**

   a. Horizontal scalability

   b. Simplicity and ease of development

   c. Independent deployment of components

   d. Allows diverse technology stacks within the same application

4. **What is a major advantage of using a microservices architecture?**

   a. Simplified communication between services

   b. Granular scalability

   c. Lower operational complexity

   d. Easier data consistency management

5. **In a monolithic architecture, when a single component requires more resources, what might be needed?**

   a. Scaling that single component independently

   b. Scaling the entire application

   c. Reducing the resources for other components

   d. Decoupling the components

6. **Which of the following can be a disadvantage of Microservices Architecture compared to Monolithic Architecture?**

   a. Faster inter-component communication

   b. Lower initial development effort

   c. Data consistency challenges

   d. Less efficient resource sharing

7. **How does ML contribute to automation?**

   a. It increases the need for human intervention in repetitive tasks

   b. It trains algorithms to avoid learning from data

   c. It allows algorithms to be trained on relevant data to automate repetitive tasks

   d. It reduces the efficiency of operations

8. **In the context of finance, ML is notably used for:**

   a. Fraud detection

   b. Paperwork reduction

   c. Physical security

   d. Manual trading

9. **What is a critical challenge introduced by the data-driven revolution of ML?**

   a. Data abundance

   b. Data privacy and ethical considerations

   c. Lack of data for analysis

   d. Complete transparency in algorithms

10. **What is a key advantage of integrating microservices in ML applications?**

    a. Model diversity and flexibility

    b. Monolithic architecture

    c. Reduced specialization in development teams

    d. Slower development cycles

Answer key

1	a
2	c
3	b
4	b
5	b
6	c
7	c
8	a
9	b
10	a

Join our book's Discord space

Join the book's Discord Workspace for Latest updates, Offers, Tech happenings around the world, New Release and Sessions with the Authors:

https://discord.bpbonline.com

CHAPTER 2
Foundation of Microservices

Introduction

Microservices architecture has revolutionized the way we design and develop software applications. Its modular, decentralized, and service-oriented approach has enabled organizations to create complex systems that are more flexible, scalable, and maintainable. In this chapter, we will explore the key tenets of microservices, highlighting their significance and the benefits they bring to **Machine Learning (ML)**.

Structure

The chapter covers the following topics:

- Understanding microservices principles
- Designing microservices for modularity and scalability
- Best practices for building microservices-based applications

Objectives

The objective of this chapter is to establish a comprehensive understanding of the fundamental concepts, principles, and best practices that underlie microservices architecture. This chapter aims to provide readers with a solid foundation by explaining the core tenets of microservices, their benefits, and their implications for designing and building modern software applications. By the end of this chapter, readers should have a clear understanding of the essential principles that form the basis of microservices architecture. In subsequent chapters, we will explore how microservices can be synergistically combined with ML techniques to create dynamic applications that can learn, adapt, and provide personalized experiences to their users.

Understanding microservices principles

Understanding the foundational principles of microservices is crucial for successful implementation and scalability. These principles guide how to design, develop, and deploy microservices in a manner that balances business needs and technical requirements. The adoption of microservices architecture involves embracing a set of principles to ensure that the system is maintainable, scalable, and resilient. By analyzing established applications like music streaming and e-commerce applications, we can gain insights into how these principles are put into practice.

Single Responsibility Principle

The **Single Responsibility Principle (SRP)** is a foundational concept in object-oriented programming and is also a fundamental principle in microservices design. Let us explore its meaning, especially in the context of microservices.

The SRP posits that a class should have only one *reason to change*. When applied to microservices, it implies that each microservice should handle only one functionality or business capability. This ensures that the services remain decoupled, maintainable, and are organized around distinct business functionalities.

Tech stack

- **Languages:** Any that support modular architecture. Some common choices include:
    o Java (with frameworks like Spring Boot)
    o Go
    o Node.js
    o Python (using Flask or Django)
- **Service Mesh and Proxy:** For managing inter-service communication and ensuring independence, for example:
    o Istio
    o Envoy
    o Linkerd

- **Cloud services:** Adopting SRP in the cloud involves deploying and managing each microservice independently. Key services to assist with this include:
  - o **AWS**
    - ▪ Lambda (serverless functions for single responsibilities)
    - ▪ **Elastic Container Service (ECS)** (container orchestration)
    - ▪ **Elastic Kubernetes Service (EKS)** (Kubernetes orchestration)
  - o **Azure**
    - ▪ Azure Functions (serverless functions)
    - ▪ **Azure Kubernetes Service (AKS)**

Examples
- **Music streaming application**
  - o **Song metadata service:** Manages details about each song, such as title, artist, and duration.
  - o **Playlist management service:** Allows users to create, modify, or delete playlists.
  - o **User profile service:** Manages user data including preferences, playlists, and listening history.
  - o **Recommendation service:** Suggests songs or playlists based on user preferences and listening habits.

Each of these services has a clear, singular responsibility, ensuring they can be developed, deployed, and scaled independently.

- **E-commerce application**
  - o **Product catalog service:** Manages product details, descriptions, and images.
  - o **Inventory service:** Keeps track of stock levels for products.
  - o **Order processing service:** Handles the process of ordering, including payment processing and order status updates.
  - o **Recommendation service:** Provides product recommendations to users based on browsing and purchase history.

Again, each service is responsible for a specific business capability, ensuring modularity and the ability to adapt to changes in that specific domain without impacting other services.

Service independence

The principle of *service independence* is central to the microservices architecture. It encompasses the idea that each microservice should be self-sufficient and operate without relying on the internal details of other services. This autonomy allows for greater flexibility, scalability, and resilience in system design.

Service independence means that each microservice is an autonomous unit that can be developed, deployed, scaled, and operated independently of other services. This independence ensures that changes to one service do not necessitate changes in others, allowing for rapid and isolated feature development and troubleshooting.

Tech stack

To achieve service independence, specific technologies and tools are utilized:

- **Containerization**
  - o **Docker:** Provides a consistent environment for microservices, ensuring they run the same regardless of where they are deployed.

- **Orchestration and scheduling**
  - o **Kubernetes:** Manages and orchestrates Docker containers, handling scaling and failover.
  - o **Docker Swarm:** An alternative to Kubernetes, native to Docker.

- **Service mesh**
  - o **Istio:** Enhances the security, observability, and network traffic management between microservices.
  - o **Linkerd:** Another service mesh tool, focusing on simplicity and performance.

- **API Gateways**
  - o **Nginx or HAProxy:** For routing requests and load balancing.
  - o **Zuul:** Provides dynamic routing, monitoring, and security.

- **Cloud services**
  - o **AWS**
    - ▪ **ECS:** A container management service that supports Docker.
    - ▪ **EKS:** Managed Kubernetes service.
  - o **Azure**
    - ▪ **AKS:** Managed Kubernetes service.
    - ▪ **Azure API Management:** Provides API gateway functionalities.

Examples

- **Music streaming application:** With millions of active users, application's backend is intricate. Using Service Independence, the platform ensures that:

- o **Ad service:** The service that delivers ads can be scaled separately during peak hours.

- o **Music streaming service:** Ensures that music streaming remains uninterrupted even if other services like recommendations or social features face issues.

- o **Playlist management:** Changes or updates to how playlists are managed will not affect how songs are streamed.

- **E-commerce application:** Application leverages microservices to handle its diverse range of operations:

  - o **Inventory service:** It can be scaled up during events like *Black Friday* without affecting the user profile or recommendations services.

  - o **Pricing service:** Regular updates to pricing algorithms or strategies do not impact product listing or order processing.

  - o **Order management:** Even if there is a new feature or update in the order management workflow, it will not impact the way products are displayed or user reviews are managed.

Service independence is a cornerstone of the microservices paradigm. By ensuring that each service is self-reliant, organizations can achieve rapid development cycles, easier troubleshooting, and more robust scalability.

Decentralized data management

Decentralized data management is a pivotal principle in microservices, which dictates how data is organized, stored, and accessed across services. It stems from the need for each microservice to own its data to remain loosely coupled and independent.

Decentralized data management means that each microservice has its own private database or data store. This ensures that data is only managed and accessed by its respective service. As a result, other services must communicate through APIs if they require access to data owned by another service. This principle ensures data consistency, isolation, and promotes service autonomy.

Tech stack

Achieving decentralized data management typically involves the following tools and technologies:

- **Databases:** A wide variety of databases can be used based on the service's specific needs:

  - o **Relational databases:** PostgreSQL, MySQL

  - o **NoSQL databases:** MongoDB, Cassandra, CouchDB

  - o **In-memory stores:** Redis, Memcached

- **Data streaming and event sourcing**
  - o **Apache Kafka:** A distributed streaming platform used for building real-time data pipelines.
  - o **EventStore:** Store for event sourcing implementations.

- **Data synchronization and integration**
  - o **Debezium:** Provides change data capture for distributed databases.
  - o **Camel:** Integration framework with a range of connectors for various databases and services.

- **Cloud services:** Cloud platforms offer managed services tailored for microservices data management:
  - o **AWS**
    - **RDS:** Managed relational databases.
    - **DynamoDB:** Managed NoSQL database.
    - **Kinesis:** Real-time data streaming.
  - o **Azure**
    - **Azure SQL database:** Managed relational database.
    - **Cosmos DB:** Managed multi-model database.
    - **Azure stream analytics:** Real-time event data processing.

Examples

- **Music streaming application:** To serve millions of users, application breaks down its data needs based on features:
  - o **User data service:** Manages user profiles, with its database storing user details, settings, and preferences.
  - o **Playlist service:** Owns a database storing playlists, songs in the playlist, and playlist metadata.
  - o **Music metadata service:** Maintains a database with information on tracks, albums, artists, and related metadata.

Each of these services, and more, will have its unique database, ensuring independence and quick data access:

- **E-commerce application:** Application's vast operations are underpinned by numerous microservices, each managing its data:
  - o **Product catalog service:** Manages a database with product details, descriptions, and images.

o **Inventory service:** Maintains a separate database tracking stock levels, warehouses, and product locations.

o **Order service:** Uses its database to keep track of customer orders, shipping details, and order statuses.

Decentralized data management ensures that each microservice has complete authority over its data, which promotes service independence and reduces the blast radius of potential issues. However, this approach also necessitates robust communication mechanisms and may introduce complexities in data consistency and integrity.

Resilient communication

In the world of microservices, the way individual services communicate with one another is vital. As a distributed system, it is not a matter of *if* a service will fail, but *when*. Resilient communication ensures that such inevitable failures do not lead to system-wide outages or deteriorated user experiences.

Resilient communication in microservices refers to the ability of services to communicate with each other in a way that can handle and recover from failures. This involves implementing patterns and strategies that ensure the system remains operational and responsive, even when certain services or communication pathways encounter issues.

Tech stack

- **Service mesh**

  o **Istio:** A fully integrated service mesh that provides traffic management, security, and observability.

  o **Linkerd:** A light-weight service mesh that gives you observability, reliability, and security without requiring any code changes.

- **API gateway**

  o **Kong:** A cloud-native API gateway that also offers functionalities like load balancing, authentication, and rate limiting.

  o **Zuul:** An edge service that provides dynamic routing, monitoring, resiliency, and more.

- **Client-side libraries**

  o **Hystrix:** A latency and fault-tolerance library, known for its circuit breaker mechanism that allows services to fail gracefully.

  o **Ribbon:** A client-side load balancer that also provides control over HTTP and TCP clients.

- **Cloud services**
  - ○ **AWS**
    - ▪ **Elastic Load Balancing (ELB)**: Automatically distributes incoming traffic across multiple targets.
    - ▪ **AWS App Mesh:** A service mesh that provides application-level networking to make applications more resilient.
  - ○ **Azure**
    - ▪ **Azure Load Balancer:** Distributes incoming traffic for high availability and resilience.
    - ▪ **Azure Service Fabric Mesh:** A fully managed service mesh, offering reliable and resilient service-to-service communication.

Examples

- **Music streaming application:** To deliver uninterrupted music streaming, Application must ensure that its services communicate resiliently:
  - ○ **Fallback mechanisms:** If a particular music stream is disrupted, application might switch to a lower-quality stream or choose a different song from the same artist or genre.
  - ○ **Retry and timeout:** If the User Profile Service does not respond in time, the application might fetch cached user data or prompt the user to retry.

- **E-commerce application:** Ensuring that millions of customers can shop even if certain features or services face issues is critical for application:
  - ○ **Circuit breakers:** If the Recommendation Service starts to fail, a circuit breaker might trip to prevent requests from reaching it, allowing it time to recover without cascading the failure.
  - ○ **Load Balancing:** Traffic to the Product Details Service is balanced across various instances to ensure no single instance gets overwhelmed.
  - ○ **Fallbacks:** If the Product Review Service is down, application might display a cached version of reviews or temporarily hide that feature, ensuring the main product page remains accessible.

Resilient communication in microservices ensures that the system remains functional and offers a good user experience even in the face of individual service failures. Tools like service meshes, API gateways, and client-side libraries, combined with patterns like circuit breakers, timeouts, and fallbacks, are instrumental in achieving this resilience.

Continuous integration and continuous deployment

Continuous integration and continuous deployment (CI/CD) is the backbone of modern software development, ensuring quick iterations and stable releases, especially within the microservices architecture. Given the interdependent nature of microservices, having a robust CI/CD process is essential:

- **CI:** This is the practice of frequently merging all developer working copies to a shared mainline. After integration, automated tests are run to detect and fix integration bugs as quickly as possible.

- **CD:** This is the direct extension of CI, ensuring that code changes are automatically built, tested, and deployed to production without human intervention.

Tech stack

- **Integration and deployment tools**
    - o **Jenkins:** An open-source automation server supporting building, deploying, and automating any project.
    - o **Travis CI:** A CI/CD service integrating with GitHub repositories.
    - o **GitLab CI/CD:** Offers functionalities for CI/CD within the GitLab platform.
    - o **CircleCI:** Offers CI/CD for web applications.

- **Containerization and orchestration**
    - o **Docker:** Enables developers to create and deploy applications inside containers.
    - o **Kubernetes:** A container orchestration platform, facilitating scaling and managing of containerized applications.

- **Configuration and deployment**
    - o **Ansible:** An IT automation tool used for configuration management, application deployment, and task automation.
    - o **Terraform:** An infrastructure-as-code software to provision and manage cloud resources.

- **Cloud services**
    - o **AWS**
        - ▪ **AWS CodePipeline:** A CI/CD service to automate build, test, and deploy phases.
        - ▪ **AWS CodeBuild:** A build service that compiles, tests, and packages code.

- **AWS ECS and EKS:** Container orchestration services integrated with AWS.

o **Azure**

- **Azure DevOps services:** Offers CI/CD, testing, and Kanban project boards.

- **AKS:** Managed Kubernetes service for deploying, managing, and scaling containerized applications.

Examples

- **Music streaming application:** Application, with its vast music library and active user base, demands a fluid CI/CD pipeline for feature releases and bug fixes:

  o **Feature flags:** Application often rolls out features to a subset of users. CI/CD helps in quickly deploying these features and rolling them back if necessary.

  o **Microservices deployment:** When a new version of the Playlist microservice is developed, it goes through CI checks and, once validated, gets deployed without affecting the rest of the ecosystem.

- **E-commerce application:** Application's global reach and diverse services necessitate a robust CI/CD mechanism:

  o **Frequent releases:** Application deploys code every few seconds. CI ensures the integrated code is robust, and CD ensures it is deployed without human intervention.

  o **Service independence:** Each service, like Order Processing or Inventory Management, has its own CI/CD pipeline, ensuring failures in one do not affect the others.

  o **Rollback mechanisms:** If a deployment introduces issues, application's CD pipelines facilitate quick rollbacks to maintain system stability.

CI/CD in the realm of microservices not only ensures rapid and stable software delivery but also reduces manual errors, improves developer productivity, and enhances user satisfaction.

Decentralized governance

Decentralized governance in the context of microservices is a foundational principle. Rather than imposing a uniform solution or technology stack for every service, teams are given the autonomy to select the best tools and technologies for their specific service's needs.

Decentralized governance allows individual teams or units within an organization to make decisions about their specific services or products. Within microservices, it refers to the idea that each service can be designed, developed, deployed, and scaled using the best-suited technologies and tools for that specific service. This contrasts with a centralized approach where decisions about technology choices are made by a single authority and enforced across all services.

Tech stack

Decentralized governance promotes the idea that there is no *one-size-fits-all* tech stack. The different services it might use are:

- **Languages:** Java, Python, Go, Node.js, or others, depending on the use case.
- **Databases:** SQL databases like MySQL or PostgreSQL; NoSQL databases like MongoDB or Cassandra; or even caching solutions like Redis.
- **Frameworks:** Spring Boot for Java, Express for Node.js, Django for Python, etc.
- **Cloud services**
  - o **AWS**
    - ▪ **RDS:** Managed relational databases service supporting PostgreSQL, MySQL, MariaDB, Oracle, and SQL Server.
    - ▪ **Lambda:** Allows you to run code without provisioning servers, supporting multiple programming languages.
  - o **Azure**
    - ▪ **Azure Cosmos DB:** A multi-model database service.
    - ▪ **Azure functions:** Supports building serverless applications with multiple programming languages.

Examples

- **Music streaming application:** Application's backend is a constellation of microservices, each potentially employing a different tech stack:
  - o **Polyglot persistence:** A microservice handling song metadata might use a relational database, while another handling user playlists might use a NoSQL database for flexibility.
  - o **Service-specific frameworks:** A service managing real-time user sessions might be written in Node.js for its event-driven nature, while another performing complex analytics might use Python for its data libraries.
- **E-commerce application:** With its vast array of services, application embodies the spirit of decentralized governance:
  - o **Varied data stores:** Application's catalog service might employ a different storage mechanism than the recommendation service.

o **Different languages for different needs:** The inventory management microservice might be written in Java for its robustness, while a service handling real-time price updates might use Go for its performance and concurrency support.

o **Service autonomy:** Each service team at application can select tools and methodologies that best suit their service's requirements, fostering innovation and efficiency.

Decentralized governance in microservices champions the autonomy of teams, allowing them to make technology decisions that best serve the specific requirements of their service. While this approach fosters innovation and can lead to more optimized solutions, it also requires strong communication and documentation practices to manage the diverse tech landscape effectively.

Designing microservices for modularity and scalability

Designing microservices for modularity and scalability is a critical aspect of creating a robust and flexible architecture that can accommodate the growing demands of modern applications. Microservices architecture breaks down complex systems into smaller, independently deployable services, allowing for efficient development, maintenance, and scalability. Here is how to approach the design of microservices to ensure modularity and scalability:

Different architecture styles in microservices

Microservices architecture can be implemented in various ways, each with its own benefits and trade-offs. Here are some different architecture styles within the microservices paradigm along with associated design patterns.

Gateway Aggregation architecture

Gateway Aggregation is a prominent architecture pattern in microservices, enabling the seamless composition of multiple services' data into a unified API. Gateway Aggregation employs an API gateway that acts as the primary point of communication for client applications. The gateway routes the client's request to relevant microservices, aggregates the responses, and then sends a consolidated response back to the client. This pattern simplifies the client's perspective, reducing the need for multiple service calls and their associated complexities. Refer to *Figure 2.1* given below:

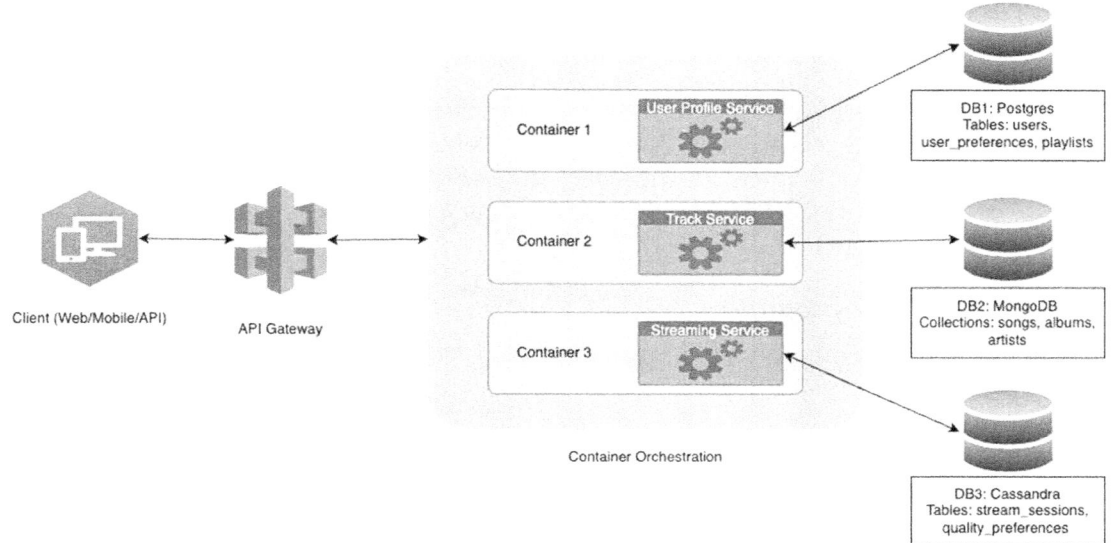

Figure 2.1: Gateway Aggregation Architecture

Design patterns

- **API Gateway pattern:** A server that is a single entry point into the system. It encapsulates the internal system architecture and provides an API tailored to each client.

- **Aggregator pattern:** The API gateway directly fetches data from individual services, aggregates the data, and sends it back to the users. This is often synchronous.

- **Chain of responsibility pattern:** The API gateway might call one service, which in turn calls another service, forming a chain.

Examples with database designs

Let us take an example of a music streaming application with following microservices: (Refer to *Figure 2.1*)

- **User profile service**
  - o **Database:** PostgreSQL
  - o **Tables:** users, user_preferences, playlists

- **Track service**
  - o **Database:** MongoDB
  - o **Collections:** songs, albums, artists

- **Streaming Service**
  - o **Database:** Cassandra
  - o **Tables:** stream_sessions, quality_preferences
- **Gateway Aggregation:** When a user retrieves a playlist, the request goes to the API gateway. It interacts with both the *user profile service* and *track service* to get playlist details and track metadata, sending a unified response.

Tech stack
- **API Gateway solutions**
  - o Zuul (commonly with Spring Cloud)
  - o Kong
  - o Apigee
  - o Express Gateway (for Node.js ecosystems)
- **Service communication:**
  - o REST APIs
  - o gRPC
  - o GraphQL
- **Databases**
  - o **Relational:** PostgreSQL, MySQL
  - o **NoSQL:** MongoDB, Cassandra, DynamoDB
  - o **In-memory:** Redis, Memcached
- **Message brokers**
  - o Apache Kafka
  - o RabbitMQ
- **Cloud services**
  - o **AWS**
    - ▪ **Amazon API Gateway:** Manages APIs.
    - ▪ **RDS and DynamoDB:** Managed relational and NoSQL database services.
    - ▪ **SQS and SNS:** Managed message queuing and pub/sub messaging services.
  - o **Azure**
    - ▪ **Azure API management:** Handles APIs.

- **Azure Cosmos DB:** Globally distributed NoSQL database.
- **Azure Service Bus:** Messaging service between applications and services.

Gateway Aggregation architecture is invaluable for presenting a simplified API to clients while managing the complexity of interactions between multiple microservices. By utilizing specific design patterns and the appropriate tech stack, applications mentioned above deliver optimized and efficient user experiences.

Event-Driven Architecture

Event-Driven Architecture (EDA) is an architectural approach where microservices in a system produce and consume events. These events indicate a change in state, and the system reacts by triggering specific actions or side effects in response.

EDA focuses on producing, detecting, consuming, and reacting to events. In microservices, EDA ensures that services can loosely couple together, communicate asynchronously, and allow for high scalability and adaptability. Refer to the following *Figure 2.2*:

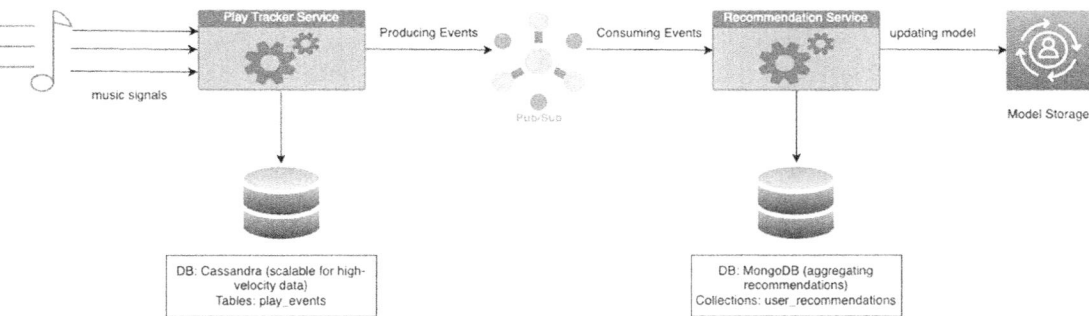

Figure 2.2: Event-Driven Architecture

Design patterns

- **Command Query Responsibility Segregation (CQRS):** Segregating operations that modify state (commands) from operations that retrieve state (queries).
- **Saga pattern:** A saga is a sequence of local transactions, where each transaction updates data within a single service. It maintains data consistency across services.

Examples with database designs

Let us take an example of a music streaming application with following microservices: (Refer to *Figure 2.2*)

- **Play tracker service**
  o **Database:** Cassandra (scalable for high-velocity data)
  o **Tables:** play_events

- **User Recommendations Service**
    - o **Database:** MongoDB (for flexible schema when aggregating recommendations)
    - o **Collections:** user_recommendations
- **Event-Driven Interaction:** When a user plays a song, the Play Tracker Service records the play event. This event is then published to an event stream. The User Recommendations Service listens for these events. Upon detecting them, it updates its recommendation model for the user.

Tech stack

- **Event-Driven Frameworks and Platforms**
    - o **Apache Kafka**
    - o **RabbitMQ**
- **Service communication**
    - o REST APIs (for synchronous)
    - o gRPC
    - o WebSockets
- **Databases**
    - o **Relational:** PostgreSQL, MySQL
    - o **NoSQL:** MongoDB, Cassandra, DynamoDB
    - o **Event Store:** Kafka Streams, EventStoreDB
- **Cloud services**
    - o **AWS**
        - ▪ **Amazon Kinesis:** Streaming data platform.
        - ▪ **AWS Lambda:** Serverless compute to run code in response to events.
        - ▪ **RDS, DynamoDB:** Managed databases.
    - o **Azure**
        - ▪ **Azure Event Hubs:** Big data streaming platform and event ingestion.
        - ▪ **Azure Functions:** Event-driven serverless computation.
        - ▪ **Azure Cosmos DB:** Globally distributed NoSQL database.

EDA in microservices is designed to handle large-scale, real-time operations seamlessly. With the rapid production and consumption of events, systems can be more reactive, scalable, and resilient. Incorporating EDA in platforms mentioned above can help manage complex workflows and user interactions efficiently.

Service mesh architecture

In the world of microservices, managing inter-service communication can become an intricate task, especially as the number of services grows. A service mesh architecture intervenes to manage this complexity and provide a range of functionalities.

A service mesh is a dedicated infrastructure layer built to facilitate service-to-service communications in a transparent, reliable, and scalable manner. It provides discovery, load balancing, failure recovery, metrics, and monitoring, without making the services aware. A service mesh also often offers more complex functionalities, such as A/B testing, canary releases, and rate limiting, see *Figure 2.3*:

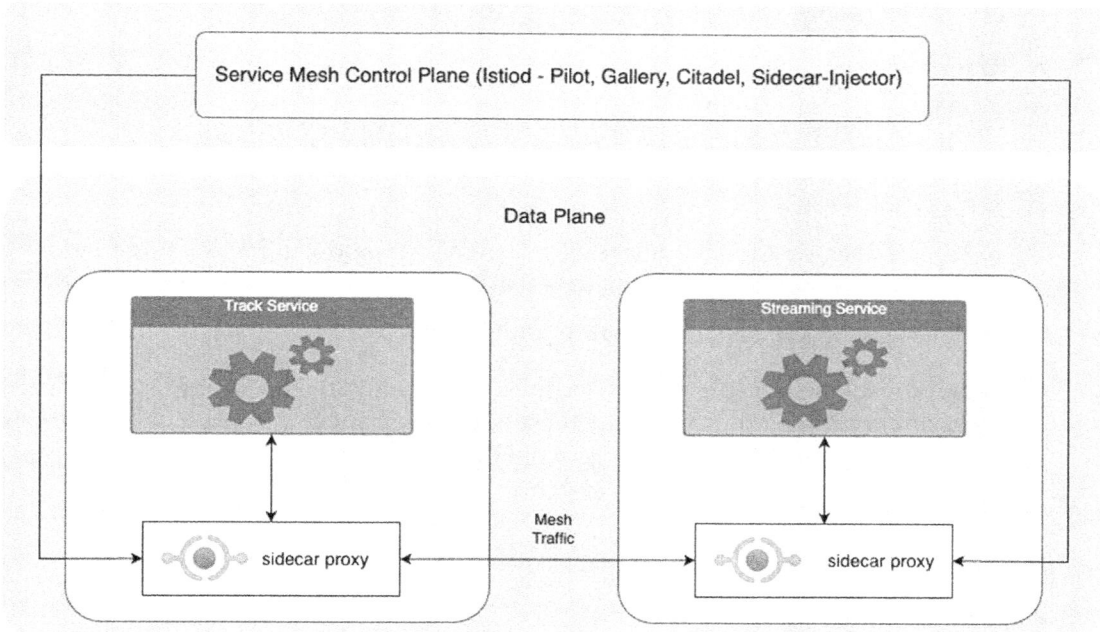

Figure 2.3: Service mesh architecture

Design patterns

- **Sidecar pattern:** In the service mesh architecture, the common pattern is to run a sidecar proxy alongside each service instance. This proxy intercepts network communication and applies mesh functionalities, effectively decoupling business logic from communication concerns.
- **Circuit breaking:** Automatically detecting failures and preventing the system from overloading.

Examples with database designs

Let us take an example of a music streaming application with following microservices: (Refer *Figure 2.3*)

In a music streaming environment, the main concern is streaming quality, user experience, and handling a large number of requests.

Microservices

- **User Profile Service**
    - o **Database:** PostgreSQL
    - o **Tables:** users, user_preferences, playlists

- **Track service**
    - o **Database:** MongoDB
    - o **Collections:** songs, albums, artists

- **Streaming service**
    - o **Database:** Cassandra (designed for scalability and can handle large amounts of data spread out across the world)
    - o **Tables:** stream_sessions, quality_preferences

- **Service mesh application:** A service mesh, for example, Istio, is applied. It ensures reliable communication between these services, handling retries, failovers, and load balancing. If the *Streaming Service* fails in one region, the mesh reroutes user requests to the nearest available instance, ensuring uninterrupted music playback. (Refer to *Figure 2.3*)

Tech stack

- **Service mesh solutions**
    - o Istio
    - o Linkerd
    - o Consul Connect

- **Proxy solutions:**
    - o Envoy
    - o HAProxy

- **Monitoring and tracing**
    - o Prometheus (for monitoring)
    - o Jaeger or Zipkin (for distributed tracing)

- **Cloud services**
  - o **AWS**
    - ▪ **AWS App Mesh:** Service mesh based on Envoy, integrates with Amazon ECS, EKS, and EC2.
    - ▪ **Amazon CloudWatch:** Monitoring and observability.
  - o **Azure**
    - ▪ **Azure Service Fabric Mesh:** Fully managed service mesh solution.
    - ▪ **Azure Monitor:** Full-stack monitoring, advanced analytics, and intelligent alerting.

Service mesh architecture stands as a backbone in a microservices environment, ensuring that the services not only communicate effectively but also have a safety net to fall back on in case of failures.

Design patterns in microservices architecture

Following are a few design patterns linked to distinct architectural styles within the microservices framework.

API Gateway pattern

The API Gateway pattern is a design pattern that plays a critical role in microservices architecture by acting as a reverse proxy to route requests, compose responses, and provide a unified API interface for clients. This gateway abstracts the underlying microservices from client applications, making it more manageable to request and receive the necessary data.

The key concepts of API Gateway pattern are:

- **Unified API interface:** The API Gateway offers a single-entry point for all client requests across multiple microservices.
- **Request routing:** Directs client requests to the appropriate service or services.
- **Response aggregation:** The gateway can consolidate data from multiple services into a single response.
- **Cross-cutting concerns:** Manages shared operational concerns such as authentication, SSL termination, rate limiting, caching, and logging.

The benefits in microservices architecture are:

- **Decoupling:** Client applications are decoupled from individual microservices, enabling microservices to evolve independently.
- **Centralized management:** A unified point to handle concerns like security, rate limiting, and analytics.

- **Performance optimization:** With caching and response aggregation, the gateway can improve response times and reduce network chatter.

- **Enhanced security:** The gateway can serve as the first line of defense, managing authentication and filtering malicious requests.

Examples: Consider a music streaming platform with multiple microservices: User Management, Playlist Management, Music Streaming, and Recommendations.

Scenario: Fetching User's home page

When a user opens the platform, the client sends a request to the API Gateway to fetch data for the home page.

- **API Gateway**
  - o Asks the User Management service for user details and preferences.
  - o Retrieves recommended tracks from the Recommendations service based on user preferences.
  - o Fetches user-created playlists from the Playlist Management service.

The API Gateway aggregates this data and provides a consolidated response to the client, which displays the user's home page with personalized playlists and recommendations.

Through the API Gateway, a single request fetches multiple pieces of data seamlessly, giving users a smooth experience.

Considerations

- **Potential bottleneck:** The API Gateway could become a system's single point of failure. To mitigate this, it's crucial to ensure its scalability and resilience.

- **Complexity:** A significant amount of logic can accumulate in the API Gateway, leading to maintenance challenges.

- **Latency:** Introducing an intermediary layer can add some latency, making it essential to ensure the gateway's efficient operation.

The API Gateway pattern centralizes and simplifies external access to microservices in a system. It enhances security, optimizes request handling, and offers a convenient point for monitoring and management. As with any architectural choice, its implementation should be done considering the specific needs of the project, keeping in mind scalability and maintainability.

Publish-Subscribe pattern

The Publish-Subscribe (often termed Pub/Sub) pattern is a messaging communication pattern where senders (publishers) of messages are decoupled from receivers (subscribers). Publishers send messages to a middle layer (often termed as a topic or a channel), and subscribers listen to these topics or channels. Since the publishers and subscribers do not interact or know about each other directly, this pattern allows for flexibility, scalability, and decoupling in system architectures.

The key concepts of Pub/Sub pattern are:

- **Publisher:** The component/service that sends or emits messages to a topic.
- **Subscriber:** The component/service that listens to a topic and consumes messages emitted to it.
- **Topic/channel:** A communication medium where messages are sent. Subscribers can listen to one or multiple topics.
- **Message broker:** A system responsible for maintaining and managing the topics/ channels and ensuring that messages are properly sent from publishers to subscribers.

The benefits in microservices architecture are:

- **Decoupling:** Microservices can evolve independently without needing to change their interfaces.
- **Scalability:** New subscribers can be added without the need for publishers to be aware of them.
- **Flexibility:** Services can subscribe or unsubscribe from topics as needed, allowing for dynamic system adjustments.
- **Fault tolerance:** Even if a subscriber service fails, the message system ensures message delivery when it's back online.

Examples: Online e-commerce platform

Imagine an e-commerce platform with several microservices, such as Order Management, Inventory Management, and Notification Service.

Scenario: Order placement

A user places an order on the platform.

The Order Management microservice processes the order and then publishes a message to the topic OrderProcessed.

The Inventory Management microservice is a subscriber to the OrderProcessed topic. Once it receives the message, it updates the inventory based on the order.

Simultaneously, the Notification Service is also a subscriber to the OrderProcessed topic. Upon receiving the message, it triggers an email notification to the user confirming the order.

Here, the Pub/Sub pattern allows the Order Management microservice to simply publish a message without concerning itself with what other services might do with that information. Inventory Management and Notification Service, on the other hand, can independently decide to act upon the order placement without directly interfacing with the Order Management service.

The considerations are as follows:

- **Message durability:** Depending on the broker and configuration, messages may be lost if no subscriber is listening. Solutions like persistent storage or durable subscriptions can be implemented.

- **Ordering guarantees:** Not all systems guarantee the order of message delivery. If order is crucial, additional strategies or tools may be needed.

- **Eventual consistency:** As systems act on messages independently and possibly at different times, the system as a whole may be in an inconsistent state for a period.

The Pub/Sub pattern offers a robust solution for building decoupled and scalable microservices architectures. With the rise of EDA, Pub/Sub has become increasingly popular and essential for many dynamic and large-scale systems.

Sidecar pattern

The sidecar pattern is a popular design pattern for microservices where each service has an accompanying component (the sidecar) that runs in the same pod or environment and augments or extends the service's responsibilities. This approach ensures that primary service can focus on its core logic while the sidecar handles ancillary tasks, like monitoring, logging, proxying, or security.

The key concepts of sidecar pattern are:

- **Primary service:** The main application or service that performs the business logic.

- **Sidecar:** The ancillary component that runs alongside the primary service to enhance, extend, or manage its operations. It shares the same lifecycle as the primary service.

- **Isolation:** The sidecar pattern promotes separation of concerns by isolating non-business related functionality from the primary service.

The benefits in microservices architecture are:

- **Separation of concerns:** The primary service remains clean, focusing on business logic, while the sidecar handles cross-cutting concerns.

- **Reusable components:** Sidecars can be reused across multiple services.

- **Enhanced modularity:** Sidecars allow features to be plugged in or removed without touching the primary service.

- **Independent scaling:** Sidecars can be scaled independently of their primary service if necessary.

Examples: Service mesh with Istio

Scenario: Imagine you have a microservices-based e-commerce application, and you want to implement a service mesh for better inter-service communication management, monitoring, and security:

- **Primary services:** Services such as User Management, Product Catalog, Order Processing, etc., each running in their individual containers.

- **Sidecar (Envoy Proxy in Istio):** Alongside each primary service container, there's an Envoy proxy container running as a sidecar.

- **Traffic management:** When services need to communicate, they don't talk directly to each other. Instead, they talk through their sidecar proxies. This allows for sophisticated routing, retries, failovers, and more.

- **Monitoring and tracing:** The sidecar proxies can collect detailed metrics and traces of the inter-service communication, providing insights into latencies, error rates, and other valuable metrics.

- **Security:** The sidecars can also manage TLS encryption for inter-service communication, ensuring data privacy and security without the primary services handling it.

The sidecar proxies, in this example, effectively abstracts away a multitude of concern from the primary services, allowing developers to focus on the business logic.

The considerations are as follows:

- **Overhead:** Sidecars can increase the resource overhead, especially in systems with numerous microservices.

- **Complexity:** The addition of sidecars can add operational and cognitive complexity.

- **Maintenance:** Keeping sidecars updated and in sync with primary services can be challenging.

The sidecar pattern is an effective way to modularize and separate cross-cutting concerns in a microservices architecture. By decoupling functionalities, it enables clean, focused microservices and provides a scalable approach to system-wide concerns. However, developers and architects should weigh the advantages against the potential overhead and complexity introduced.

Saga pattern

The saga pattern is a design pattern in microservices architectures aimed at managing long-running, distributed transactions without relying on a centralized coordinator or distributed locks. Instead of using a traditional two-phase commit, the saga pattern breaks a distributed transaction into multiple local transactions. Each of these transactions updates data in a single service and publishes an event or message to trigger the next local transaction in another service.

There are two primary ways to coordinate sagas:

- **Choreography:** Every local transaction publishes domain events that other services can listen to. No service instructs another service what to do directly.

- **Orchestration:** One service (or an external coordinator) takes charge of the distributed transaction and tells involved services what to do.

The benefits in microservices architecture are:

- **Decentralization:** Without a centralized coordinator, the system is less prone to bottlenecks and single points of failure.

- **Failure handling:** The system can implement compensating transactions to revert changes when part of the saga fails.

- **Maintainability:** Each service in the saga focuses on its local transactions, ensuring separation of concerns.

Examples: Online e-commerce platform

Imagine an e-commerce system where a user wants to place an order. The operation spans several services - Order Service, Payment Service, and Inventory Service.

Scenario: Order placement using choreography

A user places an order.

Order Service starts the saga by creating an order in a *Pending* state and then publishing an OrderCreated event.

Payment Service listens for the `OrderCreated` event. Upon receipt, it tries to process the payment. If successful, it publishes a `PaymentProcessed` event.

Inventory Service listens for the `PaymentProcessed` event. It then tries to reserve the ordered item. If successful, it publishes an `ItemReserved` event.

Order Service listens for the `ItemReserved` event and then finalizes the order by setting its state to *Completed*.

If any step fails, compensating transactions are triggered to revert the preceding steps. For example, if the inventory for an item is insufficient, the Inventory Service can emit an `ItemReservationFailed` event. The Payment Service, listening to this, would then refund any captured payment, and the Order Service could mark the order as *Failed*.

The considerations are as follows:

- **Complexity:** Implementing sagas can increase the complexity of the system due to event flows and compensating transactions.

- **Consistency:** Sagas lead to eventual consistency. It might take time before a distributed transaction is fully committed or rolled back across all involved services.

- **Event tracking:** It is essential to monitor and track the flow of events to debug issues in the system effectively.

The saga pattern offers a decentralized solution to manage distributed transactions in microservices architectures. By ensuring individual services manage their local transactions and using events for coordination, sagas provide a scalable way to achieve data consistency. However, architects and developers should be prepared for the added complexity and the challenges of eventual consistency.

Best practices for building microservices-based applications

When developing microservices-based applications, adhering to best practices ensures that the system remains scalable, maintainable, and efficient. This detailed exploration will cover these best practices, their definitions, associated tech stacks, cloud services, and real-world examples:

- **Define a clear service boundary:** Each microservice should have a clear and defined scope, often aligned with a specific business capability or domain.

  For example: In Amazon, each service handles a clear responsibility, such as order management, user profiles, and recommendations.

- **Decentralize everything:** Microservices should be autonomous, from data management to decision-making processes, allowing for faster iteration and flexibility.

  Tech stack

  o **Databases:** MongoDB, Cassandra, PostgreSQL.

  o **Event-Driven Systems:** Apache Kafka, RabbitMQ.

  o **Cloud Services:** AWS RDS, DynamoDB, Azure Cosmos DB

  For example: In Netflix, each microservice operates independently, from data storage to processing.

- **Use API Gateways**

  Centralize external access through an API gateway, which manages and routes requests to the appropriate microservice.

  Tech stack

  o **API management tools:** Zuul, Kong.

  o **Cloud services:** AWS API Gateway, Azure API Management

  For example: Twitter uses an API gateway to handle requests and distribute them across numerous services.

- **Implement Service Discovery:** Enable microservices to automatically detect and communicate with each other without hard-coded addresses.

  Tech stack

  o **Service Discovery tools:** Eureka, Consul.

  o **Cloud services:** AWS Cloud Map, Azure Service Fabric

  For example: Netflix's Eureka provides service discovery to ensure smooth inter-service communication.

- **Embrace CI/CD and automation:** Automate integration, testing, and deployment processes to ensure rapid, consistent, and reliable software releases.

  Tech stack

  o **CI/CD Tools:** Jenkins, CircleCI, GitLab CI.

  o **Cloud Services:** AWS CodePipeline & CodeDeploy, Azure DevOps

  For example: Spotify Uses CI/CD to continually test and deploy updates and features to their microservices.

- **Design for failure:** Expect and design for service failures to ensure resilience. Implement strategies like circuit breakers and fallbacks.

  Tech stack

  o **Resilience libraries:** Hystrix, Resilience4J.

  For example: Netflix uses Hystrix to detect service failures and provide fallbacks to ensure uninterrupted user experiences.

- **Implement centralized logging and monitoring:** Consolidate logs, metrics, and traces from all microservices into a centralized monitoring solution.

  Tech stack

  o **Monitoring tools:** Prometheus, Grafana.

  o **Logging solutions:** ELK Stack (Elasticsearch, Logstash, Kibana).

  o **Cloud services:** AWS CloudWatch, Azure Monitor

  For example: Uber uses centralized logging to debug issues and monitor the health of hundreds of microservices.

- **Prioritize security:** Implement security best practices at all levels - from API access, data storage, to network configurations.

  Tech stack

  o **API security:** OAuth, JWT.

  o **Network security:** Istio, Linkerd.

  o **Cloud services:** AWS Security Groups & VPC, Azure Security Center

For example: Airbnb implements OAuth for secure API access and other best practices to protect user data.

- **Ensure data consistency:** Implement strategies to handle data consistency across microservices, such as the Saga pattern.

    Tech stack

    o   **EDA:** Apache Kafka, RabbitMQ.

    For example: E-commerce platforms use the Saga pattern to handle transactions that span multiple services, like order placement and inventory deduction.

Building microservices-based applications involves much more than splitting a monolithic application into smaller parts. It requires a deep understanding of domain-specific boundaries, efficient communication between services, and the agility to adapt and evolve. Adhering to best practices ensures that the system is robust, scalable, and efficient. Real-world examples, from tech giants to startups, further underline the importance and practicality of these practices.

Conclusion

As we close this chapter, we leave with a richer, deeper understanding of microservices. We have seen that microservices are not just about technology; they represent a holistic approach to designing and building software systems that are scalable, flexible, and resilient. While the journey towards adopting microservices can be challenging, the principles, patterns, and best practices we have explored in this chapter serve as a robust guidebook for that journey.

In this chapter, we embarked on a comprehensive journey through the landscape of microservices, beginning with a solid foundation of the principles that underpin this architectural style. We explored the concept of single-responsibility services and how they promote a culture of independence and agility within development teams.

As we navigated through the different architecture styles in microservices, we saw that each approach, whether it be API Gateway, service mesh, or event-driven, has its own unique strengths and challenges. These styles are not mutually exclusive, and in many instances, they can be combined to create more robust and flexible systems.

The real-world examples and case studies, like the music streaming application, illustrated the principles and patterns discussed in this chapter. It served as a valuable bridge between theory and practice, showing that the principles we have learned are not merely academic, they are proven strategies used by leading tech companies worldwide.

The next chapter will unravel the core concepts and methodologies of ML, revealing its synergy with microservices. We will explore how ML can leverage the modular and decentralized nature of microservices to facilitate dynamic learning processes and decision-making. This exploration will cover the spectrum of ML paradigms, including supervised, unsupervised, and reinforcement learning, and how these can be integrated within microservices to create intelligent, adaptive systems.

Points to remember

- Microservices architecture has transformed software design and development.
- It emphasizes modularity, decentralization, and service orientation.
- Organizations benefit from increased flexibility, scalability, and maintainability.
- The chapter covers understanding microservices principles, designing for modularity and scalability, different architecture styles, design patterns, and best practices.
- Microservices adhere to principles like single responsibility, service autonomy, and decentralized data management.
- These principles contribute to agility, resilience, and efficient development.
- Microservices are self-contained units that encapsulate specific business functionalities. They communicate through APIs and enable independent scaling and deployment.
- Microservices interact via well-defined APIs, promoting loose coupling and flexibility.
- Communication patterns include synchronous (HTTP) and asynchronous (messaging) methods.
- Each microservice manages its own data store, minimizing dependencies.
- Challenges include maintaining data consistency and synchronization.
- Microservices can be developed, tested, and deployed independently.
- Scalability can be achieved both horizontally (instances) and vertically (resources).

Multiple choice questions

1. **What does SRP in microservices architecture emphasize?**
   a. Each service should have multiple responsibilities.
   b. Each service should encapsulate a single business capability.
   c. Services should share responsibilities for better efficiency.
   d. Responsibilities of services should be tightly coupled.

2. **How does service independence benefit microservices architecture?**
   a. It promotes tight coupling between services.
   b. It leads to centralized data management.

c. It enables modular development and scaling.

d. It eliminates the need for APIs.

3. **What does decentralize data management in microservices architecture refer to?**

   a. All services sharing a single database.

   b. Each service managing its own data store.

   c. Centralized control over data consistency.

   d. Data managed by a single monolithic service.

4. **Which pattern helps prevent cascading failures by isolating faulty services?**

   a. Retry pattern

   b. Circuit Breaker pattern

   c. Pub/Sub pattern

   d. Monolithic pattern

5. **What is the primary benefit of CI/CD in microservices development?**

   a. Slower release cycles

   b. Manual deployment process

   c. Automated testing and rapid deployment

   d. Lack of integration testing

6. **In microservices architecture, what does decentralized governance mean?**

   a. All services are governed by a central authority.

   b. Each service has its own governance policies.

   c. Governance is handled only by the development team.

   d. Governance is irrelevant in microservices.

7. **Which architecture style acts as a single-entry point for client requests, aggregating data from multiple microservices?**

   a. EDA

   b. Service Mesh Architecture

   c. Gateway Aggregation Architecture

   d. Sidecar Pattern

8. **What is the primary characteristic of the EDA in microservices?**

   a. Services communicate synchronously using REST APIs.

   b. Services communicate asynchronously via events.

    c. Services share a common monolithic database.

    d. Services only communicate through direct function calls.

9. **How does the Gateway Aggregation Architecture improve client experiences?**

    a. It increases latency by aggregating data.

    b. It reduces scalability of services.

    c. It reduces the need for APIs.

    d. It provides a unified entry point for clients to retrieve data.

10. **What is a key benefit of adopting service autonomy in microservices design?**

    a. Tight coupling between services

    b. Increased inter-service dependencies

    c. Simplified communication patterns

    d. Reduced complexity and improved scalability

Answer key

1	b
2	c
3	b
4	b
5	c
6	b
7	c
8	b
9	d
10	d

Join our book's Discord space

Join the book's Discord Workspace for Latest updates, Offers, Tech happenings around the world, New Release and Sessions with the Authors:

https://discord.bpbonline.com

CHAPTER 3
Fundamentals of Machine Learning

Introduction

In this chapter, we will explore the fundamental concepts that form the backbone of **Machine Learning (ML)**. At its core, ML is a field of **Artificial Intelligence (AI)** that focuses on building systems that can learn from and make decisions based on data. Rather than being explicitly programmed to perform a task, these systems are trained using large amounts of data and algorithms that give them the ability to learn how to perform the task. From recommendation systems to self-driving cars, ML is behind many technological conveniences we enjoy today.

Structure

The chapter covers the following topics:

- Machine Learning concepts and algorithms
- Data preprocessing and feature engineering for ML
- Model training, evaluation, and deployment

Objectives

The primary objective of this chapter is to provide readers with a comprehensive understanding of the core concepts, methodologies, and principles underlying ML. By delving into the foundational aspects of ML, the chapter aims to equip learners with the necessary knowledge and tools to approach and solve real-world problems using machine learning techniques effectively.

Machine Learning concepts and algorithms

ML is a subfield of AI that focuses on developing algorithms that enable computers to learn from and make decisions based on data. Rather than being explicitly programmed to perform a certain task, these systems are trained using large amounts of data and algorithms that give them the ability to learn how to perform the task.

Here are the key components of the definition:

- **Learning from data:** At the core of ML is the idea that we can build algorithms that learn from data. Rather than being explicitly programmed to solve a problem, a ML system is given data and works to generalize and make decisions based on that data.

- **Improving with experience:** A key aspect of ML is that these algorithms can improve performance as they are exposed to more data. This is often referred to as *training* the model. As the model receives more data, it can learn more nuanced decision boundaries, which in turn improves its ability to make accurate predictions or decisions.

- **Generalization:** The goal of a ML model is to generalize well from its training data to new, unseen data. This is different from memorization; we want the model to make accurate predictions or decisions in situations it has never seen before based on patterns it learned during training.

Types of Machine Learning

ML can largely be categorized into several types based on the learning style into the categories of supervised learning and unsupervised learning. Each of these types has its unique approach and use-cases, helping in designing models that learn and make decisions from data. In the following sections, we will delve deeper into the mechanisms and applications of supervised and unsupervised learning.

Supervised learning

Supervised learning is a ML paradigm where the model is trained on labeled data. The training data consists of input-output pairs; each training example is paired with an output label, which the model uses to learn the underlying patterns. The primary goal is to learn a mapping from inputs to outputs and make predictions on new, unseen data.

Based on the type of output or prediction task, supervised learning can be broadly categorized into the following types:

- **Classification**

  Classification is a fundamental supervised ML task. It involves predicting discrete class labels based on input data. The primary goal of classification is to determine which category or class a new data instance belongs to a training dataset containing instances where the correct class is known.

  o **Types of classification**

    ▪ **Binary classification:** This involves categorizing data into one of two classes. Example: Email spam detection (spam or not spam), Medical diagnosis (disease or no disease).

    ▪ **Multiclass classification (or multinomial classification):** This involves categorizing data into more than two classes. For example, digit recognition (0 through 9), or animal classification (dog, cat, bird, etc.).

  o **Common classification algorithms**

    ▪ **Logistic regression:** Despite its name, logistic regression is used for binary classification problems. It predicts the probability that an instance belongs to a particular class.

    ▪ **Decision trees:** Graphical models that make decisions based on asking a series of questions.

    ▪ **Random forest:** An ensemble method that creates a *forest* of decision trees and outputs the mode of the classes (classification) of individual trees.

    ▪ **Support Vector Machines (SVM):** Aims to find a hyperplane that best separates the classes in the input feature space.

    ▪ **Naive Bayes:** Based on the Bayes' theorem, particularly suitable for high-dimensional datasets.

    ▪ **k-Nearest Neighbors (k-NN):** Classifies an instance based on how its neighbors are classified.

- **Regression**

  Regression is a type of supervised learning where the goal is to predict a continuous output variable based on one or more input variables. Unlike classification, where the output is a category, regression predicts a continuous value. In regression, the output variable (or label) is a continuous value, such as weight, price, or temperature.

o **Common regression algorithms**

- **Linear regression:** It assumes a linear relationship between the input features and the output. It estimates real values (cost of houses, number of calls, total sales, etc.) based on one or multiple independent variables.

- **Polynomial regression:** This is a type of regression analysis in which the relationship between the independent variable x and the dependent variable y is modeled as *nth* degree polynomial.

- **Ridge (L2 Regularization) and Lasso Regression (L1 Regularization):** Techniques that add regularization to the linear regression. They can prevent overfitting by adding penalty terms for feature coefficients. Similar to Ridge, but can lead to zero coefficients (for example, feature selection).

o **Examples**

- House price prediction based on features like size, location, etc.

- Stock price prediction.

- Predicting a student's future test score based on past performance.

Unsupervised learning

Unsupervised learning is an ML paradigm where the model is trained on unlabeled data. Unlike supervised learning, there are no clear-cut output values in the training data, and the algorithm is tasked with discovering the underlying structure in the data, such as groups or clusters.

Common algorithms include:

- **K-Means clustering:** Groups data into 'K' number of clusters.

- **Hierarchical clustering:** Builds a tree of nested clusters by successively merging or splitting groups.

- **Principal Component Analysis (PCA):** A technique for reducing the dimensionality of data.

- **Gaussian Mixture Models (GMM):** Uses a mixture of Gaussian distributions to model data.

- **Density-Based Spatial Clustering of Applications with Noise (DBSCAN):** Clusters data based on density.

- **t-Distributed Stochastic Neighbor Embedding (t-SNE):** A technique for dimensionality reduction that is particularly well suited for visualizing high-dimensional datasets.

Examples:

- **Customer segmentation**
    - o **Input:** Features of customers, such as age, income, purchase history, etc.
    - o **Output:** Groups or clusters of customers with similar behavior or characteristics.
    - o **Explanation:** The algorithm analyzes the customer data and identifies clusters of customers with similar purchasing behaviors, which can help in targeted marketing.

- **Anomaly detection in network security**
    - o **Input:** Network activity data.
    - o **Output:** Identification of unusual patterns that do not conform to expected behavior (anomalies).
    - o **Explanation:** The algorithm learns the normal behavior from the network activity data and identifies abnormal patterns that could indicate a cyber-attack or system malfunction.

- **Topic modeling in text data**
    - o **Input:** Large collections of text documents.
    - o **Output:** A set of topics that summarize the documents.
    - o **Explanation:** The algorithm identifies common themes or topics in a large set of documents. This is often used for organizing, understanding and summarizing large datasets of textual information.

Reinforcement Learning

Reinforcement Learning (RL) is a ML paradigm where an agent learns how to behave in an environment by performing actions and observing the rewards of those actions. The agent learns to achieve a goal or to maximize some notion of cumulative reward through trial and error. In RL, the learner is not told which actions to take but is given a reward or penalty based on the actions it takes.

Common algorithms include:

- **Q-Learning:** An off-policy algorithm that learns the value of actions in each state and uses this to determine the policy.
- **Deep Q Networks (DQN):** Combines Q-Learning with deep neural networks.
- **Policy gradients:** Directly optimizes the policy function, rather than the value function.
- **Actor-Critic Algorithms:** Combines the benefits of both policy and value function approaches.

- **Proximal Policy Optimization (PPO):** A type of Policy Gradient method that has become a standard baseline for various tasks.
- **Temporal Difference (TD) Learning:** A hybrid of *Monte Carlo* ideas and **dynamic programming (DP)** ideas.

Examples:
- **Game playing**
  - o **Input:** Current state of the game (for example, position of all pieces in chess).
  - o **Output:** The next move the agent should make.
  - o **Explanation:** In these environments, the RL agent learns the optimal strategy for playing a game. For example, in chess, the agent observes the board (state), makes a move (action), and receives a reward when the move is beneficial (for example, capturing an opponent's piece) and a penalty when the move is detrimental (for example, losing a piece). The goal is to learn a policy that will result in winning the game.

- **Robot vacuum cleaner**
  - o **Input:** Sensor data from the robot (for example, camera images, lidar data).
  - o **Output:** The next action the robot should take (for example, move forward, turn left).
  - o **Explanation:** The RL agent controls the cleaner's actions to navigate around a room, avoid obstacles, and efficiently clean the floor. The state could include sensor readings that describe the cleaner's surroundings, the action is a movement command (for example, move forward, turn), and the reward could be positive when the cleaner picks up dirt, and negative when it bumps into a wall or travels over an area it has already cleaned.

Key concepts of Machine Learning

In ML, several key concepts form the foundation for creating, training, and evaluating models. These concepts, including features and labels, training and testing data, loss functions, and hyperparameters, play crucial roles in developing effective ML models. In the ensuing discussion, we will explore these fundamental concepts in more detail to understand their significance in the ML pipeline.

Features and labels

In ML, **features** and **labels** are two fundamental concepts essential to train a model. Here is a clear explanation of both:

- **Features**

  Features, also known as **attributes** or **input variables**, represent the independent variables in the model. They are the data attributes used for training the ML models. Models use features to make a prediction or classification. In a dataset, features are typically the columns that are input to the model (with the exception of the target column, which is the label).

  Example:

  Consider a dataset where the goal is to predict the price of houses. The features in this scenario might include:

  o Size of the house in square feet

  o Number of bedrooms

  o Number of bathrooms

  o Location (for example, urban, suburban, rural)

  o Age of the house

  These are the variables that the model uses to learn patterns and make a prediction. They are often denoted as X in mathematical formulations.

- **Labels**

  Labels, also known as **targets** or **output variables**, represent the dependent variable that we are trying to predict or classify. In supervised learning, each instance in the dataset is associated with a label. The ML model aims to predict the label of an instance based on its features. In a dataset, the label is typically one column and is what we are aiming to predict or classify.

  Example: Continuing with the house price prediction scenario, the label would be the actual price at which the house was sold.

  This is the variable we are trying to predict based on the features of the data. Labels are often denoted as y in mathematical formulations.

  Importance in ML:

  o In a supervised learning problem, the algorithm learns to predict the labels from the features. During the training phase, the model learns the relationship between the features and the labels using a dataset where the labels are known. This dataset is often referred to as the training dataset. Once the model has been trained, it can be used to predict the labels of new, unseen data based on their features.

  o In an unsupervised learning problem, there are no labels. The algorithm tries to learn patterns directly from the features. For example, clustering is an unsupervised learning technique where the algorithm groups data based on the features but does not have any labels to guide this grouping.

o   In reinforcement learning, the concept of features and labels is a bit different. Instead of labels, we have rewards that the algorithm tries to maximize by choosing certain actions in different states.

Knowing how to select and preprocess features properly, and understanding the nature of your labels is a fundamental skill in ML, as it significantly impacts the performance of the model.

Training and testing data

In ML, a common practice is to split the available dataset into training and testing subsets. This allows us to train a model on one subset of the data and then test it on a different, unseen subset. This is a crucial step because it helps in evaluating how well the trained model will generalize to new, unseen data. Here is an explanation of both:

- **Training data**

  The training data is the portion of the dataset used to train the ML model. The model learns to make predictions or decisions based on this data. The training data includes the features (independent variables) and the corresponding labels (dependent variables). The model learns the relationship between the features and the labels during the training process.

  Example: In a scenario where we want to predict the price of houses based on various features like size, location, and number of bedrooms, the model will use the training data to learn how these features relate to the actual prices at which houses were sold.

- **Testing data**

  The testing data is the portion of the dataset that the model has not seen during its training phase and is used to evaluate the model. It is a separate set that we hold back from our training data. The testing data includes the features but we also hold the labels for this data, which allows us to compare the model's predictions with the actual truth and hence evaluate how well the model is performing.

  Example: Continuing with the house price prediction scenario, after the model is trained on the training data, we use the testing data (for which we know the actual sale prices, but the model does not) to see how closely the model's predicted house prices align with the actual prices.

  Importance of splitting data:

  o   **Avoiding overfitting:** One of the main reasons for splitting data into training and testing sets is to avoid overfitting. Overfitting occurs when a model is trained too well on the training data but performs poorly on unseen data because it has learned the noise in the training data rather than the actual relationships between variables.

o **Generalization:** We use a separate testing dataset to evaluate how well our model will generalize to new, unseen data. A model that performs well on its training data may not necessarily perform well on new data.

o **Model evaluation:** Testing data allows us to evaluate our model rigorously. Common evaluation metrics include accuracy, precision, recall, F1 score for classification problems, and **Mean Absolute Error (MAE)**, **Mean Squared Error (MSE)**, and R-squared for regression problems.

Common split ratios:

o A common practice is to split the data into 70/30, 80/20, or 75/25 (training/testing) ratios.

o In many cases, a third set, called a validation set, is also created, and the data might be split into 70/15/15 or 60/20/20 (training/validation/testing) ratios. The validation set is used to tune hyperparameters and make decisions about the model architecture without touching the test set.

o The process of splitting the dataset into training and testing sets is fundamental in ML and is supported by various libraries like Scikit-Learn in Python with functions like `train_test_split`.

Remember that, in practice, the data should be split randomly but in a stratified manner (especially for classification problems) to ensure that the training and testing datasets have a similar distribution of classes.

Loss functions

Loss functions, also known as **cost functions** or **objective functions**, measure how well a model's predictions match the true values. In ML, we optimize our model by minimizing the value of the loss function. The choice of loss function depends on the nature of the problem, for example, whether it is a regression or classification task.

Here are some common loss functions used in ML:

• **MSE / Quadratic Loss / L2 Loss**

MSE is one of the most commonly used loss functions for regression problems in ML. Let us delve into its definition, characteristics, and some insights.

Given N observed data pairs $(x_1, y_1), (x_2, y_2) \ldots (x_N, y_N)$ and a model function f which predicts $\hat{y}_i$ for input x_i, the MSE is given by:

$$MSE = \left(\frac{1}{N}\right) \sum_{i=1}^{N} \left(y_i - \hat{y}_i\right)^2$$

where:

o y_i is the actual value of the i-th observation.

o $\hat{y}_i$ is the predicted value for the i-th observation.

Characteristics:

o **Positive definiteness:** The MSE is always non-negative, i.e., MSE≥0. An MSE of 0 indicates a perfect fit to the data, meaning the model's predictions are exactly accurate. This rarely happens in real-world applications.

o **Sensitivity to outliers:** Due to the squared term, the MSE penalizes large errors more severely than small ones. As a result, it is especially sensitive to outliers. This could be an advantage if large errors are genuinely undesirable, but a disadvantage if the presence of outliers is not indicative of a poor model.

o **Units:** The MSE has units that are the square of the original target variable, which can sometimes be hard to interpret.

o **Differentiability:** The MSE is differentiable, which is a key reason why it is favored in optimization algorithms, such as gradient descent. The gradient gives a direction and rate of change of the error, which helps in adjusting model parameters to minimize the MSE.

• **MAE / L1 Loss**

MAE is another widely used loss function, especially in regression problems. Here is an exploration of its definition, characteristics, and insights.

Given N observed data pairs (x_1, y_1), (x_2, y_2) ... (x_N, y_N) and a model function f which predicts $\hat{y}_i$ for input x_i, the MSE is given by:

$$MAE = \left(\frac{1}{N}\right) \sum_{i=1}^{N} |y_i - \hat{y}_i|$$

where:

o y_i is the actual value of the i-th observation.

o $\hat{y}_i$ is the predicted value for the i-th observation.

Characteristics:

o **Non-negativity:** MAE is always non-negative, i.e., MAE≥0. An MAE of 0 indicates that the model has perfect accuracy.

o **Less sensitive to outliers**: Unlike MSE, MAE treats all errors equally. This means it is not particularly sensitive to outliers. Large errors are not disproportionately penalized, making MAE more robust in the presence of outliers.

o **Units:** The units of MAE are the same as the units of the target variable, which can make it more interpretable than the squared units of MSE.

o **Non-differentiability at zero:** While MAE is mostly differentiable, it is not differentiable at the point of zero error (because of the absolute value function). However, in practice, this rarely causes problems for optimization algorithms.

Data preprocessing and feature engineering

Data preprocessing and feature engineering are foundational steps in the ML pipeline. They ensure that data fed into ML models is clean, relevant, and structured in a way that enhances the performance of models.

Data preprocessing involves preparing and cleaning raw data to bring it into a suitable format or structure for analysis. Proper preprocessing can significantly boost a model's performance, while neglecting this step can lead to inaccurate and unreliable models.

Feature engineering is the process of selecting, modifying, or creating new features from raw data to improve the performance of ML models. It requires domain knowledge, creativity, and a deep understanding of the ML algorithms used. This step often plays a decisive role in the success of a ML project, as the quality and relevance of features largely dictate the predictive power of the model. The main steps are covered in the next section.

Handling missing data

Handling missing data is a crucial step in the data preprocessing phase of ML. Data can have missing values due to various reasons. Missing data can distort predictions and reduce the statistical power of a model. Strategies to deal with them include:

Before handling missing values, it is essential to understand the nature of the missingness:

- **Missing Completely at Random (MCAR):** The missingness of data is entirely random and not related to any other observed or unobserved data. It is as if someone randomly deleted some of the data. Data that is MCAR does not introduce bias in the analysis, but it may reduce the power of the analysis (that is, larger confidence intervals or reduced significance levels) because there is less data.

- **Missing at Random (MAR):** The probability of data being missing is not random, but it can be predicted based on other observed data. For example, if men are more likely to tell their age than women, but this propensity is the same for all ages among men and women, then age is MAR. Handling MAR data can be a bit tricky since the missingness is systematic. Simple deletion can introduce bias.

- **Missing Not at Random (MNAR):** Data is MNAR when the absence is related to the value of the variable that is missing. A classic example is that people with high incomes might be less likely to disclose their earnings in a survey. The missingness of the income is related to the value of income itself. MNAR can introduce serious bias in the analysis if not handled properly since the missingness is related to the unobserved missing value.

Deletion

Deletion is one of the simplest methods to handle missing data. It involves removing the data points with missing values from the dataset. While this method is straightforward, it is not always the best option as it can introduce bias and reduce the power of the analysis. The primary techniques under deletion include:

- **Listwise deletion (complete case analysis):** This method removes all data for an observation (that is, a row) if any single value is missing. It is simple and does not introduce any artificial bias due to imputation. It can lead to a significant reduction in sample size, especially if the data has missing values across multiple variables. This can reduce statistical power and potentially introduce bias if the missingness is not completely at random (MCAR).

- **Pairwise deletion:** Instead of removing an entire observation, you only exclude the specific missing value in the analysis. It maximizes the available data, especially helpful when dealing with correlation or covariance calculations. However, it can lead to different results for different analyses because different subsets of the data are used for different pairs of variables.

- **Dropping variables:** If a specific variable (that is, a column) has a high percentage of missing values, it might be more practical to remove that variable entirely from the analysis. It simplifies the dataset and analysis. However, important information or patterns from that variable are lost. This method is not advisable unless a variable has an exceedingly high proportion of missing values, and it is deemed not critical to the analysis or prediction task.

When to use deletion:
- When the amount of missing data is small.
- When the missing data is MCAR, there is no specific pattern to the missing data.

When not to use deletion:
- When missing data is not MCAR, deletion can introduce bias. For example, the missingness is related to the outcome of interest.
- When the dataset is small, removing observations can further reduce its size, impacting the statistical power of subsequent analyses.

Mean/median/mode imputation

Mean/median/mode imputation is a statistical method that replaces missing values in a dataset. The approach is simple and involves filling in the missing value of a particular feature with the mean, median, or mode of the non-missing values. Let us delve into the details:

- **Mean imputation**
  - o Replace the missing values with the mean (average) of the non-missing values of that feature.
  - o Suitable for continuous data without many outliers.
  - o Drawback: Reduces variance in the dataset, and if the missingness is not at random, it can introduce bias.

- **Median imputation**
  - o Replace the missing values with the median (middle value when sorted in order) of the non-missing values of that feature.
  - o Suitable for continuous data, especially when there are outliers. The median is less sensitive to extreme values than the mean.
  - o Drawback: Like mean imputation, it can introduce bias if the missingness is systematic.

- **Mode imputation**
  - o Replace the missing values with the mode (most frequent value) of the non-missing values of that feature.
  - o Suitable for categorical data.
  - o Drawback: Can introduce bias and over-represent a particular category, especially if the proportion of missing values is high.

When to use mean/median/mode imputation:
- When the data is MCAR.
- As an initial approach to get a quick sense of the dataset's behavior with imputed values.
- When the percentage of missing data for a feature is low.

When not to use:
- When the data has a recognizable pattern of missingness (not MCAR).
- When more sophisticated imputation methods are feasible and can preserve the dataset's intrinsic correlations and structures.

Model-based imputation

Model-based imputation involves using statistical models to estimate and impute missing values based on observed (non-missing) data. This approach aims to use the relationships present in the data to predict and fill in missing values accurately. Let us delve deeper into this approach:

- **Linear regression imputation:** Involves using variables with complete cases to predict the missing values in another variable. For example, if we are trying to predict missing values in a feature Y using feature X, we would fit a regression line using X's observed values to predict Y's observed values. This line can then predict Y's missing values using X's corresponding values.

- **K-NN imputation:** The missing values of an instance (row) are imputed using the values of 'k' other instances that are most similar to that instance. Similarity is typically determined using a distance metric, such as Euclidean distance. It can be computationally expensive for large datasets.

- **Decision trees and random forests:** Trees can predict and impute missing values. A decision tree is trained on data with observed values and then used to predict missing values. Random forests, an ensemble method, can be even more effective as they average the results of multiple decision trees, thereby increasing accuracy and robustness.

- **Deep learning and neural networks:** More complex structures like neural networks can be trained on the dataset to predict missing values. Given the flexibility and capacity of neural networks, they can capture intricate patterns in the data. However, they require substantial data and computational resources.

The advantages of model-based imputation are:

- Can be more accurate than simple imputations like mean, median, or mode because they consider patterns and relationships in the data.
- Can capture nonlinear relationships.

The disadvantages of model-based imputation are:

- More computationally intensive.
- The risk of overfitting, especially if the model is too complex for the amount of data.
- Might be biased if the model is not chosen or trained appropriately.

Model-based imputation is used when:

- There is a lot of missing data.
- There are clear patterns and relationships in the data that simpler imputation methods might miss.
- The missingness is related to other variables in the dataset (not MCAR).

Model-based imputation is not used:

- For small datasets where the computational burden or risk of overfitting is high.
- When the relationships in the data are not well-understood, leading to potential model bias.

Before relying on model-based imputation, it is crucial to validate the imputation model using techniques like cross-validation. It ensures that the model generalizes well and provides reliable imputations.

Data transformation

Data transformation is a critical step in preprocessing, especially for algorithms that are sensitive to feature scales or require assumptions about the distribution of the data. By transforming features, we can ensure that the algorithm performs optimally.

Here are the details on two of the most commonly used data transformations: Normalization and Standardization, which are as follows:

- **Normalization**

    Normalization typically means adjusting values measured on different scales to a common scale. It is especially important for algorithms that rely on distance measures, like k-NN or Gradient Descent optimization in neural networks.

    Method:

    $$X^{'} = \frac{X - X_{min}}{X_{max} - X_{min}}$$

    Where:

    o X' is the normalized value

    o X is the original value

    o X_{min} is the minimum value of the feature

    o X_{max} is the maximum value of the feature

    After normalization, the data will have values between 0 and 1.

    Normalization is used when you want the data to be bounded within a specific range, typically [0,1].

- **Standardization**

    Standardization (or z-score normalization) scales the values while considering standard deviation. If the standard deviation of features is different, their range also would differ from each other. This might result in an imbalance in terms of the feature's influence on the response variable. Standardization centers the feature on zero with a standard deviation of 1, resulting in unit variance.

Method:

$$Z = \frac{X - \mu}{\sigma}$$

Where:

o Z is the standardized value

o X is the original value

o μ is the mean of the feature

o σ is the standard deviation of the feature

After standardization, the data will have a mean of 0 and a standard deviation of 1.

Most algorithms, like regression, SVM, and neural networks, benefit from standardization because it helps them converge (to find the best solution) faster.

Data encoding

In ML, data encoding is a crucial step in data preprocessing that involves converting categorical data into a format that can be fed into ML algorithms. Two common methods for data encoding are One-Hot Encoding and Label Encoding:

*   **One-Hot Encoding**

    In ML, One-Hot Encoding is a commonly used method for converting categorical data into a format that can be easily utilized by ML algorithms. The technique transforms each unique category in a feature column into a new, individual feature column containing binary values (0 or 1).

    For a feature column with n unique categories, One-Hot Encoding will generate n new binary columns. Each of these columns corresponds to a single unique category from the original column. A row in these new columns will contain a 1 if the original row contained that category, and 0 otherwise.

    Example: Suppose you have a variable Color with three categories: Red, Green, and Blue. One-hot encoding will represent this as:

    In this encoded matrix:

    o   The category Red is represented by the array [1, 0, 0]

    o   The category Green is represented by the array [0, 1, 0]

    o   The category Blue is represented by the array [0, 0, 1]

*   **Label Encoding**

    Label Encoding is a technique in ML for converting categorical variables into numerical form so that they can be provided as input to ML algorithms. Unlike One-Hot Encoding, which expands the feature space, Label Encoding converts each unique category into a unique integer, thus keeping the feature space the same size as the original column.

For a feature column with n unique categories, Label Encoding will assign a unique integer between 0 and n-1 to each category. These integers are usually assigned in the order in which the categories appear, though it is possible to customize the numbering.

Example: Consider a dataset with a Color column containing three colors: Red, Green, and Blue. Here, Red is encoded as 0, Green as 1, and Blue as 2.

Feature extraction

Feature extraction is a crucial part of the ML pipeline, involving the transformation or projection of data into a space where the ML algorithm can more easily identify patterns, correlations, or underlying structures. It aims to reduce the dimensionality of the data and to simplify the representation, preserving the most important aspects of the data.

The types of feature extraction are:

- **Principal Component Analysis (PCA):** A statistical technique to convert correlated features into a set of linearly uncorrelated features called principal components.
- **Linear Discriminant Analysis (LDA):** Used to find a combination of features that best separates different classes.
- **Autoencoders:** Neural networks used for unsupervised feature extraction.
- **t-Distributed Stochastic Neighbor Embedding (t-SNE):** A non-linear dimensionality reduction technique.
- **Word Embeddings (Word2Vec, GloVe, etc.):** Common in NLP, these models map words into a dense vector space based on their context.
- **Fourier and Wavelet Transforms:** Common in signal processing, these methods transform signals from the time domain into the frequency domain.
- **Histogram of Oriented Gradients (HOG), Scale-Invariant Feature Transform (SIFT)**, etc. These are specific to image processing and computer vision.

The advantages of feature extraction are:

- **Dimensionality reduction:** Less computationally intensive.
- **Overfitting:** Reduces the risk of overfitting by removing redundant features.
- **Interpretability:** Easier to understand and visualize the data.

The disadvantages of feature extraction are:

- **Information loss:** Risk of losing important information.
- **Computational complexity:** Some methods are computationally intensive.

- **Interpreting transformations:** The new features after extraction may not be directly interpretable.

Feature selection

Feature selection is the process of selecting a subset of important features (variables, predictors) from the original set of features, with the objective of simplifying the model, reducing computation time, and improving generalization performance. Unlike feature extraction, feature selection aims to retain the original semantics of the variables.

Types of feature selection methods are:

- **Filter methods**
  - o **Variance threshold:** Remove features with low variance.
  - o **Chi-squared test:** Statistical test for the independence of two variables.
  - o **Correlation coefficient:** Remove features that are highly correlated.

- **Wrapper methods**
  - o **Recursive Feature Elimination (RFE):** Fits a model and removes the weakest feature(s) until the specified number of features is reached.
  - o **Forward selection:** Starts with no features and adds one feature at a time until no improvement can be made.
  - o **Backward elimination:** Starts with all features and removes one feature at a time until no improvement can be made.

- **Embedded methods**
  - o **Lasso regression:** Uses L1 regularization to eliminate features by making their coefficients zero.
  - o **Random forests:** Utilizes feature importance scores.
  - o **Elastic net:** A combination of L1 and L2 regularization.

The advantages of feature selection methods are:

- **Reduced overfitting:** Fewer redundant features mean less opportunity to make decisions based on noise.
- **Improved accuracy:** Less misleading data results in a more accurate model.
- **Reduced training time:** Fewer data points reduce algorithm complexity and algorithms train faster.

The disadvantages of feature selection methods are:

- **Loss of information:** You may lose some useful signals by dropping features.
- **Dependence on domain knowledge:** Effective feature selection is often domain-

specific.

Model training, evaluation, and deployment

Model training and evaluation are two of the most fundamental steps in the machine learning pipeline. They determine how the model learns from data and how well it performs. Let us explore each step-in detail.

Model training

Model training is the process where a machine learning algorithm learns patterns from a provided dataset. It involves inputting data into an algorithm, which then adjusts its weights and biases based on the data to make predictions or classify instances.

The steps for model training are as follows:

1. **Initialization:** Depending on the algorithm, certain parameters are initialized. For example, neural networks initialize weights often with small random values.

2. **Learning process:** The data is fed into the model iteratively. The model makes predictions, and errors are calculated.

3. **Error minimization:** Based on the error, the model adjusts its internal parameters (like weights in neural networks or split criteria in decision trees). This can be done via techniques like gradient descent.

4. **Iteration:** The process continues until a certain stopping criterion is met (like a maximum number of iterations or the error rate stops improving).

Fitting models

Fitting models, also known as **model training,** is the process of adjusting the internal parameters of a ML model based on a dataset. The goal is to minimize the difference between the model's predictions and the actual data points. This difference is quantified by a loss function.

The steps for fitting models are as follows:

1. **Data preparation:** Before training, the dataset is generally divided into at least two subsets: a training set and a testing set. You might also have a validation set.

2. **Initialization:** All model parameters (weights in neural networks, coefficients in linear regression, etc.) are initialized, often randomly.

3. **Choose a Loss Function:** This function quantifies how well the model's predictions match the true data.

4. **Forward propagation:** The model makes initial predictions on the training data with the initial random parameters.

5. **Calculate loss:** The loss function is computed using the model's predictions and the actual values in the training set.

6. **Backward propagation:** Algorithms like gradient descent adjust the model parameters to minimize the loss.

7. **Iterate:** Steps 4-6 are repeated until the loss converges to a minimum value.

8. **Evaluate:** Once trained, the model's performance is evaluated using the testing set.

9. **Hyperparameter tuning:** The process may involve tuning hyperparameters, such as learning rate in gradient descent, regularization parameters, etc.

10. **Model selection:** If you are working with multiple models, you will choose the one with the best performance metrics on the validation/test sets.

Types of model fitting are:

- **Batch Gradient Descent:** Uses all training samples in each iteration.
- **Stochastic Gradient Descent (SGD):** Uses one random training sample in each iteration.
- **Mini-batch Gradient Descent:** Uses a small random subset of training samples in each iteration.

Tools for model fitting:

Python Libraries: Scikit-Learn, TensorFlow, PyTorch, etc.

Underfitting and overfitting

Underfitting and overfitting are common challenges in ML related to how well our model generalizes to new, unseen data based on its performance with the training data.

- **Underfitting:** Underfitting occurs when a model is too simple to capture the underlying structure of the data. It means the model performs poorly on the training data and will also perform poorly on new, unseen data.

  o **Characteristics of underfitting**
    - The model has high training error.
    - The model also has high test/validation errors.
    - The model does not capture the underlying trend of the data.

  o **Causes**
    - Overly simplistic model (for example, trying to fit non-linear data with a linear model).
    - Not enough features.
    - Too much regularization (for algorithms that support it).

o **Example:** If you were trying to predict the trajectory of a thrown ball and you modeled its path as a straight line, you would be underfitting because the real path (a parabola due to gravity) is more complex than your model.

- **Overfitting:** Overfitting occurs when a model is so complex that it starts to capture the noise in the training data rather than the underlying distribution. It means the model will perform very well on the training data but poorly on new, unseen data.

  o **Characteristics of overfitting**

    ▪ The model has low training error.

    ▪ The model has high test/validation errors.

    ▪ The model is tailored to the training data and captures specific quirks.

  o **Causes**

    ▪ Excessively complex model (for example, high-degree polynomial fit for slightly curved data).

    ▪ Not enough training data relative to the number of features.

    ▪ Insufficient regularization.

  o **Example:** If you were trying to fit a curve to a set of data points derived from a quadratic function, but you use a 10th-degree polynomial, the model might fit the training data points perfectly but would likely predict poorly on new data.

Bias and variance

In ML, bias and variance are crucial concepts that form the foundation of model development, dictating the trade-off between the model's accuracy and its ability to generalize. High bias can lead to underfitting, where the model is too simple to capture the underlying patterns in the data. In contrast, high variance can result in overfitting, where the model is excessively tailored to the training data, affecting its performance on new, unseen data. The understanding of bias and variance is pivotal as it guides the selection and tuning of models to achieve optimal performance:

- **Bias:** Bias refers to the error introduced by approximating a real-world problem (which may be complex) by a too-simple model. It is the difference between the average prediction of our model and the correct value.

  o **High bias:** This means the model is too simple (oversimplified) and cannot capture the underlying patterns of the data, leading to systematic and high errors in training and new data (test data).

  o **Examples:** Linear regression might exhibit high bias on non-linear data.

- **Variance:** Variance measures the variability of model prediction for different training sets. It quantifies how much the model's predictions would change if we trained it on a different training dataset.

- o **High variance:** The model is overly flexible and fits the noise in the training data, leading to very different (and potentially wild) predictions for slight changes in training data.

- o **Examples:** High-degree polynomial regression or deep neural networks without regularization might exhibit high variance.

- **Trade-off:** There is a trade-off between bias and variance. Simplifying a model might increase its bias but decrease its variance. Conversely, making a model more complex might decrease its bias but increase its variance.

The optimal model complexity will result in a balanced trade-off leading to minimal generalization error.

- **Regularization:** Regularization is a technique used in ML and statistics to prevent overfitting. Overfitting occurs when a model learns the noise in the training data, leading to poor generalization to new, unseen data. Regularization adds a penalty term to the loss function to constrain the complexity of the model.

Types of regularization:

- o L1 Regularization (Lasso)

  - ▪ Adds the sum of the absolute values of the coefficients as a penalty term to the loss function.

  - ▪ *Loss* = *OriginalLoss* + $\lambda\Sigma|\omega_i|$

  - ▪ Makes some of the coefficients zero, effectively eliminating irrelevant features.

- o L2 Regularization (Ridge)

  - ▪ Adds the sum of the squared values of the coefficients as penalty term to the loss function.

  - ▪ *Loss* = *OriginalLoss* + $\lambda\Sigma|\omega_i^2|$

  - ▪ Reduces but doesn't eliminate coefficients.

Advantages:

- o **Prevents overfitting:** By adding a penalty, regularization ensures that the model generalizes well on unseen data.

- o **Feature selection:** L1 regularization can make some feature coefficients zero, effectively selecting more important features.

Disadvantages:

- o **Underfitting:** If the regularization strength is set too high, the model may become too simple and underfit the data.

- o **Computationally intensive:** Regularization may increase the computational complexity, especially for large datasets.

Model evaluation

Model evaluation is crucial in ML to determine the performance and generalization ability of a model. Depending on the type of ML problem (classification, regression, clustering, etc.), different metrics are used. Here is a breakdown of some of the most commonly used evaluation metrics for different types of tasks.

Confusion Matrix

A Confusion Matrix is a fundamental tool in classification tasks within ML. It is a table used to evaluate the performance of an algorithm, specifically a classifier, by providing a comprehensive breakdown of the true positives, true negatives, false positives, and false negatives.

Components of a Confusion Matrix:

- **True Positives (TP):** The cases in which the model predicted *Yes* (or Positive), and the actual truth was also *Yes* (or Positive).
- **True Negatives (TN):** The cases in which the model predicted *No* (or Negative), and the actual truth was also *No* (or Negative).
- **False Positives (FP):** The cases in which the model predicted *Yes*, but the actual truth was *No*. It is also known as a *Type I error*.
- **False Negatives (FN):** The cases in which the model predicted *No*, but the actual truth was *Yes*. It is also known as a *Type II error*.

Visual Representation: Tables or heatmaps that display the number of TP, TN, FP, and FN, thus allowing for a clearer and immediate understanding of performance of the model. Refer to the following *Table 3.1*:

	Actual Positive	**Actual Negative**
Predicted Positive	True Positive	False Positive
Predicted Negative	False Negative	True Negative

Table 3.1: Visual representation of confusion matrix

Importance of the Confusion Matrix:

- **Precision:** Precision gives the ratio of correctly predicted positive observations to the total predicted positives. It can be represented as:

$$Precision = \frac{TP}{TP+FP}$$

Imagine a music streaming platform that uses a recommendation algorithm to suggest 10 songs daily to a user based on their listening history. If out of those 10 songs, the user likes 7 and dislikes 3, the precision of the recommendation for that day would be 70%.

- **Recall:** Recall, often also termed as *Sensitivity* or *True Positive Rate*, is one of the core metrics used to evaluate the performance of a classification model. It measures the capability of a model to find all the relevant cases within a dataset. It can be represented as:

$$Recall = \frac{TP}{TP+FN}$$

Suppose a user likes 100 songs of a particular genre, say Jazz. Out of these, the system recommends 70 songs to the user, and they like all of them. However, the system missed the other 30 songs the user liked and had to play manually:

TP: 70 (Songs recommended and liked by the user)

FN: 30 (Songs not recommended but liked by the user)

This means the system has a recall of 0.7 or 70% in its music recommendation for this user.

Precision is often used in tandem with recall (sensitivity). While precision focuses on the correctness of positive predictions, recall focuses on the proportion of actual positives that were correctly identified. Recall often comes at the expense of precision. A model that predicts everything as the positive class will have a recall of 1 (perfect recall). However, its precision would be very low, as it would also incorrectly classify many negative instances as positive.

The F1-score is a metric that combines precision and recall into a single number, providing a balance between them.

- **Specificity:** Specificity, often referred to as the *True Negative Rate*, is a performance metric used in binary classification. It quantifies the ability of the classifier to identify negative instances correctly. It can be represented as:

$$Specificity = \frac{TN}{TN+FP}$$

Specificity is crucial when the cost of falsely classifying a negative instance as positive is high. For example:

o **Medical diagnostics:** If a diagnostic test for a disease has low specificity, it might falsely classify healthy individuals as having the disease. This can lead to unnecessary stress, further testing, and possibly unwarranted treatment.

o **Spam email filters:** A spam filter with low specificity might place legitimate emails into the spam folder, causing users to miss important messages.

- **F1 Score:** It is the harmonic mean of precision and recall and provides a more holistic view of the model's performance, especially when the data has imbalanced classes. It can be represented as:

$$F1\ Score = 2 \times \frac{Precision \times Recall}{Precision + Recall}$$

Area Under the Receiver Operating Characteristic Curve

Area Under the Receiver Operating Characteristic Curve (AUC-ROC) is a performance metric used to evaluate the performance of binary classification models. It provides an aggregate measure of a model's performance across all possible classification thresholds. The AUC-ROC is especially useful when the classes in the dataset are imbalanced.

The **ROC** curve is a graphical representation of the true positive rate (sensitivity) versus the false positive rate (1 - specificity) for a binary classifier system as its discrimination threshold is varied.

- **True Positive Rate (TPR):** It is the proportion of actual positives that are correctly identified as such. It can be represented as:

$$TPR = \frac{TP}{TP+FN}$$

- **False Positive Rate (FPR):** It is the proportion of actual negatives that are incorrectly identified as positives:

$$FPR = \frac{FP}{FP+FN}$$

The **AUC** represents the degree or measure of separability, indicating how well the model distinguishes between the two classes:

- An AUC of 1 indicates a perfect classifier.
- An AUC of 0.5 suggests that the model's predictions are no better than random guessing.
- An AUC of 0 indicates a perfectly incorrect classifier (though, in practice, you would simply reverse the predictions to get a perfect classifier).

Root Mean Squared Error

The **Root Mean Squared Error (RMSE)** is a frequently used metric to measure the performance of a regression model. It represents the square root of the second sample moment of the differences between predicted and observed values or the quadratic mean of these differences.

Given N observed values $y_1, y_2, \dots, y_N$ and their corresponding predicted values are $\hat{y}_1, \hat{y}_2, \dots, \hat{y}_N$, the RMSE is calculated as:

$$RMSE = \sqrt{\frac{1}{N}\sum_{i=1}^{N}\left(y_i - \hat{y}_i\right)^2}$$

The interpretation is as follows:

- **Scale-dependent:** The RMSE has the same unit as the data, making it scale-dependent. A model with an RMSE of 10 when predicting house prices in the scale of hundreds of thousands might be excellent, but the same RMSE would be terrible if predicting daily temperature changes.

- **Higher penalty for larger errors:** Since errors are squared before they are averaged, RMSE gives a relatively high weight to large errors. This means that RMSE is most useful when large errors are particularly undesirable.

Normalized Discounted Cumulative Gain

Normalized Discounted Cumulative Gain (NDCG) is a metric commonly used in information retrieval and recommender systems to evaluate the quality of ranking results. It measures the performance of a recommendation system based on the true relevance of recommended items, considering both the relevance of the items recommended and their position in the recommendation list.

NDCG is especially useful in scenarios like search engines and recommendation systems where both the relevance and the order of items are crucial.

The components of NDCG are:

- **Relevance scores:** Each item in the recommendation list is assigned a relevance score (often binary in nature: either relevant or not, but can be multi-scale).

- **Discounted Cumulative Gain (DCG):** It is the sum of the relevance scores, where each score is divided by a logarithmically scaled position:

$$DCG_p = \sum_{i=1}^{p} \frac{rel_i}{(i+1)}$$

where:

o p is the position up to which we are calculating DCG.

o rel_i is the relevance of the item at position .

- **Ideal Discounted Cumulative Gain (IDCG):** It is the DCG of the ideal ranking, that is, when items are perfectly ranked by relevance. IDCG is used for normalization.

- **NDCG:** The normalization of DCG based on IDCG. If the recommendations are perfect, NDCG will be 1:

$$NDCG_p = \frac{DCG_p}{IDCG_p}$$

The interpretation is as follows:

- **Positional weight:** Items being incorrectly ranked higher (e.g., an irrelevant item ranked 1st) are penalized more than items ranked lower. This reflects user behavior, as they're more likely to interact with items at the top of a recommendation list.

- **Normalization:** By dividing DCG by IDCG, the NDCG metric is in the range [0, 1], making it easier to compare between different queries or recommendation lists.

Imagine a recommendation system that suggests five movies to a user. Let's assume binary relevance (0 for irrelevant, 1 for relevant). The system's recommendations, in order, are: 0,1,0,1,1. So, the second, fourth, and fifth movies are relevant.

The DCG for this list, up to position 5 is:

$$DCG_5 = \frac{0}{ln(2)} + \frac{1}{ln(3)} + \frac{0}{ln(4)} + \frac{1}{ln(5)} + \frac{1}{ln(6)}$$

The ideal ranking would be: 1,1,1,0,0

Calculating the IDCG gives:

$$IDCG_5 = \frac{1}{ln(2)} + \frac{1}{ln(3)} + \frac{1}{ln(4)}$$

Finally, $NDCG_5 = \frac{DCG_5}{IDCG_5}$, would give us the normalized metric for this recommendation.

Cross-validation

Cross-validation is a statistical technique used to estimate the performance of a ML model by partitioning the original sample into a training set to train the model, and a test set to evaluate it. This process is repeated multiple times, using different partitions, to obtain a more robust measure of model performance.

Process:

- **Partition the data:** The most common method of cross-validation is k-fold cross-validation. Here, the data is divided into k subsets (or "folds").
- **Model training and evaluation:** For each of the k folds, the model is trained on k−1 of these subsets and tested on the remaining subset. This process is repeated k times, each time using a different subset as the test set while the remaining data is used for training.
- **Average the results:** After iterating through all folds, the results (like accuracy, precision, recall, etc.) are averaged to provide a more generalized model performance estimate.

Benefits:

- **Robustness:** Cross-validation provides a more generalized performance measure compared to a single train-test split, as the model is trained and tested on all data points.
- **Reduced overfitting:** By averaging performance over multiple train-test splits, we mitigate the risk of overfitting to a particular subset of the data.

- **Efficient use of data:** Especially in scenarios with limited data, cross-validation ensures that all data contributes to both training and testing, making full use of available data.

Variants:
- **Stratified k-Fold Cross-Validation:** This variation ensures that each fold retains the same proportion of instances of each class as the complete dataset, which is particularly useful for imbalanced datasets.
- **Leave-One-Out Cross-Validation (LOOCV):** A special case of k-fold cross-validation where k equals the number of data points. Each data point is used once as the test set while the remaining data points form the training set.
- **Time Series Cross-Validation:** Used for time-series data where the order of data points matters. It takes into account the sequence of data to avoid lookahead bias.

Considerations:
- **Computational cost:** As the model is trained multiple times, cross-validation can be computationally expensive, especially for large datasets or complex models.
- **Choice of k:** Common choices of k are 5 or 10, but the optimal number can depend on the dataset size and variance.
- **Randomness:** To avoid biases introduced by the order of the dataset, it's often recommended to shuffle data before applying cross-validation, especially if the data has some sort of order.

Model deployment

Model deployment is the process of integrating a ML model into an existing production environment to make practical business decisions based on data. This phase marks the transition from the model as a mere experiment or prototype to a part of a working application. Deployment ensures that the model can take new input data and output predictions or decisions that are acted upon in a real-world setting.

The choice of deployment strategy often depends on a variety of factors such as speed, scale, and data privacy concerns. Here are the primary strategies for deploying ML models:

- **Cloud-based deployment**

  Advantages:
  - **Scalability:** Cloud platforms can handle large volumes of requests and can automatically allocate resources based on demand.
  - **Managed services:** Many cloud providers offer ML platforms that manage much of the deployment process for you (for example, AWS SageMaker, Google Cloud AI Platform).

o **Cost-effective:** Instead of investing in physical infrastructure, you only pay for the resources you use.

Disadvantages:

o **Latency:** Sending data to the cloud and getting predictions back can introduce latency.

o **Data privacy:** Transferring data to the cloud might be against the policies of certain organizations or regions due to privacy concerns.

- **On-premises deployment**

Advantages:

o **Data security:** Since the model and data reside in-house, it is often seen as more secure.

o **Latency:** Typically offers faster response times compared to cloud-based deployments.

o **Control:** Full control over the environment, from hardware to software.

Disadvantages:

o **Limited scalability:** Expanding capacity might require significant hardware investments.

o **Maintenance:** Need to manually handle updates, security patches, and other infrastructure concerns.

- **Edge deployment**

Advantages:

o **Real-time processing:** Best for situations that require immediate predictions, like autonomous vehicles or certain IoT devices.

o **Data privacy:** Data is processed on the device, so there's no need to transfer it elsewhere.

Disadvantages:

o **Limited computing power:** Edge devices, like mobile phones or IoT devices, might not have the same computing capabilities as servers.

o **Storage limitations:** Edge devices might not be suitable for models that require a large amount of storage.

- **Decision factors**

o **Volume of requests:** If you expect a high volume of requests, cloud-based deployment might be more suitable due to its scalability.

o **Data privacy concerns:** If data privacy is paramount, then on-premises or edge deployment might be more suitable.

o **Latency requirements:** For applications requiring immediate predictions, edge deployment might be the most appropriate.

The choice of deployment strategy depends on the specific requirements of the application, the nature of the data, and the expected volume of requests. Each strategy has its strengths and weaknesses, so it is crucial to choose the one that aligns best with the project's goals.

Conclusion

In this chapter, we have provided a comprehensive overview of the fundamental concepts and methodologies in the field of ML. The aim was to arm you with the requisite knowledge to understand, implement, and assess ML models in practical settings.

By comprehending the topics covered in this chapter, you are now well-equipped to venture deeper into the world of ML, be it in academic research or practical applications.

The next chapters will delve into more advanced topics, but the fundamentals laid out here will always serve as your guide.

Exercise

Having gained a solid understanding of the essentials and key principles of ML, it is time to transition from theory to hands-on practice. In our lab exercise, we will utilize Scikit-Learn to work with a healthcare dataset. We will assess the performance of three different classification methods: SVM, Logistic Regression and Decision Tree by plotting the ROC-AUC curves and contrasting the effectiveness of each algorithm. Let us get started:

1. Let us generate a healthcare dataset using Python with the help of the pandas and numpy libraries:

```
import pandas as pd
import numpy as np


np.random.seed(42)  # Setting the random seed for reproducibility
n_samples = 1000  # Number of samples


# Generating random data for the given parameters
df = pd.DataFrame({
    'pregnancies': np.random.randint(0, 18, n_samples),  # Assuming
    a range from 0 to 17 pregnancies
```

```
    'glucose': np.random.randint(50, 200, n_samples),    # Random
    glucose levels between 50 and 200 mg/dL

    'blood_pressure': np.random.randint(60, 140, n_samples),  #
    Random blood pressure values (in mmHg)

    'skin_thickness': np.random.randint(10, 60, n_samples),  #
    Random skin thickness (in mm)

    'insulin': np.random.randint(10, 300, n_samples),   # Random
    insulin levels

    'bmi': np.random.uniform(15, 45, n_samples),    # Random BMI
    values

    'DPF': np.random.uniform(0.1, 2.0, n_samples),   # Random
    pedigree function values

    'age': np.random.randint(20, 80, n_samples),   # Random ages
    between 20 and 80
})


# Adding the disease_present column based on the conditions specified
df['disease_present'] = np.where(
    (df['glucose'] < 70) |
    (df['glucose'] > 130) |
    (df['blood_pressure'] < 80) |
    (df['blood_pressure'] > 130),
    1, 0)


# Save the dataset to a CSV file
df.to_csv('healthcare_dataset.csv', index=False)
```

This script will generate a dataset with random values for the mentioned parameters and save it as **healthcare_dataset.csv**.

2. We will write a code that performs several steps involved in the ML pipeline, including data loading, preprocessing, model training, and evaluation. Here is an explanation with comments:

```
# Import required libraries
import numpy as np
import pandas as pd
import matplotlib.pyplot as plt
```

```python
# Read the healthcare dataset into a Pandas DataFrame
data = pd.read_csv("healthcare_dataset.csv")


# Separate features and labels: X for features and y for labels
X = data.iloc[:,0:-1].values  # All rows and all columns except the
last one
y = data.iloc[:,-1].values    # All rows and only the last column


# Split the dataset into training and test sets
from sklearn.model_selection import train_test_split
X_train, X_test, y_train, y_test = train_test_split(X, y, test_
size=0.3, random_state=4)


# Scale the features
from sklearn.preprocessing import StandardScaler
sc_X = StandardScaler()
X_train = sc_X.fit_transform(X_train)
X_test = sc_X.transform(X_test)


# Train an SVM model
from sklearn.svm import SVC
model_SVC = SVC(kernel = 'rbf', random_state=4)
model_SVC.fit(X_train, y_train)
# Get decision function scores for SVM
y_pred_svm = model_SVC.decision_function(X_test)


# Train a logistic regression model
from sklearn.linear_model import LogisticRegression
model_logistic = LogisticRegression()
model_logistic.fit(X_train, y_train)
# Get decision function scores for Logistic Regression
y_pred_logistic = model_logistic.decision_function(X_test)
```

```python
# Train a decision tree model
from sklearn.tree import DecisionTreeClassifier
model_decision_tree = DecisionTreeClassifier()
model_decision_tree.fit(X_train, y_train)
# Get predicted probabilities for Decision Tree
y_pred_proba_decision_tree  =  model_decision_tree.predict_proba(X_
test)[:, 1]


# Evaluate the models using ROC curve and AUC
from sklearn.metrics import roc_curve, auc
logistic_fpr, logistic_tpr, thresold = roc_curve(y_test, y_pred_
logistic)
auc_logistic = auc(logistic_fpr, logistic_tpr)
svm_fpr, svm_tpr, thresold = roc_curve(y_test, y_pred_svm)
auc_svm = auc(svm_fpr, svm_tpr)
decision_tree_fpr, decision_tree_tpr, thresold = roc_curve(y_test, y_
pred_proba_decision_tree)
auc_decision_tree = auc(decision_tree_fpr, decision_tree_tpr)


# Plot the ROC curve
plt.figure(figsize = (5,5), dpi = 100)
plt.plot(svm_fpr, svm_tpr, linestyle = '-', label = 'SVM (auc = %0.3f)'
% auc_svm)
plt.plot(logistic_fpr, logistic_tpr, marker = '.', label = 'Logistic
(auc = %0.3f)' % auc_logistic)
plt.plot(decision_tree_fpr, decision_tree_tpr, marker = '.', label =
'Decision_Tree (auc = %0.3f)' % auc_decision_tree)
plt.xlabel("FPR -- >")
plt.ylabel("TPR -- >")
plt.legend()
plt.show()
```

3. Analysis for the plots of ROC curves for the three models in shown in *Figure 3.1*:

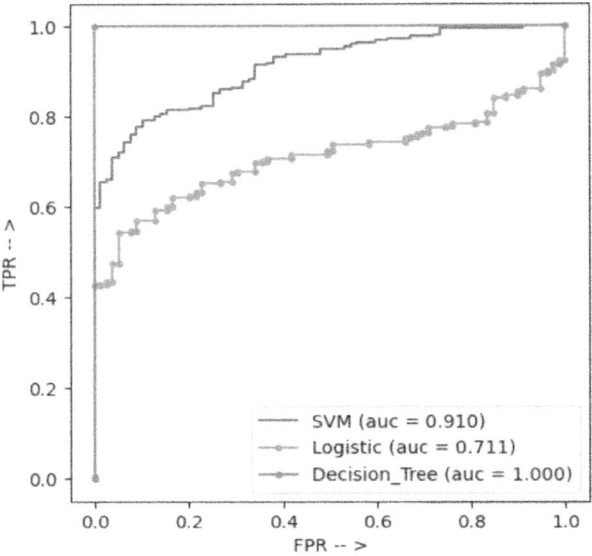

Figure 3.1: AUC-ROC Plots

Here is what these AUC scores generally suggest:

- **Support Vector Machine (SVM):** With an AUC of 0.910, the SVM model shows excellent performance. It is highly capable of distinguishing between positive and negative cases. This is a strong result and suggests that the SVM model may be a good fit for your data.

- **Logistic Regression:** An AUC of 0.711 indicates reasonable performance but leaves room for improvement. The logistic regression model seems to be less effective at distinguishing between the positive and negative classes compared to the SVM.

- **Decision Tree:** An AUC score of 1.0 for the decision tree is a perfect score. While this may seem ideal, it is generally a red flag and suggests the possibility of overfitting. The model might have learned the training data too well, including its noise and outliers, which makes it less likely to generalize well to new, unseen data.

Key terms

- **SVM:** Very good at distinguishing between classes.
- **Logistic Regression:** Fair but could be improved.
- **Decision Tree:** Likely overfitting, as it is too good to be true for most real-world scenarios.

Points to remember

- **ML types**

  o **Supervised learning:** Learning from labeled data to make predictions.

  o **Unsupervised learning:** Uncovering hidden patterns from unlabeled data.

  o **Semi-supervised and reinforcement learning:** Learning with limited labeled data and through interaction with the environment.

- **Key concepts**

  o **Features and labels:** Features are input; labels are what we're predicting.

  o **Training and testing data:** Dividing data into subsets to learn and then evaluate models.

  o **Loss functions:** Measure how well a model is performing.

- **Data preprocessing and feature engineering**

  o **Handling missing data:** Techniques like deletion, imputation are used to handle missing data.

  o **Data transformation:** Involves normalization and standardization.

  o **Data encoding:** Representing categorical data in a way that can be provided to ML models, for example, one-hot, label encoding.

- **Model training, evaluation, and deployment**

  o **Fitting models:** Training models on a dataset.

  o **Overfitting and underfitting:** Overfitting occurs when a model learns the training data too well, including its noise and outliers. Underfitting is when the model cannot capture the underlying trend of the data.

  o **Regularization:** Technique used to avoid overfitting.

  o **Model evaluation:** Uses metrics like confusion matrix, precision, recall, F1-Score, and AUC-ROC for classification models.

  o **Model deployment:** Involves making the model available for use, and it could be on-premises, cloud, or edge deployments.

- **Algorithms and model**

  o **Popular algorithms:** Such as Linear Regression, Decision Trees, Support Vector Machines, and Neural Networks.

  o **Visual representation of model performance:** For example, Confusion Matrix provides insight into the performance of classification models by visualizing true and false positives and negatives.

- **Regular Continuous Improvement**
  - o **Monitoring and maintaining models:** Essential for ensuring models remain effective and relevant.
  - o **Continuous learning and adjustment:** Necessary for adapting to new data and changing environments.

Multiple choice questions

1. **Which of the following options best describes the process of Overfitting in a ML model?**
   a. Model learns the training data perfectly but performs poorly on unseen data
   b. Model cannot capture the underlying trend of the data
   c. Model performs equally well on both training and unseen data
   d. None of the above

2. **In which type of ML does the model learn by reinforcing its actions?**
   a. Supervised learning
   b. Unsupervised learning
   c. Reinforcement learning
   d. Semi-supervised learning

3. **Which of the following is not a Data Preprocessing step in ML?**
   a. Feature engineering
   b. Model deployment
   c. Handling missing data
   d. Data transformation

4. **Which ML algorithm would be suitable for creating clusters of similar data points?**
   a. Linear regression
   b. Decision trees
   c. K-Means Clustering
   d. Logistic regression

5. **Which among the following is a common method to handle MNAR data?**
   a. Mean imputation
   b. Model-based imputation

c. Deleting rows

d. None of the above

6. **In the context of ML, what does AUC stand for?**

a. Area Under Curve

b. Average Use Case

c. Algorithmic Unseen Case

d. Area Use Case

7. **Which technique is NOT primarily used for reducing overfitting in a model?**

a. Pruning

b. Regularization

c. Adding more data

d. Increasing model complexity

8. **Which data transformation method is suitable to transform a skewed distribution to a normal distribution?**

a. Normalization

b. Log Transformation

c. One-Hot Encoding

d. Standardization

9. **In Feature Engineering, what does the process of Feature Extraction involve?**

a. Selecting a subset of original features

b. Removing irrelevant features

c. Transforming existing features to a higher dimension

d. Creating new features from existing ones

10. **In a Confusion Matrix, what does the term False Positive represent?**

a. Actual Positive and Predicted Positive

b. Actual Negative and Predicted Negative

c. Actual Positive and Predicted Negative

d. Actual Negative and Predicted Positive

Answer key

1	a
2	c
3	b
4	c
5	b
6	a
7	d
8	b
9	d
10	d

Join our book's Discord space

Join the book's Discord Workspace for Latest updates, Offers, Tech happenings around the world, New Release and Sessions with the Authors:

https://discord.bpbonline.com

CHAPTER 4
Designing Microservices for Machine Learning

Introduction

In this chapter, we begin the fascinating process of designing microservices specifically for **Machine Learning** (**ML**) applications. Building upon the foundational knowledge of microservices and ML, we delve into the intricacies of designing a scalable, flexible, and robust architecture that seamlessly integrates **Artificial Intelligence** (**AI**) capabilities.

We will focus on a hands-on example: Creating a *music recommendation system* built on a foundation of microservices. This comprehensive high-level design will cover everything from user interactions with multiple microservices to the role of an **Application Programming Interface** (**API**) gateway. We will also cover data storage strategies, data processing methodologies involving a range of ML algorithms, and updating models. To tie it all together, we will explore how to orchestrate the entire ecosystem using various architectural styles suited for microservices. This real-world example aims to provide an end-to-end view of designing a microservices-based ML application.

Structure

The chapter covers the following topics:

- Domain-driven design for ML projects
- Defining microservices boundaries

- Data flow and communication patterns
- Decomposing monolithic ML applications
- Designing the ML microservice

Objectives

The objectives of this chapter are multi-faceted and aimed at providing a comprehensive understanding of architect microservices for ML applications.

Domain-driven design for ML projects

Domain-driven design (**DDD**) is an approach that focuses on the core domain and domain logic as the primary complexity in software development. When applied to ML projects, DDD can help identify important boundaries, contexts, and entities that need to be modeled and implemented. Let us discuss the various aspects of DDD as applied to ML, using the example of a music recommendation system.

Understanding the domain

Understanding the domain is a critical first step in the design and implementation of any system, especially one as complex as a microservices-based music recommendation system. Domain understanding provides a conceptual framework that guides architectural decisions, influences the choice of ML algorithms, and impacts how microservices are defined and interact. Here is what you need to consider for understanding the domain:

- **User needs and interactions:** It is essential to comprehend the user's requirements and their interaction with the system. Users may seek recommendations based on genres, mood, or other distinct criteria. Their methods of rating songs or engaging with playlists are critical to understand.

- **Types of data:** Identify the types of data that will flow through the system. This could include user profiles, song metadata, play history, and user interactions like likes, skips, and ratings.

- **Business logic:** Determine what business logic is applicable. For example, there may be rules about the number of times a song can be recommended within a certain time frame or how *new releases* are prioritized in recommendations.

- **ML objectives:** It is imperative to establish specific goals for the ML models. Determine whether the focus is on enhancing click-through rates, boosting user engagement, or targeting a different metric. This decision will be pivotal in guiding the choice of algorithms and features to be used.

- **Scalability and performance:** It is crucial to accurately gauge the anticipated system load. Assess the number of users likely to engage with the system and the volume of data that will need processing. These factors are key in shaping your architectural choices.

- **Regulatory and compliance requirements:** It is essential to identify any data privacy regulations, such as GDPR, that the system must adhere to. The methods of storing and safeguarding user data must be clearly defined.
- **Stakeholder needs:** Consider the needs of other stakeholders like business analysts, data scientists, and system administrators who will interact with the system differently.

By gaining a thorough understanding of the domain, you can make informed decisions throughout the design and implementation process. It is the foundation upon which all other aspects of the system are built.

Bounded contexts

The concept of **bounded contexts** is vital for defining the limits of a particular subsystem or domain model within a larger system. It helps to clarify the responsibilities, entities, and even the language or terminology used within a specific part of a system. When applied to a microservices-based music recommendation system, bounded contexts can help organize the architecture into discrete, manageable pieces.

Bounded contexts are important for the following reasons:

- **Clarity:** They define the scope and responsibility of each microservice.
- **Autonomy:** They allow each microservice to evolve independently, reducing the risk of changes in one service affecting others.
- **Team collaboration:** They facilitate more effective communication within development teams by creating a shared understanding of each microservice's role.

Some examples of bounded contexts in a music recommendation system are:

- **User context**
  - o **Responsibility:** Manages user data, preferences, and authentication.
  - o **Entities:** Users, profiles, authentication tokens
  - o **Service:** User service

- **Catalog context**
  - o **Responsibility:** Manages the music catalog, including songs, artists, and albums.
  - o **Entities:** Songs, albums, artists
  - o **Service:** Catalog service

- **Playback context**
  - o **Responsibility:** Handles the streaming and playback of music tracks.

- o **Entities:** Streaming sessions, playback queue
- o **Service:** Playback service

- **Recommendation context**
  - o **Responsibility:** Provides music recommendations based on various algorithms.
  - o **Entities:** User behavior, recommendation models
  - o **Service:** Recommendation engine

- **Analytics context**
  - o **Responsibility:** Collects and analyzes user interaction data for business intelligence.
  - o **Entities:** User events, metrics, reports
  - o **Service:** Analytics service

- **Search context**
  - o **Responsibility:** Facilitates search operations for finding music or information within the platform.
  - o **Entities:** Search queries, search results
  - o **Service:** Search service

The key considerations in defining bounded contexts are:

- **Domain analysis:** Start by conducting a thorough analysis of the domain to identify different sub-domains and their relationships.
- **Context mapping:** Use context maps to visualize the bounded contexts and their interactions.
- **Ubiquitous language:** Within each bounded context, define a ubiquitous language that ensures that all team members have a shared understanding of the terminology used.
- **API design:** Design the APIs for each microservice in a way that respects the bounded context. The API should expose relevant operations to the bounded context and hide internal details.

By carefully defining bounded contexts, you can create a microservices architecture that is more maintainable, scalable, and understandable. It will also facilitate better collaboration between different teams and make it easier to onboard new developers. We will discuss more in detail about bounded contexts and microservices boundaries in the section *Defining microservices boundaries.*

Understanding entities, aggregates and value objects

In DDD, **entities**, **aggregates**, and **value objects** are core building blocks that help to create a rich and expressive domain model. Each serves a distinct purpose and plays a unique role in the system. Let us explore these concepts with their relevance and examples related to a music recommendation system:

- **Entities**: Entities, also known as **reference objects**, are objects that have a distinct identity that runs through time and states. The identity of an entity is constant, but its state can change over time.

    o **Characteristics**

        ▪ **Identity:** Each entity has a unique identity.

        ▪ **Mutability:** Entities are mutable. Their state can change, but their identity remains the same.

    o **Example in a music recommendation system**

        ▪ **User:** A User entity could have attributes like userId, username, email, and password. The userId would be unique, serving as the identity of the entity.

- **Aggregates:** An aggregate is a cluster of domain objects (entities and value objects) that can be treated as a single unit for data changes. An aggregate will have one of its component objects be the aggregate root. Any references from outside the aggregate should only go to the aggregate root.

    o **Characteristics**

        ▪ **Root entity:** Each aggregate has a root entity, which is the only point of access for modifications in the aggregate.

        ▪ **Data integrity:** The aggregate root is responsible for maintaining data integrity within the aggregate.

    o **Example in a music recommendation system**

        ▪ **Playlist:** A Playlist could be an aggregate that includes an aggregate root, playlistId, and other entities and value objects like songs, user, duration, and so on.

- **Value objects**: Value objects are immutable objects that do not have a distinct identity and are fully defined by their attributes.

    o **Characteristics**

        ▪ **Immutability**: Value objects are immutable.

        ▪ **Equitability**: Two value objects are equal if all their attributes are equal.

o **Example in a music recommendation system**

■ **Duration**: A value object that represents the duration of a song.

Combining entities, aggregates and value objects

In a music recommendation system, the following concepts are often used together:

- A user entity might own multiple playlist aggregates.
- Each playlist aggregate could contain multiple song entities and duration value objects.
- The playlist aggregate root ensures that operations like adding or removing songs maintain data integrity, such as not exceeding a maximum number of songs.

By understanding and correctly applying entities, aggregates, and value objects, you can create a robust and expressive domain model that accurately reflects the complexities and rules of your system.

If these entities and aggregates reside in different microservices, you will need a way to communicate between those services. This could be done using RESTful APIs, message queues like Kafka, or other methods.

For instance, the playlist service might need to call the user service to get details about the playlist owner or the catalog service to get details about songs. This inter-service communication can be synchronous (HTTP/REST) or asynchronous (Message Queues).

Defining microservices boundaries

Defining the boundaries of microservices is a critical design decision that impacts the architecture, development, and maintenance of your system. Properly bounded microservices enable agility, scalability, and maintainability. In an ML-based music recommendation system, let us discuss how you can define microservices boundaries.

Data and functionality

When designing a microservices-based system like a music recommendation platform, understanding how data and functionality are divided and allocated is crucial. This division will have a significant impact on the system's scalability, maintainability, and overall performance. Let us delve into the details of these two key aspects:

- **Data in microservices**
  - **Decentralized data management**: Each microservice should own its data and be the sole manipulator of its database. For example, the user service should have its database to manage user profiles and authentication details.

o **Data consistency**: While microservices allow for decentralized data, it is essential to ensure data consistency across services. Event-driven architectures or eventual consistency models can help achieve this.

o **Data types and formats**: Be explicit about the types and formats of data that will flow between services. Use standard formats like JSON or Protobuf for communication.

o **Caching**: To improve performance, consider caching frequently accessed data. For example, a playback service might cache popular songs to speed up access times.

o **Data versioning**: When a service's data schema changes, it can affect other services that depend on it. Versioning the data or the API can help manage these changes.

o **Data security**: Implement robust security measures to ensure that sensitive data, like user credentials, is encrypted and securely transmitted.

- **Functionality in microservices**

  o **Single responsibility**: Each microservice should have a single, well-defined responsibility. For example, the recommendation engine's sole function should be to generate music recommendations based on algorithms.

  o **Business logic**: Encapsulate the business logic within the appropriate service. For example, any logic related to song playback should reside in the playback service.

  o **Statelessness**: Aim to make services stateless, allowing them to be easily scaled and deployed. Any required state should be externalized to a database or cache.

  o **Service collaboration**: Services often need to collaborate to complete tasks. This collaboration should be explicit and well-defined, usually through APIs or messaging queues.

  o **Error handling**: It is essential to establish strong error-handling mechanisms within the system. Since each microservice is an isolated unit, errors should be contained within the service and not propagate to other system parts.

  o **Asynchronous processing**: For long-running tasks, consider using asynchronous processing methods to improve system responsiveness. For example, the analytics service could process data asynchronously to provide insights.

- **Integrating data and functionality**

  o **API design**: Design APIs that are intuitive and aligned with the service's data and functionality.

o **Event-driven communication**: Use events to synchronize data across services. For example, when a new song is added to the catalog service, an event can trigger the recommendation engine to update its models.

o **Data pipelines**: In an ML system, data pipelines can be created to automate data flow from collection to model training and inference.

o **Monitoring and logging**: Implementing comprehensive monitoring and logging to track how data flows through the system and how functionalities are executed.

By planning how data and functionality are distributed across microservices, you have the opportunity to create a system characterized by robustness, scalability and maintainability. This also enables better collaboration between teams and makes it easier to add new features or make changes to existing ones.

Single Responsibility Principle

The **Single Responsibility Principle (SRP)** is one of the SOLID principles of object-oriented design and programming, but its utility extends well beyond that context. In a microservices architecture, adhering to the SRP can be particularly advantageous. The principle states that a class, module, or in this case, a microservice, should have only one reason to change, meaning it should have only one job or responsibility. To better understand the application of the SRP in a microservices architecture, consider the following key points:

- **Importance of SRP in microservices**

    o **Simplicity and clarity**: A microservice that does only one thing is easier to understand, making the system more maintainable and less prone to bugs.

    o **Ease of scaling**: When a microservice has a single responsibility, it can be scaled independently based on the specific needs of that particular function.

    o **Isolation of changes**: If a change is required, it will be isolated to a single service, reducing the chance of unintended consequences elsewhere in the system.

    o **Improved fault tolerance**: When services are isolated in functionality, a failure in one service is less likely to directly impact others.

    o **Faster development and deployment**: Teams can work on different services without interfering with each other's work, and individual services can be deployed independently.

- **Application in a music recommendation system**

    o **User service**

        ▪ **Single responsibility**: Manage user profiles and handle authentication.

- - **Reason for change**: Updates to authentication mechanisms or user data schema.
  - o Catalog service
    - **Single responsibility**: Maintain the database of songs, artists, and albums.
    - **Reason for change**: Addition of new types of metadata or catalog items.
  - o Playback service
    - **Single responsibility**: Handle the streaming and playback of music.
    - **Reason for change**: Updates to streaming algorithms or supported formats.
  - o Recommendation engine
    - **Single responsibility**: Generate personalized music recommendations.
    - **Reason for change**: Introduction of new recommendation algorithms.
  - o Analytics service
    - **Single responsibility**: Collect and analyze data on user interactions.
    - **Reason for change**: Need for new types of analytics or metrics.
- **Best practices**
  - o **Clearly defined boundaries**: Make sure the boundaries and responsibilities of each microservice are clearly defined and understood by all team members.
  - o **Avoid over-isolation**: While services should be isolated, avoid making them so granular that they become difficult to manage or introduce network latency.
  - o **Consistent communication**: Use standardized protocols and data formats for communication between services to keep interactions consistent.
  - o **Documentation**: Maintain good documentation that clearly describes what each service does, aiding in both development and maintenance.
  - o **Monitoring**: Implement robust monitoring to ensure that each service is performing its defined role effectively.

Adherence to the SRP enables the design or implementation of a microservices architecture that is not only robust, scalable, and maintainable but also allows each service to independently evolve over time. This is crucial for building complex, long-lived systems like a music recommendation platform.

Cohesion and coupling

Cohesion and coupling are two fundamental software engineering concepts that have a significant impact on the design and quality of a system, especially in microservices architecture. Understanding these concepts can help design a system that is easy to manage, extend, and scale. To fully grasp how cohesion and coupling influence the design and efficacy of a microservices architecture, let us explore these concepts in more detail.

Cohesion

Cohesion refers to the degree to which the elements within a module (or a microservice) belong together. It measures how closely the functionalities provided by a service are related to each other. Understanding the nuances of high cohesion is key to appreciating its role in effective microservices architecture. Let us understand why high cohesion is pivotal:

- **Importance of high cohesion**
  o **Maintainability**: Highly cohesive services are easier to understand, manage, and update.
  o **Reusability**: Cohesive services encapsulate related functionalities together, making it easier to reuse them in different contexts.
  o **Simplified testing**: Testing becomes straightforward because the service does one thing and does it well.

Enhancing our understanding further, let us examine how high cohesion applies in a practical scenario:

- **Application in a music recommendation system**: When designing a microservices architecture, especially in the context of a music recommendation system, it is crucial to ensure that each microservice is highly cohesive. This means that each service should have a well-defined, singular focus, performing a specific set of tasks related to its designated functionality. High cohesion within a microservice leads to easier maintenance, better scalability, and more efficient development.

  Consider, for instance, the recommendation engine in a music recommendation system. This engine should be highly cohesive, focusing solely on generating music recommendations based on different algorithms. It should not be concerned with, say, user authentication or song playback. By maintaining this focus, the recommendation engine can be optimized for its primary task, ensuring high performance and reliability in delivering personalized music suggestions to users.

Coupling

Coupling refers to the degree of dependency between different modules or services. In a microservices architecture, it is crucial to minimize coupling to ensure that services are as independent as possible. To appreciate the significance of coupling in a microservices architecture, it is important to understand its impact on system design and functionality. The crucial aspects of low coupling are as follows:

- **Importance of low coupling**
  - o **Independence**: Low coupling ensures that services can operate, evolve, and scale independently.
  - o **Fault isolation**: A failure in one service will have minimal impact on other services.
  - o **Ease of deployment**: Services can be deployed independently, making it easier to roll out updates and new features.

To illustrate this concept in a real-world scenario, let us look at an example:

- **Application in a music recommendation system**: For example, the user service and catalog service in a music recommendation system should be loosely coupled. While the user service may need to query the catalog service to get song details, this interaction should be done in a way that changes to the catalog service do not necessitate changes in the user service, and vice versa.

- **Strategies for achieving high cohesion and low coupling**
  - o **SRP**: Ensure that each service has a single, well-defined responsibility to improve cohesion.
  - o **API-layer communication**: Use well-defined APIs for interaction between services to reduce coupling.
  - o **Event-driven architecture**: Use asynchronous, event-driven communication to further decouple services.
  - o **Data ownership**: Each service should own its data to reduce dependencies and thereby coupling.
  - o **Versioning**: Implement versioning for services and their APIs to allow for changes without affecting other services.

- **Best practices**
  - o **Regular refactoring**: As the system evolves, regularly refactor services to ensure they remain highly cohesive and loosely coupled.
  - o **Monitoring and metrics**: Use monitoring tools to identify bottlenecks or dependencies that could increase coupling.
  - o **Documentation**: Keep updated documentation that clearly outlines the responsibilities and interfaces of each service.

By prioritizing high cohesion within each service and ensuring low coupling between them, you can develop a microservices architecture that is not only robust and flexible but also simpler to manage. This approach is particularly vital for intricate systems such as a music recommendation platform.

API contracts

API contracts are a crucial element in the design and implementation of a microservices-based system. Essentially, an API contract is an agreement that describes the technical details of how services will interact with each other. This includes the endpoints, request/response formats, authentication mechanisms, and rate-limiting policies. Let us begin by examining the key reasons why API contracts are vital:

- **Importance of API contracts**
  - o **Consistency**: API contracts ensure that all teams have a clear understanding of how services will interact, leading to a more cohesive and consistent architecture.
  - o **Loose coupling**: By adhering to a well-defined API contract, services can evolve independently without affecting other system parts.
  - o **Versioning**: API contracts often include version information, allowing different services to interact even as they evolve.
  - o **Security**: Contracts can specify authentication and authorization mechanisms, ensuring that only permitted services can access certain functionalities.
  - o **Scalability**: With clearly defined contracts, it is easier to scale the system horizontally and vertically.

- **Components of API contracts**
  - o **Endpoints**: Define the URLs at which services can be accessed.
  - o **HTTP methods**: Specify the HTTP methods (GET, POST, PUT, DELETE, and so on) that can interact with the service.
  - o **Request/response schema**: Outline the structure of request and response payloads, usually in JSON or XML format.
  - o **Status codes**: List the HTTP status codes the service can return and what each means.
  - o **Headers**: Specify any required or optional HTTP headers.
  - o **Rate limiting**: Include details about the number of allowed requests per unit time.
  - o **Authentication**: Detail the authentication mechanisms, such as *API keys, OAuth tokens,* or *JWT*.

- **Best practices**
  - o **Documentation**: Keep the API contract well-documented and ensure it is accessible to all relevant team members.

o **Validation**: Use automated tools to validate that the client and the service adhere to the contract.

o **Versioning**: Always version your API contracts to handle changes gracefully.

o **Error handling**: Provide clear error messages that adhere to the contract, making debugging easier.

- **Application in a music recommendation system**: In a music recommendation system, different services like the user service, catalog service, and recommendation engine would each have their own API contracts:

o **User service**: May expose endpoints for user authentication, profile creation, and profile management.

o **Catalog service**: Could have endpoints for retrieving song, artist, and album details.

o **Recommendation engine**: Might offer endpoints to fetch song recommendations based on user behavior or other criteria.

Establishing well-defined API contracts is essential for ensuring consistent, secure, and scalable interactions among the various services in your music recommendation system. Such contracts streamline development and deployment processes and enhance the system's resilience and maintainability.

Data flow and communication patterns

Data flow and communication patterns are vital when designing microservices, especially for an ML-based music recommendation system. The right patterns can enhance scalability, fault tolerance, and data consistency. The following section explores the key aspects to be considered.

Data pipelines

Data pipelines are essential for managing data flow from various sources to destinations where it can be stored, analyzed, or processed further. In a microservices architecture, particularly one designed for ML applications like a music recommendation system, data pipelines ensure that data is efficiently moved and transformed.

Let us delve into the components and functionalities of data pipelines, crucial for orchestrating data flow in microservices architectures, especially in ML contexts like a music recommendation system:

- **Key components of data pipelines**

o **Data ingestion**: Collecting data from various sources. This could be user activity logs, song metadata, or real-time streaming data.

o **Data storage**: Storing the ingested data in a suitable storage solution. It could be a SQL database, NoSQL database, or a data lake.

o **Data processing**: The raw data is processed and transformed. This could involve cleaning the data, feature extraction, and other preprocessing steps necessary for ML algorithms.

o **Data analysis/model training**: This is where ML models are trained using the processed data.

o **Model deployment**: After model training and validation, the model is deployed to a production environment.

o **Data output/consumption**: The final step is to use the model to make predictions or recommendations. This could also involve presenting the data or insights via dashboards or reports.

o **Orchestration**: This involves managing the data flow through all these stages. Tools like *Apache Airflow* or *Kubeflow* can be used for this purpose.

- **Importance of data pipelines**

  o **Automation**: Data pipelines automate manual processes, increasing efficiency and reducing error.

  o **Scalability**: Well-designed pipelines can handle increasing volumes of data seamlessly.

  o **Reproducibility**: They ensure that data transformations and analyses are reproducible, facilitating debugging and iterative development.

  o **Real-time processing**: Modern data pipelines can process data in real-time, enabling features like real-time analytics or recommendations.

  o **Data quality**: Through automated validation and cleaning steps, pipelines can improve data quality.

- **Tools for managing data pipelines in microservices for ML**

  o **Data ingestion**

    ▪ **Apache Kafka**: For streaming data and building real-time data pipelines.

    ▪ **Fluentd**: For collecting and moving log data from various sources.

  o **Data storage**

    ▪ **HDFS/Amazon S3**: For storing large volumes of unstructured data.

    ▪ **PostgreSQL/MySQL**: For structured data storage.

    ▪ **MongoDB**: For NoSQL storage needs.

o Data processing

- **Apache Spark**: For large-scale data processing.

- **Apache Flink**: For real-time stream processing.

o Machine Learning libraries

- **Scikit-learn**: For traditional ML algorithms.

- **TensorFlow/PyTorch**: For deep learning tasks.

o Model deployment

- **MLflow**: For managing the ML lifecycle.

- **Kubeflow**: For deploying ML workflows on Kubernetes.

o Orchestration

- **Apache Airflow**: For workflow orchestration.

- **Kubeflow pipelines**: For complex ML workflows.

o Monitoring and logging

- **Prometheus**: For monitoring system metrics.

- **Grafana**: For creating dashboards based on those metrics.

- **ELK Stack**: Elasticsearch, Logstash, and Kibana for searching, analyzing, and visualizing log data in real time.

o API gateway

- **Kong**: For managing APIs between microservices.

- **NGINX**: As a reverse proxy and API gateway.

- **Use/application in a music recommendation system**

  o **Tracking user activity**: Collecting data about which songs users listen to, how long they listen, and any actions like likes or skips.

  o **Catalog updates**: Regularly updating the song, album, and artist data in the system.

  o **Recommendation model training**: Aggregating and preprocessing data to train ML models for song recommendation.

  o **Analytics**: Processing data to generate insights on user behavior, popular songs, or system performance metrics.

- **Best practices**

  o **Modular design**: Make each step in the pipeline an independent module to facilitate updates and maintenance.

o **Monitoring and alerts**: Implement comprehensive monitoring and set up alerts for failures or issues.

o **Version control**: Keep track of versions for both data and the code that processes it.

o **Testing**: Regularly test the pipeline to ensure it meets all functional and performance requirements.

o **Data backup**: Maintain backups of critical data to prevent loss.

With a strategic selection and seamless integration of these tools, you can develop data pipelines that not only exhibit robustness and scalability but also adeptly cater to the intricate demands and complexities inherent in ML applications, particularly within a microservices framework.

Synchronous versus asynchronous communication

In a microservices architecture, choosing between synchronous and asynchronous communication is vital. Both have pros and cons, and the best choice often depends on the specific requirements of your system.

Let us explore these two types of communication.

Synchronous communication

In synchronous communication, the calling service (or client) waits for a response from the called service. HTTP/REST APIs are common examples of synchronous communication. After understanding that HTTP/REST APIs are common forms of synchronous communication, let us delve into its advantages and disadvantages, along with exploring specific use cases in a music recommendation system where this type of communication is particularly effective:

• **Advantages**

o **Simplicity**: It is easier to understand and implement.

o **Immediate feedback**: The client gets an immediate response, which can be beneficial for certain types of operations.

• **Disadvantages**

o **Coupling**: It increases the level of coupling between services.

o **Latency**: Waiting for a response can introduce latency into the system.

o **Availability**: If one service is down, all services that depend on it could be affected.

- **Use cases in a music recommendation system**
  - o **User login**: Authenticating a user should be synchronous to immediately inform the user of the status.
  - o **Song search**: Fetching search results can be done synchronously to provide quick feedback.

Asynchronous communication

In asynchronous communication, the calling service sends a message to a message queue and then continues its processing. The called service picks up the message from the queue and processes it. A few examples include *Kafka*, *RabbitMQ*, and other message brokers.

- **Advantages**
  - o **Decoupling**: Services are more loosely coupled, allowing for greater flexibility.
  - o **Scalability**: Enables better handling of load surges and improves system scalability.
  - o **Fault tolerance**: If a service is down, the message stays in the queue until it can be processed.

- **Disadvantages**
  - o **Complexity**: It is more challenging to implement and understand.
  - o **Eventual consistency**: Immediate consistency is not guaranteed, which might be an issue for some use-cases.

- **Use cases in a music recommendation system**
  - o **Analytics**: Collecting data on what songs users listen to can be done asynchronously not to affect the user experience.
  - o **Recommendation updates**: When a new song is added to the catalog, the recommendation models could be updated asynchronously.

    Many real-world systems use a mix of both *synchronous* and *asynchronous* communication.

  - o **API gateway**: Synchronous APIs could be exposed to the client while the services behind the gateway communicate asynchronously.
  - o **Event-driven architecture**: Components react to changes in the system by consuming events from a message queue but might use synchronous calls for specific tasks.

- **Considerations for choice**
  - o **Latency sensitivity**: If immediate feedback is required, synchronous might be better.

o **Throughput requirements**: For high-throughput systems, asynchronous can be more suitable.

o **Availability needs**: Asynchronous systems can offer better fault tolerance.

o **Consistency requirements**: Synchronous systems are often easier to make strongly consistent.

By carefully considering the needs of your system, especially in a complex domain like a music recommendation service, you can make an informed choice between synchronous and asynchronous communication. This will influence your system's architecture, scalability, and overall user experience.

Message queues and event streams

Message queues and event streams are vital components in distributed systems, especially microservices architectures. Message queues and event streams enable services in distributed systems, particularly in microservices architectures, to communicate in a decoupled manner. This approach enhances system scalability, responsiveness, and resilience. Let us discuss their definitions, differences, and popular tools.

Message queues

A message queue is an asynchronous service-to-service communication method where messages are sent from a producer service and consumed by a consumer service. Once a message is consumed, it is removed from the queue. To gain a deeper understanding of message queues, let us look at some of the popular tools used to implement them, their key characteristics, and typical use cases where they are effectively employed:

- **Popular tools**

  o RabbitMQ

  o Amazon **Simple Queue Service (SQS)**

  o ActiveMQ

- **Key characteristics**

  o **Point-to-point**: A message a producer sends is consumed by one consumer.

  o **Asynchronous**: Producers can add requests to the queue without waiting for them to be processed.

  o **Decoupling**: The producer and the consumer are decoupled, meaning the producer does not need to know about the consumer's state or vice versa.

  o **Persistent or non-persistent messages**: Messages stored can be durable or nondurable.

o   **Blocking or polling consumption**: Consumers can either wait for messages or poll the queue periodically.

- **Use cases**

    o   **Order processing**: When a user places an order, a message is sent to a queue, and an order processing service consumes messages from this queue to process them.

    o   **Task queues**: For running background jobs or scheduled tasks.

Event streams

Event streams are a continuous flow of events ordered in time. They allow multiple consumers to subscribe to events and process them in a decoupled fashion.

To further understand event streams and their role in modern distributed systems, let us explore the commonly used tools for event streaming, their defining characteristics, and some practical use cases where they prove particularly beneficial:

- **Popular tools**

    o   Apache Kafka

    o   Amazon Kinesis

    o   Azure Event Hub

- **Key characteristics**

    o   **Publish-Subscribe**: Producers publish events to the stream, and multiple consumers can subscribe to and process those events.

    o   **Distributed**: Events can be partitioned across different nodes, allowing for high throughput and scalability.

    o   **Immutable log**: Messages are immutable and stored for a defined retention period.

    o   **Real-time**: It is designed for low-latency, high-throughput scenarios.

- **Use cases**

    o   **Real-time analytics**: It consumes raw events and aggregating them for real-time analytics.

    o   **Data lakes**: It stores raw events in an event stream to be consumed by different services for various purposes.

    o   **Event sourcing**: It stores state changes as events in an immutable log.

- **Differences between message queues and event streams**

  o **Durability**: While both systems can offer durable storage, event streams (like *Kafka*) are designed to store data for longer periods, making it possible to reprocess past events.

  o **Multiple consumers**: In event streams, multiple consumers can read the same event independently. In message queues, once a message is consumed, it is removed or marked as *processed* in the queue.

  o **Ordering**: Event streams inherently ensure order, as events are sequenced as they arrive. While some message queues can ensure order, it is not an inherent feature.

  o **Event sourcing**: Event streams can serve as the backbone for event sourcing architectures, where the state of a system is determined by events rather than a fixed *current state*.

- **Use in microservices**

  o **Decoupling**: Both message queues and event streams decouple services, allowing them to operate independently.

  o **Event-driven architectures**: Using message queues or event streams enables the creation of event-driven microservices, where services react to events rather than being told what to do.

  o **Scalability**: Both systems allow for horizontal scalability, making it easier to handle increased loads by adding more instances of services.

  o **Resilience**: If one service fails, messages or events can still be added to the queue or stream, ensuring data is not lost and can be processed once the service is restored.

In a microservices architecture, especially for systems that need to handle high loads, real-time data, or complex workflows, using message queues or event streams is often crucial for ensuring efficient, scalable, and decoupled operations.

- **Application in a music recommendation system**

  o **Message queues**: It could be used for tasks like updating a user's profile, processing a song upload, or generating a daily playlist for each user.

  o **Event streams**: It could be used for real-time analytics of user behavior, like songs played, skipped, or added to favorites. This data can be used for real-time recommendation updates.

Both message queues and event streams can be fundamental in building robust, scalable, and flexible microservices architectures, especially for complex systems like a music recommendation service.

API gateways

API gateways serve as the entry point for external consumers of microservices, acting as a reverse proxy that routes requests to appropriate microservices. They play an essential role in microservices architectures by providing a unified API endpoint and handling various cross-cutting concerns.

To delve deeper into the significance and functionality of API gateways in microservices architectures, let us examine their key features, popular solutions, and how they can be effectively utilized in a system like a music recommendation platform. Additionally, we will explore the advantages and considerations of using API gateways:

- **Key features of API gateways**
  - o **Routing**: Routing directs incoming API calls to appropriate microservices.
  - o **Load balancing**: It distributes the load among multiple instances of a service.
  - o **Authentication and authorization**: It verifies the identity of users and checks their permissions before routing the request.
  - o **Rate limiting**: Rate limiting controls the number of requests a user can make within a specified time frame.
  - o **Caching**: It stores frequently accessed data to reduce the load on individual services and speed up responses.
  - o **Monitoring and logging**: It collects metrics and logs for analyzing API usage and performance.
  - o **Request and response transformation**: It alters incoming and outgoing messages, for example, by adding, modifying, or deleting headers or body content.

- **Popular API gateway solutions**
  - o **Kong**: An open-source, modular, and scalable API gateway with a wide range of plugins.
  - o **NGINX**: NGINX is often used as a reverse proxy and load balancer but can also function as an API gateway.
  - o **AWS API Gateway**: A fully managed service that makes it easy to create, publish, and maintain APIs at any scale.
  - o **Apigee**: An API platform and gateway for developing, managing, and securing APIs.
  - o **Azure API Gateway**: Provides capabilities to create, publish, secure, and analyze APIs.

- **Use/application in a music recommendation system**
  - o **Routing**: Route requests like **Get Recommended Songs** to the **Recommendation Service**, **Create Playlist** to the **Playlist Service**, and **Search** to the **Catalog Service**.
  - o **Authentication**: Authenticate users before allowing them to access their playlists, favorite songs, or use other premium features.
  - o **Rate limiting**: Limit how many songs a free-tier user can skip within a certain time frame.
  - o **Monitoring**: Collects metrics on the most popular songs or features, response times, and error rates.

- **Advantages and considerations**
  - o **Advantages**
    - ▪ **Simplifies client-side logic**: Clients need to interact with just one endpoint instead of multiple services, thereby reducing complexity and potential errors in client-side integration.
    - ▪ **Centralizes cross-cutting concerns**: Issues like authentication, logging, and security are managed centrally by the API gateway, rather than being duplicated across each microservice.
    - ▪ **Allows for easier scaling and maintenance**: Individual microservices can be scaled independently.
  - o **Considerations**
    - ▪ **Single point of failure**: If the API gateway goes down, it can affect the entire system. High availability and fault tolerance are crucial for API gateways because they ensure continuous system operation and minimize disruptions. If the API gateway, acting as the primary access point for all microservices, becomes unavailable, it can halt the entire system's functionality.
    - ▪ **Complexity**: As the central piece of your architecture, it can become complex and hard to manage if not carefully designed and maintained.
    - ▪ **Latency**: Additional processing steps in the gateway can introduce latency.

By carefully selecting and configuring an API gateway, you can manage and scale your microservices more effectively, enhancing both developer productivity and user experience.

Decomposing monolithic ML applications

Decomposing a monolithic ML application into a set of microservices can be a challenging yet rewarding process. Doing so allows for better scalability, maintainability and can speed up the development cycle. The following section provides some guidelines on how to approach this task:

Identifying modules and components

Identifying modules and components is critical for decomposing a monolithic application into cohesive, loosely coupled microservices. This is especially true for ML applications, where the complexities can quickly escalate.

Given the intricate nature of ML applications, such as a music recommendation system, it becomes even more essential to methodically identify modules and components. This process aids in effectively breaking down a monolithic application into cohesive, loosely coupled microservices. Let us consider the steps involved in this identification process and look at some examples specific to an ML music recommendation system:

- **Steps to identify modules and components**
  - o **Review the existing system architecture**: If you are working on decomposing an existing monolithic application, start by thoroughly understanding its architecture. Look at the class diagrams, database schemas, and the code to understand how different functionalities are grouped.
  - o **Identify business domains**: Look at the business requirements and identify the different business domains involved. For an ML-based music recommendation system, for example, the domains might include user management, music catalog, recommendations and analytics.
  - o **Understand data flows**: Understand how data moves within your application. For ML systems, pay special attention to how data is collected, processed, used for training, and inference.
  - o **Map out features to domains**: List all the features that your application provides, and try to map them to the identified business domains. For example, **User login**, **Password reset** would come under **User Management**, whereas **Get song recommendations** would come under **Recommendations**.
  - o **Identify shared components**: There may be components like **Authentication** or **Logging** that are used across multiple business domains. Identify these as they may be good candidates for becoming independent services.
  - o **Look for high-cohesion, low-coupling**: The aim is to identify components that do a specific set of tasks and do them well (high-cohesion) but have minimal dependencies on other components (low-coupling).

o   **Dependency analysis**: Analyze dependencies between different parts of the code. Use tools that can automatically generate dependency graphs, if available.

o   **Consult with stakeholders**: Often, the business requirements and limitations can influence the service boundaries. Make sure you consult with both technical and business stakeholders to gather their insights.

- **Examples for ML music recommendation system**

    o   **User management**: Manages user accounts, profiles, and authentication.

    - **Modules**: User Registration, User Authentication, Profile Management

    - **Components**: User database, OAuth handlers

    o   **Music catalog**: Manages information about songs, albums, and artists.

    - **Modules**: Song Management, Artist Management, Album Management

    - **Components**: Catalog database, Genre tags

    o   **Recommendations**: Generates and serves music recommendations.

    - **Modules**: Recommendation Engine, Feedback Loop

    - **Components**: ML models (for example, ALS, KNN), Feature extraction, Training data collection

    o   **Analytics**: Collects and analyzes user interaction data for insights.

    - **Modules**: Data collection, data analysis

    - **Components**: Event logs, data visualization

    o   **Shared components**: Handles functionalities that are common across different services.

    - **Modules**: Logging, security

    - **Components**: Log storage, API gateway for authentication

Now, you should have a clear map of what each microservice will look like, what its responsibilities will be, and how it will interact with other services. This is a crucial first step in breaking down a monolithic ML application into a microservices architecture.

Designing the ML microservice

Having thoroughly covered the foundational principles of designing microservices for ML applications, it is time to get hands-on. We will work on a lab exercise to practically architect a music recommendation system. This exercise will span everything from high-level architectural planning to the intricate details of API and database design. Let us discuss and break down the architecture step-by-step, starting with a high-level overview and then diving into the details for a more comprehensive understanding. Refer to the following figure:

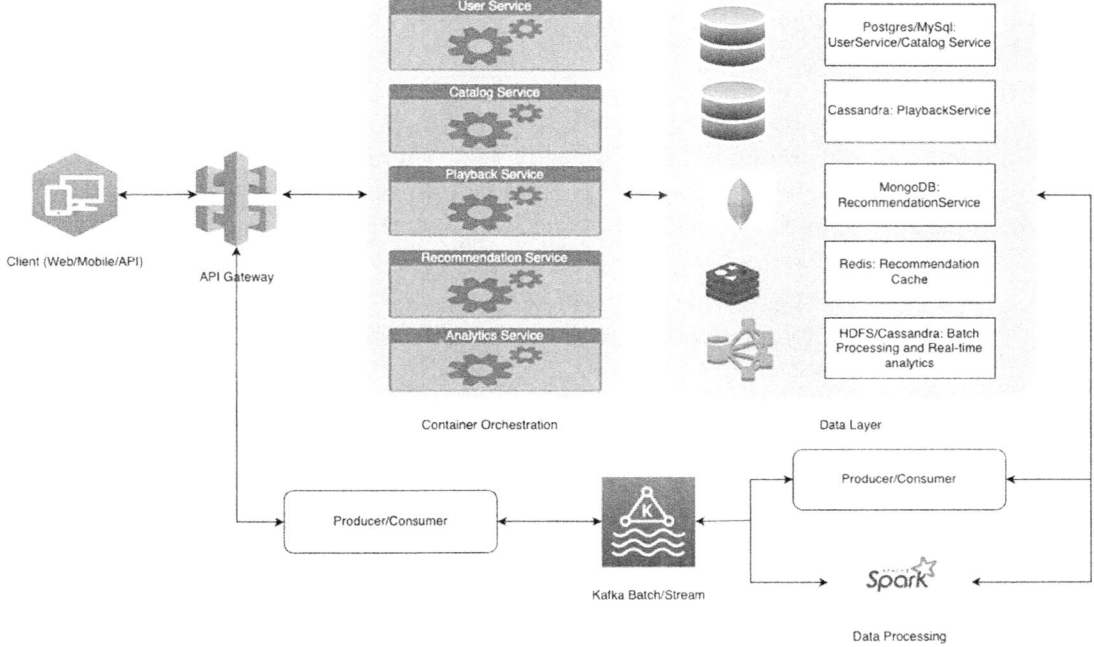

Figure 4.1: *High-level architecture for music recommendation system*

Here is a breakdown of the components covered in *Figure 4.1*:

- **Frontend**: The user interface where interactions begin.
- **API Gateway**: Manages and routes incoming API requests to the corresponding services.
- **Microservices**: User service, catalog service, playback service, recommendation service and analytics service handle the core functionalities.
- **Databases**: PostgreSQL for user/catalog service, MongoDB for recommendation service, and cassandra for playback service. We can also introduce Elasticsearch for search functionalities within the catalog service.
- **Analytics service**: Collects, analyzes, and data feeds into BI tools like *Apache Superset* for visualization.
- **Recommendation engine**: Houses the ML models and algorithms, and uses Redis for caching.
- **Data pipeline (Kafka)**: Manages real-time data streaming.
- **Kubeflow**: It orchestrates the ML workflow.

Each component is designed to be loosely coupled but highly cohesive, allowing for easier scaling, development, and maintenance.

API gateway

An API gateway often serves as a single-entry point for client applications, aggregating data from multiple services into a single composite response. This pattern is commonly used in microservices architectures to simplify the client code and reduce the number of requests between the client and server. Let us walk through the process of how an API gateway operates in a microservices architecture, illustrating the sequence of interactions from the frontend to various backend services:

- **Frontend to API gateway**: The frontend makes a single request to the API gateway, asking for an aggregated response that might include user info, music info, and recommendations.

- **API gateway to user service**: The API gateway sends a request to the user service to get user-related information.

- **API gateway to catalog service**: Simultaneously, the API gateway sends another request to the catalog service to fetch the catalog information, such as available songs or albums.

- **API gateway to playback service**: Another request might be sent to the playback service to get details about the currently playing song, its status, and so on.

- **API gateway to recommendation engine**: Finally, the API gateway queries the recommendation engine to get music recommendations based on the user's history or preferences.

- **Aggregation in API gateway**: The API gateway waits for all these responses, aggregates them, and sends a single composite response back to the frontend.

Benefits

To fully appreciate the advantages of using an API gateway in a microservices architecture, let us discuss the key benefits it offers:

- **Reduced number of requests**: Instead of the frontend making multiple requests to different services, it makes just one request, reducing load and complexity.

- **Simplified client**: The frontend does not need to know about all the different services, making the client code simpler.

- **Centralized logic**: Having an API gateway allows you to centralize some of the operational complexities like rate limiting, authentication, and so on.

Inter-service communication

Inter-service communication is a critical aspect of any microservices architecture. Knowing when to use synchronous versus asynchronous communication can have a big impact on the system's performance and reliability.

Key interactions

To better understand the methods and patterns of inter-service communication, let us examine some key interactions within such an architecture, highlighting whether they employ synchronous or asynchronous communication and the implications of each choice on system performance:

- **API gateway to user/catalog/playback/recommendation services**: These interactions are synchronous using HTTP/HTTPS. The API gateway waits for responses from these services to aggregate and return to the frontend.

- **Recommendation engine to analytics service**: This interaction is asynchronous. When a recommendation is made, the event is sent to a Kafka topic. The analytics service consumes this data but the recommendation engine does not wait for a response.

- **Playback service to analytics service**: This could also be asynchronous. For example, when a song is played, the event could be sent to a Kafka topic for analytics, without waiting for any acknowledgment.

- **Analytics service to data pipeline**: This is asynchronous. Processed or raw data is sent to a data pipeline for further processing or storage.

The choice between synchronous and asynchronous depends on whether the calling service needs to wait for the called service to complete its task. In scenarios where it is not necessary to wait (like logging analytics data), asynchronous methods are preferable as they are more scalable and decoupled.

Event bus

An event bus is a communication system that allows different parts of a system to publish and subscribe to events in a decoupled fashion. This is especially useful in microservices architectures, where services often need to communicate with each other but should remain loosely coupled for better scalability and maintainability. In a ML-based music recommendation system, an event bus can serve multiple purposes. Refer to the following figure:

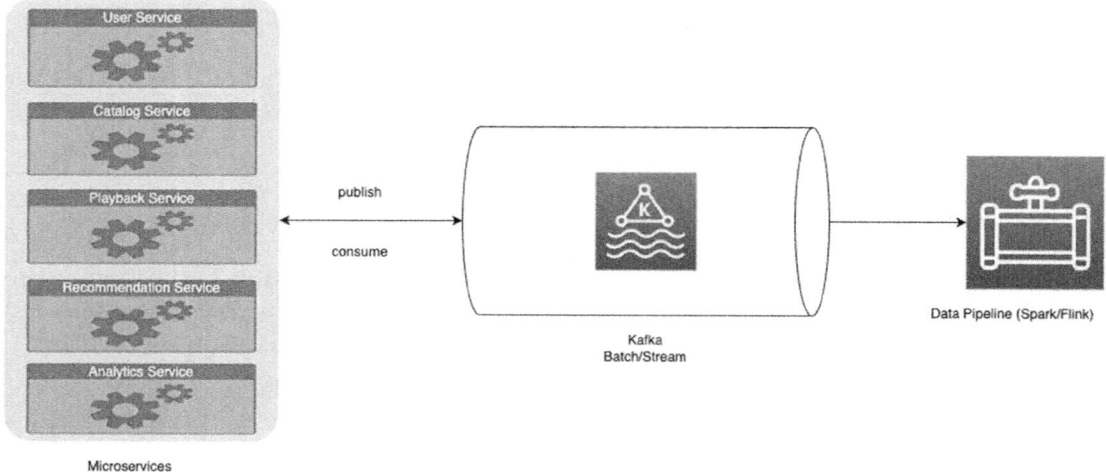

Figure 4.2: *Event bus*

The key roles of an event bus, covered in *Figure 4.2*, are as follows:

- **Event publishing**: Microservices like user service, catalog service, and playback service publish events to the event bus. These events could include user actions, song playbacks, or catalog updates. Services can publish events when certain actions occur, such as a new song being added or a user liking a song.

- **Event bus (Apache Kafka)**: It is the centralized hub for all events. It receives events from various services and makes them available for consumption.

- **Consuming services**: Services like the analytics service and recommendation engine consume events from the event bus for various purposes like analytics and generating recommendations. Services can subscribe to these events and execute actions when they occur, like updating a recommendation model.

- **Data pipeline**: The event bus also feeds into the data pipeline where Spark or Flink can process the data for advanced analytics or ML models.

Some typical events in a music recommendation system are as follows:

- **SongPlayedEvent**: It is triggered when a song is played.
- **SongLikedEvent**: It is triggered when a user likes a song.
- **NewSongAddedEvent**: It is triggered when a new song is added to the catalog.
- **UserRegisteredEvent**: It is triggered when a new user registers.

Here is what a **SongPlayedEvent** might look like:

```
{
  "event_type": "SongPlayed",
```

```
  "timestamp": "2023-08-25T12:34:56Z",

  "user_id": "1234",

  "song_id": "5678",

  "duration": "180"

}
```

Data pipeline

A data pipeline is a set of data processing elements connected in series, where the output of one element is the input of the next. It plays a critical role in ML projects, especially in microservices architecture. Refer to the following figure:

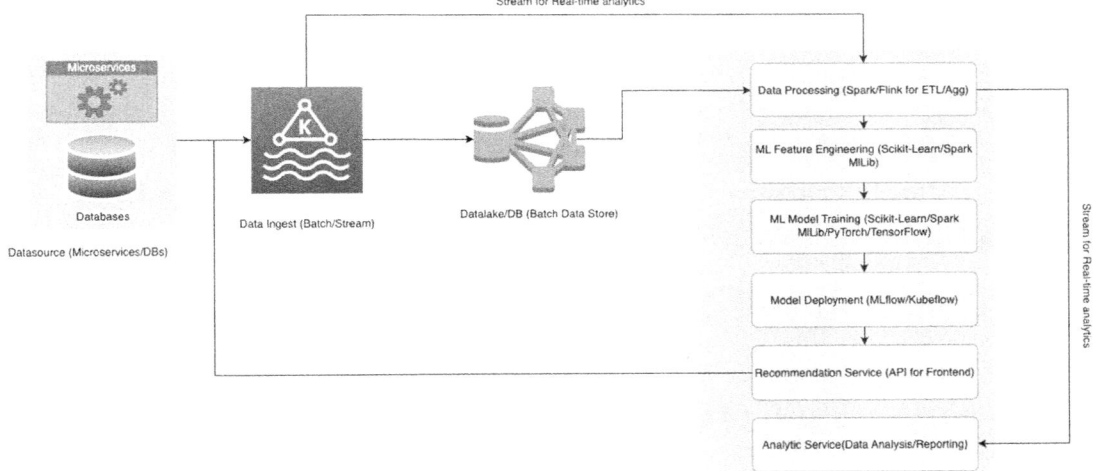

Figure 4.3: *Data pipeline*

Here is a breakdown of various stages and activities involved in a data pipeline for a music recommendation system:

- **Data ingest**: Collects data either in batch or real-time from microservices and/or databases. Batch data goes into a Data Lake or Database, and real-time data goes into a Kafka Topic.

- **Apache Spark**: Batch data is processed and transformed. Feature engineering for Machine Learning also happens here.

- **ML algorithms**: Using the features, ML models are trained. Algorithms like ALS, k-NN, k-means could be used.

- **Model deployment**: The trained model is deployed for serving using tools like Kubeflow or MLflow.

- **Recommendation engine**: The deployed model serves real-time recommendations.
- **Real-time queue (Kafka Topic)**: Collects real-time events like song plays and likes.
- **Stream processing (Apache Flink/Spark Stream)**: Processes the real-time data stream.
- **Analytics service**: This performs data analysis and reporting.

Data ingestion

It involves the process of collecting and importing data from various sources into a system where it can be stored, processed, and analyzed. In the context of real-time and batch data collection, different approaches and technologies are employed to handle diverse data types and requirements effectively.

- **Real-time data collection**
  - o User interactions like song plays, likes, and searches are captured in real-time.
  - o These events are immediately sent to a real-time event streaming platform like Kafka.

    User Interactions | Kafka Producer | Kafka Topic (real-time queue)
- **Batch data collection**
  - o For non-real-time needs, data like song metadata, user profiles are collected in batch mode.
  - o This data could be ingested into a data lake or directly into a database.

    Data Sources | ETL Jobs | Data Lake / Database

Data processing

Data processing involves handling and transforming the ingested data into a useful format for analysis and decision-making. The data processing stage is typically divided into two main categories:

- **Stream data processing**
  - o Real-time data in Kafka topics is consumed by a stream processing framework like Apache Flink or Spark Streaming.

    Kafka topic | Apache Flink | Processed Stream
- **Batch processing**
  - o Batch data can be processed by batch processing frameworks like Apache Spark.

o   Heavy transformations, aggregations, and feature engineering can happen here.

Data Lake / database | Apache Spark | Processed data

ML algorithm processing

This stage encompasses several key steps crucial in transforming raw data into actionable insights and involves specific processes and tools to ensure effectiveness and efficiency.

- **Feature engineering**
    o   Features for ML models are generated from the processed data.
    o   This could be done in Spark MLlib, scikit-learn, or directly in a database with SQL queries.

    Processed data | Feature engineering | Feature vectors

- **Model training**
    o   ML algorithms are applied to the feature vectors to train models.
    o   Algorithms like **Alternating Least Squares (ALS)**, **k-Nearest Neighbors (k-NN)**, or k-means can be used.
    o   Kubeflow or MLflow can be used for workflow orchestration.

    Feature vectors | ML algorithms | Trained model

- **Model deployment**
    o   The trained model is then deployed to a model server for real-time or batch scoring.
    o   Kubeflow or MLflow can again be used here.

    Trained model | Model server

Data serving

This stage is where the value of all previous processes comes to fruition, as it involves the actual application of the trained ML models to provide real-time services and insights:

- **Recommendation engine**
    o   The deployed model is used to serve recommendations in real-time.
    o   It could be exposed as a REST API for synchronous requests or use Kafka for asynchronous delivery.

    Model server | API / Kafka | Recommendations

- **Analytics and monitoring**

    o All activities, including model performance, user interaction, and system health, are monitored.

    o Tools like Prometheus for system health, and Grafana or Apache Superset for analytics can be used.

This pipeline ensures seamless data flow from ingestion to serving, allowing for both real-time and batch processing. This flexibility is crucial for the dynamic requirements of ML models, especially in a microservices architecture.

Microservices API layers

The microservices API layers serve as the interface between the services and the outside world. They expose a set of endpoints that allow for data ingestion, manipulation, and retrieval. In the following section, we will explain the API layers for each microservice in our music recommendation system example.

User service

This manages user-related functionalities such as sign-up, login, and profile management:

- **API endpoints**

    o **POST/users/register**

      ▪ **Description**: Registers a new user.

      ▪ **Input**: Username, password, email

      ▪ **Output**: User ID, JWT token

      ▪ **Status codes**: 201 Created, 400 Bad Request, 409 Conflict

    o **POST/users/login**

      ▪ **Description**: Authenticates an existing user.

      ▪ **Input**: Username, password

      ▪ **Output**: JWT token

      ▪ **Status codes:** 200 OK, 401 Unauthorized

    o **GET/users/{id}**

      ▪ **Description**: Retrieves user details.

      ▪ **Input**: User ID (from path)

      ▪ **Output**: User details

      ▪ **Status codes**: 200 OK, 404 Not Found

   o **PUT**/**users**/**{id}**
- **Description**: Updates user details.
- **Input**: User ID (from path), updated user details
- **Output**: Updated user details
- **Status codes**: 200 OK, 400 Bad Request, 404 Not Found

   o **DELETE**/**users**/**{id}**
- **Description**: Deletes a user.
- **Input**: User ID (from path)
- **Output**: Confirmation message
- **Status codes**: 204 No Content, 404 Not Found

Playlist service

It manages user playlists, including creating, updating, and deleting playlists:

- **API ndpoints**
  - **POST**/**playlists**
    - **Description**: Creates a new playlist for a user.
    - **Input**: User ID, playlist name, list of song IDs
    - **Output**: Playlist ID
    - **Status codes:** 201 Created, 400 Bad Request

  - **GET**/**playlists**/**{id}**
    - **Description**: Retrieves the details of a playlist.
    - **Input**: Playlist ID (from path)
    - **Output**: Playlist details
    - **Status codes**: 200 OK, 404 Not Found

  - **PUT**/**playlists**/**{id}**
    - **Description**: Updates an existing playlist.
    - **Input**: Playlist ID (from path), updated playlist details
    - **Output**: Updated playlist details
    - **Status codes**: 200 OK, 400 Bad Request, 404 Not Found

  - **DELETE**/**playlists**/**{id}**
    - **Description**: Deletes a playlist.
    - **Input**: Playlist ID (from path)

- **Output**: Confirmation message
- **Status codes**: 204 No Content, 404 Not Found

Catalog service

This manages the music catalog and provides search functionality:

- **API endpoints**
  - o **GET /catalog/songs**
    - **Description**: Lists songs available in the catalog.
    - **Input**: Optional filters like genre, artist, and so on.
    - **Output**: List of songs
    - **Status codes**: 200 OK
  - o **GET/catalog/artists**
    - **Description**: Lists artists available in the catalog.
    - **Input**: None
    - **Output**: List of artists
    - **Status codes**: 200 OK
  - o **GET/catalog/albums**
    - **Description**: Lists albums available in the catalog.
    - **Input**: Optional filters like artist
    - **Output**: List of albums
    - **Status codes**: 200 OK

Recommendation engine

It houses the ML models and provides music recommendations based on user behavior.

- **API endpoints**
  - o **GET/recommendations/{userId}**
    - **Description**: Provides music recommendations for a user.
    - **Input**: User ID (from path)
    - **Output**: List of recommended song IDs
    - **Status codes**: 200 OK, 404 Not Found

Analytics service

This collects and analyzes user interaction data for improving the recommendation model.

- **API endpoints**
  - o **POST/analytics/track**
    - ▪ **Description**: Tracks user interactions like song plays, skips, likes, and so on.
    - ▪ **Input:** User ID, event type, song ID
    - ▪ **Output:** Confirmation message
    - ▪ **Status codes:** 201 Created, 400 Bad Request

Data pipeline service

This handles ETL tasks, data cleansing, and feature engineering for the ML models.

- **API endpoints**
  - o **POST/pipeline/train**
    - ▪ **Description**: Triggers a new model training process.
    - ▪ **Input**: None
    - ▪ **Output**: Job ID, estimated time of completion
    - ▪ **Status codes**: 202 Accepted
  - o **GET/pipeline/status**
    - ▪ **Description**: Retrieves the status of the last training job.
    - ▪ **Input**: None
    - ▪ **Output**: Job status
    - ▪ **Status codes**: 200 OK, 404 Not Found

These are the detailed API layers for each microservice in our example. They define what functionalities are exposed by each service and how they can be accessed. Each endpoint is designed with RESTful principles, ensuring they are intuitive and easily consumable.

Conclusion

Our discussion on this chapter has been an insightful journey through the various aspects that go into architecting a robust, scalable, and flexible ML system. In our discussion, we focused on several crucial aspects of implementing microservices in ML systems. We started by emphasizing DDD, which is vital for creating microservices tailored to specific ML needs. This led us to explore the principles of single responsibility, cohesion, and coupling, which are instrumental in effectively defining the boundaries of each microservice. Furthermore, we delved into the complexities of data flow and communication within these systems, examining the roles of data pipelines, synchronous and asynchronous communication methods, as well as the utilization of message queues, event streams, and API gateways.

Finally, we tackled the challenge of decomposing monolithic ML applications, discussing strategies to transition from a monolithic to a microservices architecture, with a focus on modularization and service governance. This comprehensive approach is designed to enhance the scalability, flexibility, and efficiency of ML systems.

In the next chapter, we will thoroughly examine a methodical strategy for creating, building, and implementing a scalable, efficient, and robust music recommendation engine. This approach utilizes a microservices architecture and incorporates various contemporary technologies.

Exercise

Having a robust database design is crucial for system performance, scalability, and maintainability. You need to design databases, tables/schema for our example of a music recommendation system.

Points to remember

- **Understanding DDD**
  - o Recognize the importance of aligning microservice design with business domains.
  - o Identify bounded contexts, entities, aggregates, and value objects for clear domain modeling.

- **Defining microservices boundaries**
  - o Apply the SRP to ensure each microservice handles one specific aspect of the system.
  - o Focus on high cohesion within services and low coupling between services.
  - o Develop clear API contracts to facilitate service-to-service communication.
  - o Implement versioning strategies for backward compatibility and smooth transitions.

- **Data flow and communication patterns**
  - o Understand the significance of data pipelines in microservices architectures.
  - o Differentiate between synchronous and asynchronous communication and choose appropriately based on use-case.
  - o Utilize message queues and event streams for efficient, decoupled data handling.
  - o Implement API gateways to centralize external requests and simplify client interactions.

o Ensure load balancing and fault tolerance to maintain system reliability and efficiency.

- **Decomposing monolithic ML applications**

    o Methodically identify modules and components within a monolithic system for gradual decomposition.

    o Plan the transition to microservices with a focus on minimizing disruption and maintaining data integrity.

    o Implement effective monitoring and governance for newly created microservices.

- **Practical application with a music recommendation system**

    o Apply the discussed principles in designing a music recommendation system as a real-world example.

    o Design an API layer, API gateway, and choose databases that best fit the needs of each microservice.

    o Incorporate an event bus and data pipeline to handle event-driven data flows and processing.

- **Role of an event bus in data pipelines**

    o Use an event bus like Apache Kafka for managing real-time data flows and asynchronous communication.

    o Facilitate data processing through tools like Apache Spark or Flink, consuming data from the event bus.

- **Database choices for services**

    o Tailor database selection to the specific needs of each service, considering factors like data structure, query patterns, and scalability.

Multiple choice questions

1. **What principle emphasizes that a microservice should have only one responsibility?**

    a. Polyglot persistence

    b. API first

    c. Single Responsibility Principle

    d. Continuous integration

2. **In DDD, what encapsulates a specific set of responsibilities and domain logic?**

    a. Entity

b. Bounded context

c. Aggregate

d. Value object

3. **Which is not a typical responsibility of an API gateway in a microservices architecture?**

a. Load balancing

b. Data encryption

c. Request routing

d. Model training

4. **In a microservices architecture, what facilitates asynchronous communication between services?**

a. API gateway

b. Event bus

c. Docker

d. Bounded context

5. **Which database is ideal for time-series data in a music streaming microservice?**

a. MySQL

b. Cassandra

c. MongoDB

d. InfluxDB

6. **In a microservices architecture, what ensures services are loosely coupled?**

a. Synchronous communication

b. Centralized database

c. Event-driven architecture

d. Monolithic design

7. **What is the role of an API gateway in a microservices architecture?**

a. To provide a single-entry point for all client requests

b. To handle database migrations

c. To directly manage user authentication

d. To serve as the primary data storage solution

8. **Which database is commonly used in microservices for caching recommendations?**

    a. PostgreSQL

    b. MongoDB

    c. Cassandra

    d. Redis

9. **Which design principle is crucial for managing data consistency across microservices?**

    a. Event sourcing

    b. API versioning

    c. Rate limiting

    d. Circuit breaker

10. **In the context of microservices for ML, what is the purpose of data pipelines?**

    a. To manually process data

    b. To secure data transmissions

    c. To automate data flow from collection to model inference

    d. To serve as the only storage option

Answer key

1	c
2	b
3	d
4	b
5	d
6	c
7	a
8	d
9	a
10	c

Join our book's Discord space

Join the book's Discord Workspace for Latest updates, Offers, Tech happenings around the world, New Release and Sessions with the Authors:

https://discord.bpbonline.com

CHAPTER 5

Implementing Microservices for Machine Learning

Introduction

In our previous discussions, we designed a music recommendation engine. It is an application designed to understand users' musical tastes, suggesting songs that they might enjoy. The application is expected to handle potentially thousands of song suggestions, learn from users' feedback, and continuously evolve. The sheer amount of data from users' listening histories, the need for real-time recommendations, and the scalability requirements make the design and choice of technology critical.

Core features revisited:

- **User profiles**: A repository of users' tastes, preferences, and listening histories.
- **Song database**: A vast database of songs, categorized by genre, artist, release year, and other metadata.
- **Recommendation algorithm**: The *brain* of the engine, which uses **Machine Learning (ML)** models to curate song recommendations based on a user's profile and feedback.

Structure

To implement the music recommendation engine as a series of microservices, we will explore the following topics:

- Developing ML microservices with essential technologies
- Creating scalable and distributed ML pipelines
- Orchestrating microservices with containerization

Objectives

This chapter aims to provide you with a comprehensive understanding of how to design, develop, and deploy ML microservices within the context of a music recommendation engine.

By working through the examples and applying the practices, you will have the knowledge and skills needed to build your own scalable, efficient, and robust ML microservices.

Developing ML microservices with essential technologies

This section focuses on implementing ML microservices for a music recommendation engine. Starting with a high-level design, we delve into the specifics of building scalable, modular, and robust services using popular frameworks such as Flask and FastAPI. We will also explore how to create data access layers, interact with databases, and integrate external services to provide a seamless user experience.

There are several reasons why microservices are advantageous for our music recommendation engine:

- **Scalability**: Microservices can scale horizontally. If our recommendation service witnesses a surge in usage, we can simply spawn more instances of that service without disturbing other components.
- **Flexibility in technology choices**: Different components can be built using different technologies best suited for the job. For example, the recommendation algorithm might be best implemented in Python due to the rich ML ecosystem, while another service handling user management could be written in Java or Go.
- **Continuous deployment and integration**: Microservices allow us to update individual services without needing to overhaul the entire application. This is particularly beneficial for ML models, which may need frequent updates.
- **Resilience**: Failures are isolated. If the recommendation service crashes or has an issue, it would not bring down the whole application.

- • **Optimized resource allocation**: ML models can be resource-intensive, especially deep learning models. By isolating them into their services, we can allocate resources more effectively based on the demands of each service.

Flask for ML microservices

Flask is a lightweight, flexible, and modular web framework built on Python. It provides the essentials to get a web application up and running, making it ideal for prototypes and scalable production applications. Its straightforward syntax and extensibility make it popular for various applications, including microservices.

In our music recommendation engine, Flask is a quick and effective solution to expose our ML models as RESTful web services. It allows us to create endpoints where consumers can send requests to get song recommendations, submit feedback, or even request bulk suggestions for multiple users at once.

In the design phase, we discussed using databases like MySQL/Postgres, MongoDB, Redis, Solr, Cassandra, and HDFS for different microservices. However, to keep things simple and focused in this chapter, we will demonstrate code snippets using MySQL as the database for all **Data Access Object (DAO)** layers. You are encouraged to treat implementing a full-fledged system using multiple databases as an advanced exercise to enhance the microservices further.

You will need to install the **mysql-connector-python** package to interact with a MySQL database. To install the package, run:

```
pip install mysql-connector-python
```

As we delve deeper into the practical implementation of our microservices architecture, we now turn our attention to the creation of specific services utilizing the DAO pattern. The services we will discuss, demonstrate how to efficiently manage and interact with our database, ensuring a robust and scalable microservices framework:

1. **User service with DAO:** The code snippet provided in this section demonstrates how to set up the Flask application, define the DAO class for database interactions, and create API endpoints for user registration and login functionalities.

   ```
   from flask import Flask, jsonify, request


   app = Flask(__name__)


   # Mock User database
   import mysql.connector


   class UserDao:
   ```

```python
    def __init__(self):
        self.conn = mysql.connector.connect(
            host='localhost',
            user='root',
            password='your_password',
            database='your_database'
        )
        self.cursor = self.conn.cursor()

    def add_user(self, username, password):
        sql = "INSERT INTO users (username, password) VALUES (%s, %s)"
        val = (username, password)
        self.cursor.execute(sql, val)
        self.conn.commit()

    def check_user(self, username, password):
        sql = "SELECT password FROM users WHERE username=%s"
        val = (username, )
        self.cursor.execute(sql, val)
        result = self.cursor.fetchone()

        if result and result[0] == password:
            return True
        return False


userDao = UserDao()


@app.route('/register', methods=['POST'])
def register():
    data = request.json
    username = data['username']
    password = data['password']
    userDao.add_user(username, password)
    return jsonify({'status': 'registered'})
```

```python
@app.route('/login', methods=['POST'])
def login():
    data = request.json
    username = data['username']
    password = data['password']
    if userDao.check_user(username, password):
        return jsonify({'status': 'logged in'})
    else:
        return jsonify({'status': 'login failed'}), 401
```

2. **Catalog service with DAO:** Define the DAO class for database operations, and create API endpoints for querying the song catalog. This part is vital for handling song data and providing efficient access to it within the microservices ecosystem.

```python
from flask import Flask, jsonify, request

app = Flask(__name__)

import mysql.connector

class CatalogDao:
    def __init__(self):
        self.conn = mysql.connector.connect(
            host='localhost',
            user='root',
            password='your_password',
            database='your_database'
        )
        self.cursor = self.conn.cursor()

    def get_songs(self):
        sql = "SELECT * FROM songs"
        self.cursor.execute(sql)
        return self.cursor.fetchall()
```

```
        def get_song_by_id(self, song_id):
            sql = "SELECT * FROM songs WHERE id=%s"
            val = (song_id, )
            self.cursor.execute(sql, val)
            return self.cursor.fetchone()


catalog_dao = CatalogDao()


@app.route('/songs', methods=['GET'])
def get_songs():
    return jsonify({'songs': catalog_dao.get_songs()})


@app.route('/songs/<song_id>', methods=['GET'])
def get_song_by_id(song_id):
    song = catalog_dao.get_song_by_id(song_id)
    if song:
        return jsonify({'song': song})
    else:
        return jsonify({'message': 'Song not found'}), 404
```

3. **Playback service with DAO:** For the playback service, a DAO layer may interact with a file system or a blob storage service to fetch the song files. For this example, it is assumed that the DAO knows where to find the song files:

```
from flask import Flask, send_file


app = Flask(__name__)


class PlaybackDao:
    def get_song_file(self, song_id):
        # In a real application, you would fetch the song file based
        on the ID
        return 'some_song.mp3'


playbackDao = PlaybackDao()
```

```
@app.route('/play/<song_id>', methods=['GET'])
def play_song(song_id):
    song_file = playbackDao.get_song_file(song_id)
    return send_file(song_file, as_attachment=True)
```

4. **Recommendation service with DAO:** The recommendation service DAO could be more complex, involving multiple database tables or even calling external services. Here, it is simplified for demonstration.

Implementing a more complex DAO for the recommendation service would offer greater flexibility and options for leveraging multiple data sources or services. You can extend the recommendation service with a DAO that involves multiple *database tables* and potentially calls an external service.

We will simulate the following three tables here:

- **UserPreferences**: This stores user preferences

- **SongMetadata**: This stores song metadata

- **RecommendationLog**: This keeps a log of the recommendations made

And one external service:

- **ExternalRecommender**: This is a mock of an external recommendation system

DAO layer

```
# Mock database tables and external services for demonstration


# User preferences "table"
class UserPreferencesDao:
    def __init__(self):
        self.preferences = {}


    def add_preference(self, user_id, preference):
        self.preferences[user_id] = preference


    def get_preference(self, user_id):
        return self.preferences.get(user_id, None)


# Song metadata "table"
class SongMetadataDao:
    def __init__(self):
```

```python
        self.songs = [
            {'id': 1, 'title': 'Song A', 'artist': 'Artist 1'},
            {'id': 2, 'title': 'Song B', 'artist': 'Artist 2'},
        ]

    def get_song(self, song_id):
        return next((song for song in self.songs if song['id'] ==
        song_id), None)


# Recommendation log "table"
class RecommendationLogDao:
    def __init__(self):
        self.log = []

    def add_log(self, user_id, recommendation):
        self.log.append({'user_id': user_id, 'recommendation':
        recommendation})


# External recommender "service"
class ExternalRecommender:
    def get_recommendation(self, user_id):
        # Simulate calling an external recommendation service
        return {'id': 1, 'title': 'External Song A', 'artist':
        'External Artist 1'}
```

Flask service with DAO integration

```python
from flask import Flask, jsonify, request
from sklearn.neighbors import KNeighborsClassifier
import numpy as np


app = Flask(__name__)


userPreferencesDao = UserPreferencesDao()
songMetadataDao = SongMetadataDao()
recommendationLogDao = RecommendationLogDao()
```

```
externalRecommender = ExternalRecommender()


# Sample KNN model for demonstration
knn = KNeighborsClassifier(n_neighbors=3)
knn.fit(np.array([[0, 1], [1, 0], [1, 1], [0, 0]]), np.array([1, 2, 1,
2]))


@app.route('/recommend', methods=['POST'])
def recommend():
    data = request.json
    user_id = data['user_id']
    user_data = np.array([data['features']])

    # Use KNN model for recommendation
    song_id = knn.predict(user_data)[0]

    # Log the recommendation
    recommendationLogDao.add_log(user_id, song_id)

    # Get song metadata
    song = songMetadataDao.get_song(song_id)

    return jsonify({'recommendation': song})


@app.route('/recommend/external', methods=['GET'])
def recommend_external():
    user_id = request.args.get('user_id')

    # Call external recommendation service
    recommendation = externalRecommender.get_recommendation(user_id)

    # Log the recommendation
    recommendationLogDao.add_log(user_id, recommendation['id'])
```

```
        return jsonify({'recommendation': recommendation})


if __name__ == '__main__':
    app.run(port=5005)
```

In this example, the **/recommend** endpoint uses a **K-nearest neighbors (KNN)** model to make song recommendations based on user features. On the other hand, the **/recommend/external** endpoint simulates a call to an external recommendation service. Both routes log the recommendations made to a mock **RecommendationLog** database table through the DAO.

This is simple example demonstrates how to structure your code for more complex scenarios, including multiple tables and external service calls.

Recommendation service DAO using MySql DB: Here, we will use one table for user preferences (**user_preferences**) and another for recommendation logs (**recommendation_log**):

```
import mysql.connector


class RecommendationDao:
    def __init__(self):
        self.conn = mysql.connector.connect(
            host='localhost',
            user='root',
            password='your_password',
            database='your_database'
        )
        self.cursor = self.conn.cursor()


    def add_log(self, user_id, recommendation):
        sql = "INSERT INTO recommendation_log (user_id,
        recommendation) VALUES (%s, %s)"
        val = (user_id, recommendation)
        self.cursor.execute(sql, val)
        self.conn.commit()


    def get_user_preferences(self, user_id):
        sql = "SELECT preferences FROM user_preferences WHERE user_
        id=%s"
```

```
        val = (user_id, )
        self.cursor.execute(sql, val)
        return self.cursor.fetchone()
```

5. **Analytics service with DAO:** This service is essential for gathering, storing, and analyzing data. The provided code details the setup of the Flask application, the construction of the DAO class for database operations, and the creation of endpoints to manage analytics data.

```python
from flask import Flask, jsonify, request


app = Flask(__name__)


import mysql.connector


class AnalyticsDao:
    def __init__(self):
        self.conn = mysql.connector.connect(
            host='localhost',
            user='root',
            password='your_password',
            database='your_database'
        )
        self.cursor = self.conn.cursor()


    def add_data(self, new_data):
        sql = "INSERT INTO analytics_data (data_field) VALUES (%s)"
        val = (new_data, )
        self.cursor.execute(sql, val)
        self.conn.commit()


    def get_data(self):
        sql = "SELECT * FROM analytics_data"
        self.cursor.execute(sql)
        return self.cursor.fetchall()
```

```
analyticsDao = AnalyticsDao()

@app.route('/analytics', methods=['POST'])
def collect_data():
    data = request.json
    analyticsDao.add_data(data)
    return jsonify({'status': 'data collected'})

@app.route('/analytics', methods=['GET'])
def get_analytics():
    return jsonify({'data': analyticsDao.get_data()})
```

FastAPI for Machine Learning microservices

Let us move on to implementing the services using FastAPI. FastAPI is an excellent choice for building web APIs with built-in support for data validation, JWT authentication, and more. We will assume that the DAO layer is already implemented as discussed earlier.

First, make sure you have FastAPI and Uvicorn installed. If not, you can install them using pip:

```
pip install fastapi uvicorn
```

Let us start by implementing the catalog service, focusing on the endpoint that returns a single song by its ID.

FastAPI Catalog Service

First, import the necessary modules and initialize your FastAPI app:

```
from fastapi import FastAPI, HTTPException

from pydantic import BaseModel


app = FastAPI()

catalog_dao = CatalogDao()
```

Next, define a Pydantic model (*Pydantic model* is somewhat specific to the Pydantic library, which is used often with FastAPI for data validation and serialization) to describe a song:

```
class Song(BaseModel):
    id: int
```

```
    title: str

    artist: str
```

Now, you can create an **application programming interface (API)** endpoint to fetch a single song by its ID:

```
@app.get("/catalog/song/{song_id}", response_model=Song)

def get_song_by_id(song_id: int):

    song = catalog_dao.get_song_by_id(song_id)

    if song is None:

        raise HTTPException(status_code=404, detail="Song not found")

    return {"id": song[0], "title": song[1], "artist": song[2]}
```

Here, we use FastAPI's path parameters to capture the **song_id** from the URL. We also specify a **response_model**, which is a Pydantic model describing the shape of the response.

Finally, to run your FastAPI application, save it in a file (for example, **main.py**) and execute the following command:

```
uvicorn main:app --reload
```

This will start the FastAPI application. You can test the **/catalog/song/{song_id}** endpoint by navigating to **http://127.0.0.1:8000/catalog/song/1** (replace 1 with an actual song ID in your database).

Now, you have the catalog service implemented in both Flask and FastAPI, each with an API endpoint that fetches a song by its ID using the DAO layer.

Let us implement other services using FastAPI. We will build upon the existing DAO layers and provide FastAPI implementations for each of the services.

FastAPI User Service

For the user service, we will create endpoints for adding a new user and checking the existence of a user with a specific username and password.

Here is how you can add these routes to your FastAPI application:

```
class User(BaseModel):

    username: str

    password: str


@app.post("/user/add", response_model=User)
```

```
def add_user(user: User):

    user_dao = UserDao()

    user_dao.add_user(user.username, user.password)

    return {"username": user.username, "password": user.password}


@app.post("/user/check", response_model=User)

def check_user(user: User):

    user_dao = UserDao()

    if user_dao.check_user(user.username, user.password):

        return {"username": user.username, "password": user.password}

    else:

        raise HTTPException(status_code=401, detail="Unauthorized")
```

FastAPI Playback Service

For the playback service, let us assume you have a method in your DAO that updates playback information. The service will contain an endpoint for updating playback status. Take a look at the following code:

```
class PlaybackInfo(BaseModel):

    song_id: int

    user_id: int

    status: str  # Could be "PLAY", "PAUSE", etc.


@app.post("/playback/update", response_model=PlaybackInfo)

def update_playback(info: PlaybackInfo):

    playback_dao = PlaybackDao()

    playback_dao.update_playback(info.user_id, info.song_id, info.status)

    return {"song_id": info.song_id, "user_id": info.user_id, "status":
    info.status}
```

FastAPI Recommendation Service

For the recommendation service, we will create an endpoint to add a new recommendation log for a user and get recommendations for a user. Take a look at the following code:

```python
class Recommendation(BaseModel):

    user_id: int

    recommendation: str  # Could be a list of song IDs, genres, etc.


@app.post("/recommendation/add", response_model=Recommendation)

def add_recommendation(rec: Recommendation):

    recommendation_dao = RecommendationDao()

    recommendation_dao.add_log(rec.user_id, rec.recommendation)

    return {"user_id": rec.user_id, "recommendation": rec.recommendation}


@app.get("/recommendation/user/{user_id}", response_model=Recommendation)

def get_recommendation(user_id: int):

    recommendation_dao = RecommendationDao()

    recommendation = recommendation_dao.get_user_preferences(user_id)

    if recommendation is None:

        raise HTTPException(status_code=404, detail="Recommendation not
        found")

    return {"user_id": user_id, "recommendation": recommendation[0]}
```

FastAPI Analytics Service

For the analytics service, you could have an endpoint that logs data for analytics purposes, shown as follows:

```python
class AnalyticsData(BaseModel):

    data_field: str  # Could be anything, depending on your analytics
    requirements


@app.post("/analytics/add", response_model=AnalyticsData)

def add_analytics_data(data: AnalyticsData):
```

```
analytics_dao = AnalyticsDao()

analytics_dao.add_data(data.data_field)

return {"data_field": data.data_field}
```

Remember to import your DAO classes and any other required classes or libraries.

To run your FastAPI application, save it in a file (for example, **main.py**) and execute the following command:

```
uvicorn main:app --reload
```

This will give you a FastAPI application with endpoints for user, playback, recommendation, and analytics services, each backed by its respective DAO layer.

Creating scalable and distributed ML pipelines

In this section we will discuss the importance of scalability and distribution in the context of ML, emphasizing the need for adaptable, high-performance pipelines in modern data environments. The goal is to provide you with insights into developing ML pipelines that can grow and evolve in response to increasing data demands and computational complexity.

Scalable Machine Learning pipelines using Kubeflow

Scalability is the ability of a system to handle an increased load gracefully. In a microservices environment, especially one that has ML components, scalability is often a challenging but crucial requirement. As your user base grows, or as you add more features and complexity to your ML models, your architecture should be capable of growing and adapting without causing a significant degradation in performance or reliability.

Kubeflow

Kubeflow is a Kubernetes-native platform for end-to-end ML workflows. It provides various components for each stage of an ML pipeline and aims to make deployments of ML workflows on Kubernetes simple, portable, and scalable. Here is how Kubeflow facilitates the implementation of scalable ML pipelines:

- **Modular pipelines**: Kubeflow pipelines allow you to define and deploy modular, composable, and portable ML workflows. You can create individual pipeline components and stitch them together into a full workflow.

- **Resource management**: Running on Kubernetes, Kubeflow inherently possesses powerful resource management and orchestration capabilities.

- **Auto-scaling**: Kubernetes' native auto-scaling features can be utilized by Kubeflow, letting you automatically adjust the number of ML pipeline replicas based on CPU or memory usage.

- **Rich UI**: Kubeflow provides a rich set of visualizations for your ML workflows, enabling easy monitoring and debugging.

Deploying Kubeflow on AWS involves multiple steps, such as setting up an **Amazon Elastic Kubernetes Service** (**Amazon EKS**) cluster, deploying Kubeflow, and finally running your ML workflows.

The prerequisites are as follows:

- AWS account
- AWS CLI installed and configured
- **eksctl** CLI tool installed
- **kubectl** installed

The steps involved to deploy Kubeflow on AWS are as follows:

1. **Create an EKScluster**: First, you will need to create a Kubernetes cluster using Amazon EKS. You can do this with the **eksctl** command-line tool:

   ```
   eksctl create cluster --name my-kubeflow-cluster --region us-west-2
   --nodes 2
   ```

   This command will create a cluster with 2 nodes in the **us-west-2** region. You can adjust these settings as needed.

2. **Verify cluster creation**: After the cluster is created, make sure that your **kubectl** context is set to the new cluster:

   ```
   kubectl config current-context
   ```

3. **Deploy Kubeflow**: Now it is time to deploy Kubeflow. Use the **kfctl** CLI for this.

   a. Download the latest version of **kfctl** from the Kubeflow releases page.

   b. Download the configuration file for AWS deployments:

   ```
   wget https://raw.githubusercontent.com/kubeflow/manifests/v1.2-
   branch/kfdef/kfctl_aws.v1.2.0.yaml
   ```

4. **Apply the configuration**: This step will take some time as it sets up all the Kuberflow components:

   ```
   kfctl apply -V -f kfctl_aws.v1.2.0.yaml
   ```

5. **Access Kubeflow dashboard**: Access the Kubeflow dashboard to manage and monitor your ML workflows by forwarding the Istio ingress gateway service to your local machine using the command:

```
kubectl port-forward svc/istio-ingressgateway -n istio-system 8080:80
```

You can now access the dashboard at **http://localhost:8080**.

6. **Run your pipelines**: You can now upload and run your Kubeflow pipelines, as well as other ML workloads.

Additional AWS features

AWS provides several services that you might want to integrate with your Kubeflow deployment:

- **Amazon Simple Storage Service (Amazon S3)**: For scalable storage of datasets and ML model files.

- **Amazon Relational Database Service (Amazon RDS)**: For relational databases to store structured data.

- **Amazon SageMaker**: For training and deploying ML models, which can be integrated into your Kubeflow pipelines.

Deploying Kubeflow on AWS enables you to leverage the robustness and scalability of AWS services, along with the ML orchestration capabilities of Kubeflow. This combination provides a strong foundation for building scalable and maintainable ML pipelines.

Creating a Kubeflow pipeline that includes all the services like user service, catalog service, playback service, recommendation service, and analytics service would be an extensive task. However, we can outline how you could construct such a pipeline.

Let us assume each service has a specific role:

- **User service**: Manages user data and authentication
- **Catalog service**: Handles the music catalog
- **Playback service**: Takes care of music playback
- **Recommendation service**: Provides music recommendations
- **Analytics service**: Analyzes user behavior

Kubeflow pipeline outline

Following outline includes essential stages, from data ingestion to monitoring and logging, each playing a crucial role in the end-to-end process of our ML application. These steps ensure a comprehensive approach to handling data, training models, and deploying them efficiently, ultimately facilitating a robust ML lifecycle:

1. **Data ingestion**: Pulls raw data for each service.

2. **Data preprocessing**: Cleanses and transforms raw data.

3. **Model training (For recommendation service)**: Trains the recommendation model.

4. **Model evaluation**: Evaluates the trained model.

5. **Model deployment**: Deploys the trained model to a serving layer.

6. **Analytics processing**: Processes user data for analytics.

7. **User update**: Updates user profiles based on analytics and recommendations.

8. **Catalog update**: Updates the music catalog based on analytics.

9. **Monitoring and logging**: Stores logs and monitoring metrics for debugging and traceability.

Having outlined the steps of our comprehensive Kubeflow pipeline, we now transition into the practical implementation. The following code snippet exemplifies the realization of these steps, starting from data ingestion all the way to monitoring and logging:

```python
from kfp import dsl

from kfp.components import func_to_container_op


# Define individual steps using container functions

@func_to_container_op

def data_ingestion():

    # Code to ingest data

    return "Data Ingested"


@func_to_container_op

def data_preprocessing():

    # Code to preprocess data

    return "Data Preprocessed"


@func_to_container_op

def model_training():

    # Code to train the recommendation model

    return "Model Trained"
```

```python
@func_to_container_op
def model_evaluation():
    # Code to evaluate the model
    return "Model Evaluated"


@func_to_container_op
def model_deployment():
    # Code to deploy the model
    return "Model Deployed"


@func_to_container_op
def analytics_processing():
    # Code to process analytics
    return "Analytics Processed"


@func_to_container_op
def user_update():
    # Code to update user data
    return "User Updated"


@func_to_container_op
def catalog_update():
    # Code to update the catalog
    return "Catalog Updated"


@func_to_container_op
def monitoring_logging():
    # Code for monitoring and logging
    return "Monitoring and Logging Done"
```

```
# Create a pipeline

@dsl.pipeline(name='FullPipeline')

def full_pipeline():

    ingestion = data_ingestion()

    preprocessing = data_preprocessing().after(ingestion)

    training = model_training().after(preprocessing)

    evaluation = model_evaluation().after(training)

    deployment = model_deployment().after(evaluation)

    analytics = analytics_processing().after(deployment)

    user = user_update().after(analytics)

    catalog = catalog_update().after(user)

    monitor = monitoring_logging().after(catalog)


# Compile the pipeline

if __name__ == '__main__':

    import kfp.compiler as compiler

    compiler.Compiler().compile(full_pipeline, 'full_pipeline.yaml')
```

This is an example outline; you will need to add the actual code that carries out these operations inside each container function. This pipeline is linear for simplicity; however, in a real-world scenario, some of these tasks would be parallelized.

Once this YAML pipeline definition is compiled, it can be uploaded to the Kubeflow pipelines UI and run from there. You can also parameterize it further to accept inputs.

Let us consider the **model_training** function as an example. In a real-world scenario, this function might perform various tasks like loading data from a database or data lake, preprocessing it, and then training a ML model. Following is a simple example where the function trains a basic recommendation model using collaborative filtering with the **surprise** library.

First, you may need to install the **surprise** package in your Kubeflow pipeline environment or your container. This can often be done by specifying the package in a **requirements.txt** file that you include with your pipeline.

Here is how the function might look:

```python
from surprise import Dataset, SVD, accuracy

from surprise.model_selection import train_test_split


@func_to_container_op

def model_training():

    # Load built-in dataset from surprise library for demonstration

    data = Dataset.load_builtin('ml-100k')

    trainset, testset = train_test_split(data, test_size=.25)


    # Use SVD algorithm for training

    algo = SVD()


    # Train the model

    algo.fit(trainset)


    # Perform predictions

    predictions = algo.test(testset)


    # Calculate RMSE (Root Mean Square Error)

    rmse = accuracy.rmse(predictions)


    # For a production pipeline, you would save the model to disk or a
    database here


    return f"Model Trained with RMSE: {rmse}"
```

This simple example is far from a complete production scenario, but hopefully, it gives you an idea of how to include actual code in your Kubeflow pipeline steps. You could replace the simple **Dataset.load_builtin('ml-100k')** call with logic to pull your actual data from wherever it resides (for example, a database, a data lake, a distributed file system like HDFS, and so on).

To include this function in your pipeline, you could simply replace the existing **model_ training** function definition in the pipeline code provided earlier.

Remember that you will also need to ensure that any libraries you use (like **surprise** in this case) are installed in the containers that run your pipeline steps. This can usually be done by specifying a custom container image or a **requirements.txt** file.

Inter-service communication

Inter-service communication is a critical part of microservices architecture, particularly in a complex system like your music recommendation engine with multiple services (user, catalog, playback, recommendation, analytics). Let us discuss some of the commonly used paradigms for inter-service communication.

HTTP/REST

The simplest and most straightforward way to get services to communicate with each other is through HTTP/RESTful APIs. This paradigm is synchronous and best suited for straightforward CRUD operations where one service directly requires information or action from another service.

An example in Python using Flask and requests is as follows:

```python
# In Recommendation Service

from flask import Flask, jsonify

import requests


app = Flask(__name__)


@app.route('/recommendations')

def get_recommendation():

    user_id = '123'

    # Call the User Service to get user information

    response = requests.get(f'http://user-service:5000/users/{user_id}')

    user_info = response.json()

    # Process the recommendation based on user_info

    recommended_song = "Song A"

    return jsonify({'recommended_song': recommended_song})
```

```
if __name__ == '__main__':

    app.run(port=5001)
```

Message brokers

Message brokers like Kafka or RabbitMQ are typically used for asynchronous communication between services. In a Kafka-based system, services produce messages to a topic, and other services consume messages from that topic.

In example using Kafka, you need to install a Kafka Python client:

```
pip install kafka-python
```

Producer (for example, in user service): Set up a Kafka producer for sending messages, in this case, user updates, to a specified Kafka topic.

```
from kafka import KafkaProducer


producer = KafkaProducer(bootstrap_servers='localhost:9092')

producer.send('user_updates', key='user123', value='New user registered')
```

Consumer (for example, in analytics service): Set up and use a Kafka consumer to receive and process messages from the **'user_updates'** topic.

```
from kafka import KafkaConsumer


consumer = KafkaConsumer('user_updates',

                         bootstrap_servers='localhost:9092')


for message in consumer:

    print(f"Received message: {message.value.decode('utf-8')}")
```

Event-driven architecture

In an event-driven system, services communicate with each other by producing and consuming events. This is generally an extension of the message broker paradigm, with more emphasis on decoupling services. Events are usually consumed by multiple services that execute different actions in parallel.

Some examples using Kafka are:
- Producer (in catalog service after a new song is added):
  ```
  producer.send('new_song_added', value='New song XYZ added')
  ```

- Consumers (in recommendation service and analytics service):

```
consumer = KafkaConsumer('new_song_added',
                         bootstrap_servers='localhost:9092')


for message in consumer:
    if message.value.decode('utf-8') == 'New song XYZ added':
        # Recommendation Service updates its model
        # Analytics Service logs the event
```

By using such paradigms, you can establish robust communication between the services in your music recommendation engine. Each approach has its own merits and the best choice often depends on specific requirements such as latency, throughput, and complexity.

Load balancing

Load balancing is a critical component for any scalable system. As your user base grows and the demand on your services increases, a single instance of a service will not be enough to handle all the requests efficiently. Load balancing helps in distributing incoming application or network traffic across multiple servers, thereby improving responsiveness and availability of applications.

The strategies for load balancing are:

- **Round robin**: Each server is selected in turns.
- **Least connections**: The server with the fewest active connections is chosen.
- **Hash-based**: Requests are distributed based on a key you define, such as the client IP address or request URL.
- **Resource-based**: Directs traffic to the server with the most available resources.

Load balancing in microservices

Load balancing can be implemented at different levels, including **domain name system (DNS)** load balancing, hardware-based, or software-based like using Nginx, HAProxy, or built-in load balancers provided by cloud providers like AWS ELB.

Load balancing with Kubernetes

If you are deploying your microservices in a Kubernetes cluster, you have several built-in options for load balancing:

- **ClusterIP**: Exposes the service on a cluster-internal IP.
- **NodePort**: Exposes the service on each Node's IP at a static port.
- **LoadBalancer**: Provisions an external IP to act as a load balancer.

Here is a simple example of a Kubernetes service definition with load balancing:

```
apiVersion: v1

kind: Service

metadata:

  name: recommendation-service

spec:

  selector:

    app: recommendation

  ports:

    - protocol: TCP

      port: 80

      targetPort: 8080

  type: LoadBalancer
```

This will automatically provision a cloud load balancer if your cluster is running in a cloud provider that supports this, and route incoming traffic to all pods with the label **app=recommendation**.

API Gateways like Kong, AWS API Gateway, and others provide a comprehensive solution for routing and load balancing your microservices. The API Gateway acts as a reverse proxy to accept all API calls, aggregate the various services required to fulfill them, and return the appropriate result. They can provide features like API composition, rate limiting, security, analytics, and more.

Load balancing with AWS API Gateway

Suppose you have two instances of your recommendation service, and you want to balance the load between them. You can achieve this by creating a new VPC link with AWS API Gateway and attaching the two instances of recommendation service to it.

Here is how you can set it up using AWS CLI:

1. **Create a VPC link**

```
aws apigateway create-vpc-link --name "recommendation-vpc-link"
--target-arns "arn:aws:elasticloadbalancing:region:account-
id:loadbalancer/target-group-arn"
```

2. **Create a new API**

```
aws apigatewayv2 create-api --name "RecommendationAPI" --protocol-
type "HTTP"
```

3. **Create a route**

```
aws apigatewayv2 create-route --api-id "your-api-id" --route-key "GET
/recommendations" --target "integrations/your-integration-id"
```

4. **Create an integration**

```
aws apigatewayv2 create-integration --api-id "your-api-id" --integration-
type "HTTP_PROXY" --integration-method "GET" --integration-uri
"http://your-service-url/recommendations" --connection-type "VPC_
LINK" --connection-id "your-vpc-link-id"
```

Once you have set up this API Gateway, incoming requests to **https://your-api-gateway-url/recommendations** will automatically be load balanced between the two instances of the recommendation service.

Load balancing with Kong

Kong also allows you to load balance traffic by distributing incoming requests across multiple backend services. Following is a simplified example of how you can set up load balancing using Kong's Admin API:

1. **Add a service in Kong**

```
curl -i -X POST --url http://localhost:8001/services/ --data
'name=recommendation-service' --data 'url=http://recommendation-
service-address'
```

2. **Add a route to the service**

```
curl -i -X POST --url http://localhost:8001/services/recommendation-
service/routes --data 'paths[]=/recommendations'
```

3. **Configure load balancing**

Kong can automatically load balance traffic as long as you specify multiple **url** or **host** names when adding your service. You can update the service to include multiple hosts as follows:

```
curl -X PATCH http://localhost:8001/services/recommendation-service
--data 'url=http://host.one,http://host.two'
```

After this configuration, Kong will balance the load between **host.one** and **host.two**.

By using an API Gateway, you not only benefit from load balancing but also gain additional features like API composition, logging, security, and more, all configurable in a centralized service.

Real-time vs. batch processing in microservices architecture

In a microservices architecture, especially one that includes ML, the processing of data can be categorized into two types: real-time and batch processing. Both have their advantages and use-cases, and understanding the differences can guide you to make an informed decision for your specific needs.

Real-time processing

In real-time processing, each incoming request is processed immediately and individually, and a response is returned as quickly as possible. Real-time processing is commonly used in applications that require instant decision-making.

Advantages

The advantages of real-time processing are as follows:

- **Low latency**: Quick response time is the most significant advantage.
- **Personalization**: Real-time data can be used for making personalized recommendations.
- **Resource efficient**: Consumes resources only when there is a request to process.

Example use-cases

The examples of use cases are as follows:

- Fraud detection
- Real-time analytics
- Personalized recommendations

Real-time processing with FastAPI

Here is a FastAPI example to provide real-time music recommendations for a given **user_id**. We will mock the ML model with a simple function:

```
from fastapi import FastAPI


app = FastAPI()


# Simulate a machine learning model

def get_real_time_recommendation(user_id: int):

    # Normally, this function would call a trained ML model
```

```
    return f"Recommended song for user {user_id} is Song123"
```

```
@app.get("/real-time-recommendation/{user_id}")

async def real_time_recommendation(user_id: int):

    recommendation = get_real_time_recommendation(user_id)

    return {"recommendation": recommendation}
```

To run the FastAPI application, save the code in a file called **main.py** and execute **uvicorn main:app --reload** from the terminal. Then you can access the real-time recommendation API at **http://127.0.0.1:8000/real-time-recommendation/{user_id}**.

Batch processing with Apache Spark and HDFS

The first step is to ensure HDFS and Spark are properly set up and running. You can then upload your **user_behaviors.csv** to HDFS using the **hadoop fs -put** command:

```
hadoop fs -put /localpath/to/user_behaviors.csv /hdfspath/to/user_behaviors.
csv
```

Now, you can read this file into a Spark DataFrame and proceed with the batch processing.

The following example includes a basic ML model for generating music recommendations. The example uses Apache Spark's MLlib for training a basic k-means clustering model. We will use features like **listening_time**, **genre_preference**, and **user_activity** to cluster the users. The recommended song will be the most popular song in each cluster.

For demonstration purposes, let us assume our CSV file **user_behaviors.csv** has columns for **user_id**, **listening_time**, **genre_preference**, and **user_activity**. Take a look at the following code:

```
from pyspark.sql import SparkSession

from pyspark.ml.clustering import KMeans

from pyspark.ml.feature import VectorAssembler


# Initialize a Spark session

spark = SparkSession.builder \

    .appName('MusicRecommendationBatchProcessing') \

    .getOrCreate()


# Read dataset from HDFS
```

```
hdfs_path = "hdfs://localhost:9000/hdfspath/to/user_behaviors.csv"
df = spark.read.csv(hdfs_path, header=True, inferSchema=True)

# Prepare data for ML model
feature_cols = ['listening_time', 'genre_preference', 'user_activity']
vec_assembler = VectorAssembler(inputCols=feature_cols, outputCol="features")
df_kmeans = vec_assembler.transform(df).select('user_id', 'features')

# Train k-means model
kmeans = KMeans().setK(3).setSeed(1)
model = kmeans.fit(df_kmeans)

# Make predictions
predictions = model.transform(df_kmeans)

# Simulate popular song for each cluster
# In a real-world scenario, you'd look up the most popular songs in each
cluster based on user behavior
popular_songs = {0: "SongA", 1: "SongB", 2: "SongC"}

# Generate recommendations
def get_batch_recommendations(df):
    recommendations = []
    for row in df.rdd.collect():
        user_id = row['user_id']
        cluster = row['prediction']
        recommendations.append((user_id, popular_songs[cluster]))
    return recommendations

# Get recommendations
batch_recommendations = get_batch_recommendations(predictions)
```

```
# Save to HDFS
```

```
output_hdfs_path = "hdfs://localhost:9000/hdfspath/to/recommendations"
```

```
spark.createDataFrame(batch_recommendations, ["user_id", "song_id"]).write.
csv(output_hdfs_path)
```

In this example, we outline a series of steps that demonstrates a process of implementing ML in a batch processing environment using Apache Spark and HDFS:

1. Read the data from HDFS.
2. Transform the data to the required format (features column) using **VectorAssembler**.
3. Train a k-means clustering model on these features.
4. Make cluster predictions for each user.
5. Map each cluster to a popular song.
6. Generate recommendations based on these mappings.
7. Save the recommendations back to HDFS.

This simplified example provides a good starting point for implementing ML in a batch processing environment with Apache Spark and HDFS.

Caching strategies in scalable ML pipelines

Caching can be a critical part of a scalable ML pipeline, especially when dealing with large datasets or computationally expensive tasks. Effective caching can reduce latency and improve the overall user experience.

In an ML pipeline, caching can be useful in multiple places:

- **Feature transformation**: After transforming raw data into a suitable format for ML, this processed data can be cached for future use.

- **Model inference**: The results from model inference can also be cached if the same input is expected to be queried multiple times.

- **User preferences**: In a music recommendation system, user preferences do not change with every single request. Caching the user's preferences can reduce the computation time.

Caching methods

Various methods are available for caching in microservices architecture. Here we will focus on Redis as a caching layer. For example, caching model inference results with Redis.

Let us consider an example using Python with the **redis** package. This example assumes that you have a function called **recommend_songs(user_id)** that returns song recommendations for a given user ID. We will cache its results. Take a look at the following code:

```python
import redis
import json
import time

# Connect to Redis server
r = redis.Redis(host='localhost', port=6379, db=0)

def recommend_songs(user_id):
    # Simulate some heavy computation to generate recommendations
    time.sleep(2)
    return ["Song1", "Song2", "Song3"]

def get_recommendations_with_caching(user_id):
    # Use user_id as the cache key
    cache_key = f"recommendations:{user_id}"

    # Try to get cached result first
    cached_result = r.get(cache_key)
    if cached_result:
        print("Cache hit!")
        return json.loads(cached_result)

    # If not in cache, generate recommendations
    print("Cache miss!")
    recommendations = recommend_songs(user_id)

    # Store the result in cache for 1 hour
    r.setex(cache_key, 3600, json.dumps(recommendations))
```

```
        return recommendations
```

```
# Test the function
```

```
print(get_recommendations_with_caching("user123"))   # Cache miss!
```

```
print(get_recommendations_with_caching("user123"))   # Cache hit!
```

In this example, the function **get_recommendations_with_caching()** first checks if the recommendations for a given **user_id** are already in the Redis cache. If yes, it returns the cached result; otherwise, it calculates the recommendations using **recommend_songs()**, caches the result, and then returns it.

Cache invalidation

Cache invalidation is another critical aspect. You should define strategies for invalidating the cache entries whenever the underlying data changes. In Redis, the **setex** function sets an expiry time for each cache entry, which is one way to handle invalidation.

Caching is an essential aspect of building scalable ML pipelines. By storing the intermediate results or frequently requested data in a fast-access data store like Redis, you can significantly improve the system's responsiveness and efficiency. However, you must also manage cache invalidation effectively to ensure that the system remains accurate and up-to-date.

Through the various code segments and architectural components discussed above, we have collectively demonstrated the development of a music recommendation system. This compilation of practical examples serves as a foundational blueprint for constructing a scalable and sophisticated music recommendation pipeline, incorporating a multitude of services and technologies.

Orchestrating microservices with containerization

So far, we have built a complex architecture with multiple microservices, which can become hard to manage quickly. This is where containerization comes in. Containers package up code and all its dependencies so the application runs consistently. Docker is a popular containerization platform, and Kubernetes is widely used for orchestration.

Dockerizing microservices

Each microservice can be containerized into its own Docker image, making it easy to deploy and scale.

1. **Create dockerfiles:** For each service, you create a **Dockerfile**. Here is an example for the **UserService**:

```
# Use an official Python runtime as a base image
FROM python:3.8-slim-buster


# Set the working directory
WORKDIR /usr/src/app


# Copy the current directory contents into the container at /usr/src/
app
COPY . .


# Install required packages
RUN pip install --no-cache-dir -r requirements.txt


# Run app.py when the container launches
CMD ["python", "app.py"]
```

Similarly, you would have Dockerfiles for **CatalogService**, **RecommendationSer-vice**, **AnalyticsService**, and the **API Gateway**.

2. **Build Docker images:** Build Docker images for each service. Take a look at the following code:

```
docker build -t user-service .
docker build -t catalog-service .
docker build -t recommendation-service .
docker build -t analytics-service .
docker build -t api-gateway .
```

3. **Run docker containers:** To run these images as containers, refer to the following code:

```
docker run -p 5001:5001 user-service
docker run -p 5002:5002 catalog-service
docker run -p 5003:5003 recommendation-service
docker run -p 5004:5004 analytics-service
docker run -p 5000:5000 api-gateway
```

Kubernetes for orchestration

With Docker, you have containerized your services. Now, use Kubernetes to manage these containers at scale:

1. **Kubernetes YAML configurations:** For each service, create a Kubernetes YAML configuration file to specify how the service should be deployed and run. Here is an example for the **UserService**:

```
apiVersion: v1
kind: Service
metadata:
  name: user-service
spec:
  selector:
    app: user-service
  ports:
    - protocol: TCP
      port: 5001
---
apiVersion: apps/v1
kind: Deployment
metadata:
  name: user-service
spec:
  replicas: 3
  selector:
    matchLabels:
      app: user-service
  template:
    metadata:
      labels:
        app: user-service
    spec:
      containers:
      - name: user-service
```

```
image: user-service:latest
ports:
- containerPort: 5001
```

2. **Deploy to Kubernetes:** Apply these configurations to your Kubernetes cluster:

```
kubectl apply -f user-service.yaml
kubectl apply -f catalog-service.yaml
kubectl apply -f recommendation-service.yaml
kubectl apply -f analytics-service.yaml
kubectl apply -f api-gateway.yaml
```

This will deploy your microservices and make them accessible via services in your Kubernetes cluster. Kubernetes will ensure that a specified number of replicas for each service is always running.

We have now dockerized each microservice and used Kubernetes to orchestrate them. This adds a layer of abstraction over our services, enabling easy scaling, load balancing, and inter-service communication. This is a foundational step in deploying your scalable music recommendation engine. With this setup, you can easily extend functionalities and ensure high availability.

Setting up the environment on AWS

Deploying your microservices architecture on AWS involves several services like Amazon EKS for Kubernetes orchestration, Amazon RDS for database needs, and Amazon S3 for storage. Following is a high-level overview of how to do this:

1. **AWS EKS cluster:** You will first need to create an Amazon EKS cluster. Here are simplified steps:

   a. **Install and configure AWS CLI and eksctl**: Make sure you have the **AWS CLI** and **eksctl** command line tool installed and properly configured.

   b. **Create EKS cluster**: You can use **eksctl** to create a cluster:

   ```
   eksctl create cluster \
   --name my-cluster \
   --region us-west-2 \
   --nodegroup-name my-nodes \
   --node-type t2.micro \
   --nodes 3
   ```

2. **Deploy services to EKS:** After creating the cluster, you can deploy your services.

a. **Set Kubernetes context**: Make sure your **kubectl** context is set to the newly created cluster.

```
aws eks update-kubeconfig --name my-cluster
```

b. **Deploy services**: Use **kubectl** to deploy your services, just as you would in a local Kubernetes setup:

```
kubectl apply -f user-service.yaml
kubectl apply -f catalog-service.yaml
# ... and so on for other services
```

3. **Using Amazon RDS for databases:** Amazon RDS simplifies the database setup, operation, and scaling. For your music recommendation engine, let us assume you have chosen MySQL as the database.

Create a new RDS instance

a. **Go to the RDS console**: Navigate to the RDS section in the AWS management console.

b. **Launch a new database instance**: Choose **Create Database**, select **MySQL**, and follow the setup wizard. Be sure to note the endpoint, username, and password.

Update microservices configuration

Your microservices' database configurations will have to be updated to connect to this RDS instance. In your code where you define the database connection, update the endpoint, username, and password to match your RDS instance. Take a look at the following code:

```
import pymysql


# Establish a database connection
connection = pymysql.connect(
    host='your-rds-endpoint.amazonaws.com',
    user='your-username',
    password='your-password',
    db='your-database',
    charset='utf8',
)
```

4. **Using Amazon S3 for file storage:** Amazon S3 is a scalable object storage service. In the context of your music recommendation engine, this could be used to store songs, album art, or any other static files.

Create an S3 bucket

a. **Go to S3 console**: Navigate to the S3 section in the AWS management console.

b. **Create a new bucket**: Click **Create Bucket**, give it a name, and follow the setup wizard.

Integrate S3 into microservices

AWS provides SDKs for various programming languages that make it easy to interact with S3. The following is an example using Python's boto3.

First, you need to install the **boto3** package:

```
pip install boto3
```

Here is a simple example that uploads a song to an S3 bucket:

```
import boto3


# Initialize a session using Amazon S3
s3 = boto3.client(
    's3',
    aws_access_key_id='your-access-key-id',
    aws_secret_access_key='your-secret-access-key',
    region_name='your-region'
)


# Upload a new file
s3.upload_file('song.mp3', 'your-bucket-name', 'song.mp3')
```

Integrating Amazon RDS and S3 into your microservices architecture simplifies the management and scalability issues associated with databases and file storage. With RDS and S3, you can focus on building features for your music recommendation engine rather than worrying about infrastructure management.

5. **Service discovery and load balancing:** Service discovery and load balancing are critical components of any distributed system. In the AWS ecosystem, you can use services like Amazon Route 53 for DNS based service discovery and **Amazon Elastic Load Balancer** (**Amazon ELB**) for load balancing. Let us dive into how these services can be used in your music recommendation engine project.

Amazon ELB for load balancing

Elastic load balancing distributes incoming traffic across multiple targets, such as Amazon EC2 instances, containers, and IP addresses, in one or more availability zones.

Setting up ELB

a. **Create a load balancer**: Navigate to the EC2 dashboard and select **Load Balancers** from the sidebar. Click on **Create Load Balancer**.

b. **Configure load balancer**: Choose the type of load balancer (application or network), specify the protocol and port for listener configuration, and follow the setup wizard.

c. **Target group**: Configure a target group consisting of the EC2 instances where your microservices are running.

d. **Attach to EKS**: If you are using EKS, update your Kubernetes service definition to use the AWS ELB annotations.

```
apiVersion: v1
kind: Service
metadata:
  annotations:
    service.beta.kubernetes.io/aws-load-balancer-type: "nlb"
  name: my-service
spec:
  type: LoadBalancer
  ports:
    - port: 80
      targetPort: 8080
```

Amazon Route 53 for service discovery

Amazon Route 53 provides highly available and scalable DNS, domain name registration, and routing services.

Setting up Route 53

a. **Create a hosted zone**: Navigate to the Route 53 dashboard, and create a new hosted zone. Enter your domain details.

b. **Set up records**: Create DNS records for each of your services. For example, you could create a CNAME record to route traffic from **api.yourdomain.com** to your load balancer's DNS name.

c. **Integrate with your application**: Update your microservices to use the new domain names for inter-service communication.

Here is how a service in your application could communicate with another service:

```
import requests
```

```
def get_song_details(song_id):
    url = f"http://api.yourdomain.com/catalog-service/songs/{song_id}"
    response = requests.get(url)
    return response.json()
```

By implementing these AWS services for load balancing and service discovery, you can build a robust, scalable, and fault-tolerant microservices architecture for your music recommendation engine.

6. **Continuous integration/continuous deployment pipeline**

   Continuous integration and continuous deployment (CI/CD) are critical for automating the deployment of your applications. In a microservices architecture like your music recommendation engine, CI/CD can be especially useful for streamlining development, testing, and deployment. AWS services like AWS CodePipeline and AWS CodeBuild can be used to create a robust CI/CD pipeline.

   Setting up AWS CodePipeline

   AWS CodePipeline is a continuous integration and continuous delivery service that automates the build, test, and deploy phases of your release process.

   Creating a pipeline

   a. **Navigate to CodePipeline**: Open AWS management console and navigate to the CodePipeline service.

   b. **Create pipeline**: Click **Create pipeline**, name it, and associate it with the code repository where your microservices' source code resides.

   c. **Add stages**: Define the stages of the pipeline like Source, Build, Deploy.

   d. **Source stage**: Connect to your version control system (like GitHub, Bitbucket, or AWS CodeCommit).

   e. **Build stage**: Use AWS CodeBuild to compile the code, run tests, and create deployable docker containers.

   f. **Deploy stage**: Deploy to your Amazon ECS or EKS cluster, automatically updating the services with the new containers.

   Setting up AWS CodeBuild

   AWS CodeBuild is a fully managed build service that compiles your source code, runs tests, and produces artifacts that are ready to deploy.

Configure build stage

a. **Navigate to CodeBuild**: In the AWS management console, go to the CodeBuild service.

b. **Create BuildProject**: Click **Create build project**, name it, and associate it with the build specifications.

c. **Buildspec**: Define a **buildspec.yaml** file that outlines the build commands and artifact definitions. Here is a simplified example:

```
version: 0.2

phases:
  install:
    runtime-versions:
      docker: 18
  pre_build:
    commands:
      - echo Logging in to Amazon ECR...
      - aws ecr get-login-password --region $AWS_DEFAULT_REGION |
        docker login --username AWS --password-stdin $AWS_ACCOUNT_
        ID.dkr.ecr.$AWS_DEFAULT_REGION.amazonaws.com
  build:
    commands:
      - echo Build started on `date`
      - echo Building the Docker image...
      - docker build -t your-image-name .
  post_build:
    commands:
      - echo Build completed on `date`
```

By setting up a CI/CD pipeline with AWS CodePipeline and CodeBuild, you can automate the tedious tasks involved in deploying and scaling your microservices. Whenever you commit code, the pipeline automatically builds, tests, and deploys your applications, ensuring a stable and up-to-date environment. This makes it easier to iterate and rapidly deliver features in your music recommendation engine.

Conclusion

Throughout our discussion, we delved deep into the intricacies of designing and implementing ML microservices with a focus on a music recommendation engine. We walked through different architectural considerations, choosing frameworks like Flask and

FastAPI, and implementing various services like user, catalog, playback, recommendation, and analytics.

We also touched upon creating scalable and distributed ML pipelines, with **Kubeflow** playing a pivotal role. Topics like real-time, batch processing, data transformation, and caching strategies were examined in detail.

Additionally, we explored containerization and orchestration using Docker and Kubernetes. To bring it all together, we discussed how these technologies can be deployed on AWS, covering services like ELB, Route 53 for DNS, and AWS CodePipeline and CodeBuild for CI/CD.

This should serve as a strong foundational guide for anyone looking to build similar services or architectures, whether they are specific to music recommendations or adaptable to other ML applications.

In the next chapter, we will explore the complexities of handling data effectively, ensuring its accuracy and quality for enhanced model predictions. This next chapter will provide you with a comprehensive understanding of data management practices, vital for the success of any ML microservice.

Assignment

Based on our extensive discussion, here are some assignments that can help readers further deepen their understanding and skills in designing, developing, and deploying ML microservices.

Basic assignments

1. **Implementing additional microservices**: Extend the existing architecture by implementing additional microservices, such as a search service or a ratings service, using either Flask or FastAPI.

2. **Database diversification**: Although we used MySQL for simplicity, try implementing the DAO layer using a mix of databases like MongoDB for catalog services, Redis for caching, and PostgreSQL for user data.

3. **API Gateway**: Implement an API gateway to handle and route requests to the appropriate microservices.

Intermediate assignments

1. **Kubeflow components**: Build additional Kubeflow components and pipelines for features like A/B testing or real-time retraining of the ML models.

2. **Event-driven architecture**: Integrate an event-driven architecture using Kafka to pass messages between services, especially for real-time updates or analytics.

3. **Batch processing**: Implement batch processing of the recommendation logic using Apache Spark and store the processed data in HDFS.

Advanced assignments

1. **Monitoring and logging**: Set up a monitoring and logging mechanism using Prometheus and Grafana to monitor the health and performance of your microservices.

2. **Scalability**: Test the scalability of the entire system by simulating high traffic using tools like Apache JMeter or Locust, and make any necessary adjustments to the architecture.

3. **Multi-cloud deployment**: Try deploying your microservices on a different cloud provider like Azure or GCP and compare the differences in performance, cost, and ease of use.

4. **Full CI/CD pipeline**: Extend the CI/CD pipeline to include automated testing, security checks, and rolling updates.

These assignments range from foundational tasks to more complex challenges, covering various facets of building and deploying a robust and scalable music recommendation engine. They should help you reinforce the concepts and practices discussed while adding valuable hands-on experience.

Points to remember

• **Modular microservice design**: Emphasize the importance of building each service, like user, catalog, or analytics, in a modular and scalable manner using Flask or FastAPI.

• **Effective data management**: Highlight the role of **data access objects (DAOs)** in efficiently managing database interactions across different services.

• **Kubeflow for scalable ML pipelines**: Stress on using Kubeflow for constructing scalable ML pipelines in a Kubernetes environment.

• **Inter-service communication**: Recall the use of HTTP/RESTful APIs and message brokers like Kafka for robust communication between services.

• **Load balancing and containerization**: Remember the significance of load balancing strategies and containerization (using Docker and Kubernetes) for managing and scaling services.

• **Real-time vs batch processing**: Note the differences and applications of real-time and batch processing within microservices architecture.

• **Caching strategies**: Caching, especially in high-load environments, can significantly improve response times and system efficiency.

Multiple choice questions

1. **What is the primary purpose of using Flask in building ML microservices?**

   a. Data visualization

   b. Web application development

   c. ML model training

   d. Database management

2. **In the context of ML microservices, what role does a DAO play?**

   a. Data visualization tool

   b. Database interaction facilitator

   c. ML algorithm

   d. User interface designer

3. **Which of the following is a key benefit of using Kubeflow in ML pipelines?**

   a. Enhanced security

   b. Improved data visualization

   c. Scalability and orchestration

   d. Reduced computational power

4. **What type of communication is primarily used in a Kafka-based system?**

   a. Synchronous

   b. Asynchronous

   c. Sequential

   d. Parallel

5. **How does containerization benefit microservices architecture?**

   a. By simplifying data analysis

   b. By enhancing ML models

   c. By facilitating deployment and scalability

   d. By improving data visualization

6. **Which framework is preferred for real-time processing in microservices architecture?**

   a. Flask

   b. FastAPI

   c. Django

   d. Ruby on Rails

7. **What is a primary use case for batch processing in ML microservices?**

   a. Instant decision-making

   b. Real-time data streaming

   c. Processing large datasets

   d. User interface interactions

8. **In scalable ML pipelines, what is a significant role of caching?**

   a. Data storage

   b. Reducing latency

   c. Model training

   d. Data visualization

9. **What is the primary function of an API gateway in microservices architecture?**

   a. Data analysis

   b. Routing and load balancing

   c. ML model deployment

   d. User authentication

10. **Which aspect is crucial for the management of distributed microservices?**

    a. Data visualization techniques

    b. User interface design

    c. Load balancing strategies

    d. Algorithm optimization

Answer key

1	b
2	b
3	c
4	b
5	c
6	b
7	c
8	b
9	b
10	c

Join our book's Discord space

Join the book's Discord Workspace for Latest updates, Offers, Tech happenings around the world, New Release and Sessions with the Authors:

https://discord.bpbonline.com

CHAPTER 6
Data Management in Machine Learning Microservices

Introduction

Data management is a critical component in the construction of **Machine Learning (ML)** microservices. Efficient data management ensures that the services have access to accurate, high-quality, and well-organized data, leading to more reliable and precise model predictions. The goal of this chapter is to guide the reader through various aspects of data management, including ingestion, storage, processing, and versioning, with practical examples from the music recommendation engine case study. By the end of this chapter, you should be proficient in implementing robust data management solutions for ML microservices.

In our *music recommendation engine* example, managing data effectively is crucial. The interaction logs, user profiles, song metadata, and other forms of data should be well-organized and accessible. Efficient data management will enable the various microservices, like the analytics service and recommendation service, to function seamlessly and provide users with accurate and timely recommendations.

Structure

In this chapter, we delve into the design and management of ML microservices, exploring the nuances of data ingestion and storage, emphasizing the pivotal role each stage plays in optimizing the efficiency and dependability of the ML microservices:

- Handling data ingestion and storage
- Data versioning and lineage tracking
- Batch and real-time data processing for ML applications

Objectives

The primary goal of this chapter is to equip you with a deep understanding of complex data management principles in the context of ML microservices, specifically focusing on the application within a music recommendation engine as an illustrative example. We aim to delve into the intricacies of data ingestion and storage, emphasizing how these critical processes enhance the robustness of ML microservices. The exploration includes a detailed examination of Apache Parquet and its advantages for efficient large-scale data management, the role of Hadoop in handling vast datasets, the significance of data versioning for maintaining integrity and reliability, and the crucial functions of Apache Kafka and Apache Spark in enabling both batch and real-time data processing. Through this structured investigation, we aspire to provide practical insights and methodologies for implementing scalable and resilient data management solutions, utilizing cutting-edge technologies to bolster the performance and reliability of ML microservices.

Handling data ingestion and storage

ML microservices thrives on the efficient and timely acquisition, ingestion, and storage of data. The data that powers these services can come from various sources and in different formats. Ensuring that this data is properly ingested and stored is paramount to the functionality and efficiency of the service. Let us explore this facet in the context of our music recommendation engine.

Data sources

Data sources are pivotal, as they fuel the recommendation engine with the raw information needed to draw insightful conclusions and generate user-specific recommendations. In the context of the music recommendation engine, delving deeper into each data source provides us with a comprehensive understanding of the varying nature, characteristics, and utilization of the data. Each source, with its unique characteristics and application, contributes significantly to the engine's ability to deliver personalized music recommendations. Here is a closer look at these sources and how they are utilized:

- **Streaming data**
  - o **Nature**: This data is dynamic and transient, representing user activities and interactions with the service in real-time.
  - o **Example**: When a user plays a song, pauses it, or skips to the next one, these actions are captured as streaming data.

o **Use**: This data is crucial for understanding user preferences and behaviors, allowing the recommendation model to adjust and fine-tune its suggestions based on the most recent interactions.

- **User profiles**

  o **Nature**: Typically static, it encompasses user-specific information, preferences, and historical data.

  o **Example**: A user's age, location, preferred genres, and play history are stored as part of the user profile.

  o **Use**: This foundational data helps in initializing the recommendation model with baseline preferences and serves as a reference point for further adaptations.

- **Song metadata**

  o **Nature**: Static data about songs, artists, and albums, providing context and additional information.

  o **Example**: Information like song title, artist name, album name, genre, and release date are examples of song metadata.

  o **Use**: This data enriches the context of the recommendation engine, enabling it to make more informed and relevant suggestions by considering the attributes of the songs.

- **External APIs**

  o **Nature**: Dynamic and potentially diverse, this data source provides additional contextual information from external services.

  o **Example**: An API from a concert ticketing platform could provide information about upcoming concerts of the user's favorite artists.

  o **Use**: By integrating external data sources, the recommendation engine can offer enriched, context-aware recommendations, enhancing user engagement and experience.

Utilization of data sources

To extract maximum value, the recommendation engine must seamlessly integrate and utilize these diverse data sources. For instance:

- A user's real-time interactions (streaming data) can immediately influence the recommendations, providing dynamic adaptability.
- The static data points from user profiles and song metadata serve as a base, contributing to the initial setup of user preferences in the recommendation model.

- The integration of external APIs can supplement the core recommendation logic with additional context, presenting users with unique and diverse suggestions.

Understanding the nuances of each data source and its role within the recommendation engine is fundamental. By strategically leveraging streaming data, user profiles, song metadata, and external APIs, we can significantly enhance the recommendation engine's accuracy and relevance, providing a more personalized and enriched user experience.

Data ingestion

Data ingestion is the process of importing, transferring, loading, and processing data for immediate use or storage in a database. In the context of our music recommendation engine, this involves pulling in data from various sources like user interactions, music metadata, user profiles, and so on. Here, various methods and technologies can be utilized to perform data ingestion:

Batch ingestion

Batch ingestion involves collecting and storing data over a period and then processing it all at once at scheduled intervals.

The characteristics of batch ingestion are as follows:

- **Volume**: Typically deals with high volumes of data.
- **Latency**: High latency due to scheduled processing times, not suitable for real-time insights.
- **Efficiency**: More efficient in processing large volumes of data.
- **Complexity**: Generally, less complex due to dealing with static data.

The following are its use cases in music recommendation engine:

- In the music recommendation engine, batch ingestion can be employed to process user interaction logs, music metadata updates, and user profile updates that are not time-sensitive.
- It is especially suitable for training and updating recommendation models with new interaction data, which does not require real-time processing.

The advantages of batch ingestion are as follows:

- **Efficiency**: More resource-efficient for processing large datasets.
- **Simplicity**: Easier to manage due to the absence of concurrency and ordering issues.
- **Scalability**: Can handle growing amounts of data by adjusting batch sizes and scheduling.

The following are the technologies and tools related to batch ingestion:

- **Apache Hadoop**: Effective for storing and processing large datasets in a distributed environment.
- **Apache Spark**: Suitable for performing complex transformations and computations on batch data.
- **SQL databases**: Useful for storing the results of batch analytics and aggregations.

Refer to the following example:

```
# Example using Apache Spark for batch processing

from pyspark.sql import SparkSession

spark = SparkSession.builder.appName("BatchProcessing").getOrCreate()

data = spark.read.csv('hdfs://user_interactions.csv')

# Perform transformations and actions, for example, aggregations, filtering,
etc. on the data
```

Refer to the following considerations:

- **Scheduling**: Deciding the appropriate time intervals for running batch jobs is crucial to balance load and timeliness.
- **Error handling**: Errors during batch processing need to be handled effectively to avoid reprocessing of the entire batch.
- **Resource management**: Allocating adequate resources is essential to handle the processing load during batch execution.

Music recommendation engine

This section exemplifies how the batch ingestions principles are crucial in a real-world application like music recommendation engine in enhancing the engine's ability to offer personalized music recommendations through systematic data analysis and application. The following key areas illustrate this impact:

- **Model training**: Batch ingestion is fundamental for training models where historical data is ingested in batches to train the recommendation models.
- **Data aggregation**: It is used for aggregating user interactions and preferences over time to gain insights into user behavior and preferences.
- **User profile update**: Periodically updating user profiles with batch-processed data to incorporate the latest interactions and preferences.

In the music recommendation microservice, batch jobs could be scheduled to run during off-peak hours to update user profiles, retrain models, and process new music metadata without affecting the real-time performance of the system.

Real-time ingestion

Real-time ingestion involves continuously capturing and processing data immediately as it arrives to provide insights or drive actions in near real-time.

The characteristics of real-time ingestion are as follows:

- **Volume**: Deals with high-velocity data, often in smaller volumes per item.
- **Latency**: Extremely low latency is required for near-instantaneous processing.
- **Complexity**: Higher due to the need to handle concurrency and order preservation.

Use cases in music recommendation engine are given as follows:

- For a music recommendation engine, real-time ingestion is crucial for capturing user interactions, play counts, and other real-time user behavior which could be used to provide immediate recommendations and insights.
- This approach is suitable for processing streaming data, such as user clicks, plays, or pauses, for real-time analytics and personalized user interactions.

The advantages of real-time ingestion are as follows:

- **Timeliness**: Allows for immediate insights and reactions.
- **Personalization**: Enables highly personalized user experiences based on real-time behavior.
- **Anomaly detection**: Useful for detecting anomalies and triggering instant alerts or actions.

The technologies and tools related to real-time ingestion are as follows:

- **Apache Kafka**: A distributed streaming platform suitable for building real-time data pipelines and streaming apps.
- **Apache Flink**: A stream-processing framework, is great for real-time analytics and monitoring.
- **Redis**: In-memory data structure store, used as a database, cache, and message broker.

Refer to the following example:

```
# Example using Apache Kafka for real-time data ingestion

from kafka import KafkaProducer

producer = KafkaProducer(bootstrap_servers='localhost:9092')

producer.send('user_interactions', b'user1,play,song1')
```

Refer to the considerations:

- **Ordering**: Maintaining the order of real-time data is critical for accurate processing.
- **Scalability**: Must be able to scale to handle potentially large volumes of incoming data.
- **Data persistence**: Consideration about whether and how to store the real-time data for later use.

Music recommendation engine

This section exemplifies how the real-time ingestions principles are crucial in a real-world application like music recommendation engine in enhancing the user experience, offering insights into behavior, and ensuring the system's optimal performance, all vital for the dynamic environment of a music recommendation engine. The following key areas illustrate this impact:

- **Real-time recommendations**: Real-time ingestion is vital to provide instant recommendations based on the user's current actions and behavior.
- **User engagement analysis**: Allows analyzing user engagement and behavior in real-time to fine-tune the user experience.
- **Live monitoring**: Essential for monitoring system health and user interactions live.

In implementing real-time ingestion in the music recommendation engine, maintaining a balance between processing latency and system load is crucial. It can be combined with batch processing for updating models and user profiles while serving real-time insights and recommendations to the users.

Data storage

Data storage solutions are foundational for managing and organizing data effectively. They provide the means to store, retrieve, and manage data in various forms, essential for the seamless functioning of ML microservices.

Types of data storage are as follows:

- **Relational databases**: Use tables to store data and are suitable for structured data. For example, MySQL, PostgreSQL.
- **NoSQL databases**: Suitable for unstructured or semi-structured data. For example, MongoDB, Cassandra.
- **Distributed file systems**: Suitable for storing large volumes of unstructured data. For example, Hadoop HDFS.
- **Object storage**: Stores data as objects and is suitable for unstructured data. For example, Amazon S3.

Relational databases

It uses a structure called a table to organize data in rows and columns. Each row represents a record, and each column represents a field.

The use of relational databases in music recommendation engine are as follows:

- Store user information, music metadata, and user-music interaction in a structured format.
- Ensures data integrity and relationships between different entities like users and songs.

For example, MySQL, PostgreSQL:

```
CREATE TABLE users (id INT AUTO_INCREMENT PRIMARY KEY, username VARCHAR(255));

INSERT INTO users (username) VALUES ('user1');
```

The advantages of relational databases are as follows:

- ACID properties (atomicity, consistency, isolation, durability).
- Supports complex queries and transactions.

NoSQL databases

NoSQL databases are non-relational or distributed databases that enable the storage and processing of a large amount of unstructured data and support dynamic schemas, offering high scalability and flexibility. They are optimized for specific data models such as document, key-value, wide-column, and graph, allowing high-level data manipulation using various data models like JSON and XML.

The uses of NoSQL databases in music recommendation engine are as follows:

- Store and manage user interactions, logs, and semi-structured data.
- Suitable for storing large volumes of rapidly changing data.

For example, MongoDB, Cassandra.

```
db.user_interactions.insert({user_id: 1, action: 'play', song_id: 'song1'});
```

The advantages of NoSQL databases are as follows:

- Schema-less
- Horizontal scalability

Distributed file systems

It manages files across multiple machines, allowing storage of large volumes of data across many nodes.

The uses of distributed file systems are as follows in music recommendation engine:

- Store large datasets like music files and user logs in a distributed manner.
- Facilitate parallel processing of data for model training.

For example, Hadoop HDFS.

```
hdfs dfs -put song.mp3 /user/songs/song.mp3
```

The advantages of this system are fault tolerance and scalability.

Object storage

It stores data as objects and is suitable for storing large amounts of unstructured data.

The uses in music recommendation engine are as follows:

- Store music files, images, and other multimedia content.
- Serves as a scalable storage solution for large assets.

For example, Amazon S3.

```
import boto3

s3 = boto3.client('s3')

s3.upload_file('song.mp3', 'mybucket', 'song.mp3')
```

Refer to the following considerations:

- **Scalability**: The storage solution must scale to accommodate growing data.
- **Accessibility**: Quick and reliable data access is crucial.
- **Consistency**: Maintaining data consistency across different storage solutions is vital.
- **Data security**: Protecting sensitive information is paramount.

In the context of music recommendation engine:

Using a combination of these storage solutions can significantly optimize the storage, retrieval, and management of data, facilitating the efficient functioning of the recommendation engine.

A cohesive integration of various storage solutions is instrumental in building a robust music recommendation engine, allowing it to leverage the strengths of each storage type for enhanced performance and reliability.

Each storage type serves a distinct purpose in managing different data forms in the music recommendation engine, enabling it to handle diverse data efficiently. By leveraging the strengths of each storage solution, developers can ensure optimal data storage, processing, and retrieval, enhancing the overall performance and functionality of the ML microservices in the music recommendation engine.

Distributed storage: Hadoop

Hadoop is a distributed processing framework designed for large data sets across computer clusters, scaling from single servers to thousands of machines. Its primary storage, **Hadoop Distributed File System (HDFS)**, breaks large files into smaller blocks (default 128 MB) and replicates them for fault tolerance. Key reasons for Hadoop's preference in big data applications like music recommendation engines include:

- **Scalability**: Handles growing data volumes efficiently, crucial for expanding user bases.

- **Cost-effectiveness**: Uses inexpensive hardware for storage, offering low cost per terabyte.

- **Fault tolerance**: Automatically replicates data across nodes, ensuring reliability and uninterrupted service.

- **Flexibility**: Stores all data types (structured, semi-structured, unstructured), allowing comprehensive data analysis and accurate recommendations.

- **Parallel processing**: Divides tasks for fast processing of large datasets, vital for quick, efficient recommendation generation.

- **Open source**: Allows customization, beneficial for tailoring performance to specific needs.

- **Rich ecosystem**: Includes tools like Hive, Pig, HBase, and a supportive developer community, enhancing capabilities and support.

- **Data locality**: Moves computation to data, not vice versa, speeding up processing and enhancing efficiency.

Hadoop excels in managing the complex needs of big data projects, offering scalability, cost efficiency, and performance, making it ideal for applications such as music recommendation systems.

Hadoop Distributed File System architecture

Reflecting on the architecture and components of HDFS detailed above, it is evident how the system's design ensures robustness, scalability, and fault tolerance. These characteristics make HDFS exceptionally suitable for a wide range of big data applications, from music recommendation engines to complex data analysis tasks. The key components and functions include:

- **NameNode**: Acts as the master server, managing metadata and the file system's structure. It tracks files, directories, and storage blocks, but does not store the actual data. The NameNode handles client requests and manages file operations.

- **DataNode**: These are the storage nodes, holding data blocks as instructed by the NameNode or clients. DataNodes handle data storage, retrieval, and replication, reporting their status to the NameNode. They typically run on commodity hardware and are key to the system's operation.

- **Block**: HDFS splits data into blocks (default 128 MB), each replicated independently across DataNodes to ensure data safety and availability.

- **Secondary NameNode**: Contrary to its name, it does not replace the NameNode. Instead, it manages background tasks like merging the edit log with the file system image, helping to optimize the NameNode's startup and performance.

- **Client**: Interfaces with the HDFS, requesting metadata from the NameNode and handling direct file operations with DataNodes.

- **Replication and fault tolerance**: HDFS replicates each data block (default factor: 3) across multiple DataNodes, automatically handling replication for node failures to maintain data integrity and availability.

- **Federated HDFS**: Enhances scalability by allowing multiple NameNodes to manage separate namespaces within a cluster. Each namespace has its own NameNode, supporting larger clusters and more files.

HDFS's design focuses on managing large volumes of data with high throughput, fault tolerance, and scalability, essential for processing and storing data efficiently in large-scale applications.

Data formats supported by Hadoop

Hadoop supports various data formats, each with specific benefits for different tasks:

- **Text file**: Human-readable, ideal for data requiring readability without needing compression.

- **Sequence file**: A binary format efficient for storing and accessing smaller files.

- **Avro**: A compact binary format, excellent for data serialization and exchange across different languages, ideal for inter-language data transfer in Hadoop.

- **Parquet and ORC**: Columnar formats optimized for heavy read operations, perfect for large, read-heavy datasets in analytics and data warehousing, offering superior performance and compression.

- **Protobuf/Thrift**: Binary formats for efficient serialization of structured data.

- **JSON**: Human-readable, supporting hierarchical data, good for evolving data schemas while maintaining readability.

- **CSV**: Simple and readable, best for smaller datasets where readability outweighs performance and compression concerns.

For a music recommendation engine, a columnar format like *Apache Parquet* is recommended. It enhances compression and read performance, crucial for analytics-driven applications.

Parquet supports schema evolution, accommodating application changes over time. In real-time processing contexts, combining Avro (for efficient data serialization and writes) with Parquet (for optimized reads) could be effective.

Interacting with Hadoop Distributed File System

Users and applications can interact with HDFS using a variety of methods, including the Hadoop Shell command, Hadoop's Java API, and web interfaces like Hue.

Code sample: Using Python's HDFS package:

```
from hdfs import InsecureClient

# Connecting to WebHDFS by providing HDFS namenode host and webhdfs port
(default 50070)

client = InsecureClient('http://namenode_host:50070', user='hdfs_user')


# Writing Data to HDFS

with open('localfile.txt', 'rb') as file:

    client.write('/user/hdfs_user/hadoopfile.txt', file)


# Reading Data from HDFS

with client.read('/user/hdfs_user/hadoopfile.txt') as reader:

    content = reader.read()
```

Data format: Apache parquet

Apache parquet is a columnar storage file format optimized for use with big data processing frameworks. It is efficient both for storage and processing, especially for complex nested data structures.

The advantages are as follows:

- **Schema evolution**: Parquet supports modifications to the schema, allowing new columns to be added, and old ones to be deprecated, making it adaptable to the evolving needs of the application.
- **Column pruning**: When queries are run, only the necessary columns of data are read from storage. This reduces the I/O operations and thus enhances the performance of read operations, vital for analytics workloads.
- **Enhanced compression**: Due to its columnar nature, it allows more efficient compression, which saves storage space and also reduces the time and resources used to read from and write to the storage.

Here is a simple example of how you might write a Pandas **DataFrame** to a Parquet file in Python:

```
import pandas as pd

df = pd.DataFrame({
    'user_id': [1, 2, 3],
    'song_id': ['song1', 'song2', 'song3'],
    'interaction_type': ['play', 'like', 'dislike']
})

df.to_parquet('interactions.parquet', index=False)
```

Microservices

This section exemplifies how Apache Parquet is applied within the architecture of microservices. This highlights its role in enhancing data processing and storage capabilities in microservice architectures. The following key areas illustrate this impact:

- The **analytics service** can use Apache Parquet to store aggregated data points needed for analysis.
- The **recommendation service** can leverage Parquet to store features that are used to generate music recommendations.

By leveraging Apache Parquet, our music recommendation engine can enhance data processing speed and efficiency, especially beneficial for analytical processes within the microservices, making it an integral part of the engine's effective data management.

Storing Parquet files

In Hadoop, storing Parquet files in the HDFS is a common practice, especially for big data applications. HDFS can store large volumes of data across multiple nodes in a distributed fashion, providing fault tolerance and high availability. Refer to the following code:

```
hadoop fs -copyFromLocal localfile.parquet /user/hadoop/hadoopfile.parquet
```

Amazon S3 is also a popular choice for storing Parquet files due to its scalability, durability, and ease of access. It is especially useful when using cloud-based data processing services like Amazon EMR. Refer to the following code:

```
import boto3

s3 = boto3.client('s3')

s3.upload_file('localfile.parquet', 'mybucket', 'myparquetfile.parquet')
```

Choice of storage

The choice between Hadoop and S3 or another storage solution depends largely on the specific needs, architecture, and existing infrastructure of the project. For instance, a cloud-native approach might favor S3, while an on-premises big data environment might leverage Hadoop.

Analytics service and recommendation service

Both services can utilize Parquet files stored either in Hadoop or S3. For instance, the analytics service can efficiently read the necessary columns from the Parquet files to generate insights, while the recommendation service can read user interaction logs to generate recommendations.

For example, recommendation service reading from Parquet:

```
import pyarrow.parquet as pq

# Assuming the Parquet file is stored in Hadoop or S3

table = pq.read_table('path_to_parquet_file_in_hadoop_or_s3')

data_frame = table.to_pandas()
```

The combination of Apache Parquet's columnar storage efficiency and the robustness of Hadoop or the flexibility of S3 results in a powerful synergy, enabling scalable and efficient data storage and processing solutions for ML microservices.

Data versioning and lineage tracking

Data versioning and lineage tracking are crucial for maintaining the integrity, reliability, and reproducibility of data in a scalable ML microservices environment, especially in our music recommendation engine.

Data versioning

Data versioning is key in managing data changes over time, essential for tracking modifications and maintaining consistent, reliable models in ML.

Following are the key data versioning tools:

- **Data version control (DVC)**
  - o **Use case**: Ideal for ML projects requiring tracking of data and code changes.
  - o **Function**: Uses Git for versioning; supports various storage options (S3, GCS, Azure, SSH).
  - o **Advantages**: Integrates well with ML workflows; storage agnostic.

- **Delta Lake**
  - o **Use case**: Best for large, mutable big data scenarios needing ACID transactions.
  - o **Function**: Provides ACID transactions on top of data lakes; compatible with Apache Spark™ and similar APIs.
  - o **Advantages**: Offers schema enforcement, supports batch/streaming workloads, and in-built data versioning.

- **Amazon S3 with versioning**
  - o **Use case**: Suitable for AWS-based projects with object-level versioning needs.
  - o **Function**: Automatically assigns a unique version ID to stored objects in S3 buckets.
  - o **Advantages**: Scalable, secure, managed service with access controls.

- **Git-Large File Storage (LFS)**
  - o **Use case**: Useful for smaller datasets needing data and code versioning.
  - o **Function**: Replaces large files in Git repos with text pointers, stores content on a server.
  - o **Advantages**: Seamlessly integrates with Git.

- **MLflow**
  - o **Use case**: Ideal for managing the full ML lifecycle, including experiment tracking, model versioning, and deployment.
  - o **Function**: Facilitates comprehensive tracking of experiments to log and query model metadata, supports project management, and model serving. It uniquely emphasizes effective monitoring of model performance and experiment metrics, which is crucial for optimizing ML workflows.
  - o **Advantages**: Open-source, compatible with any ML library, includes a UI for experiment visualization.

We choose the right tool depending upon:

- **Scalability**: Ensure the tool can handle your data's size and complexity.
- **Integration**: It should integrate with existing tech stack and workflows.
- **Usability**: User-friendly to reduce learning and adaptation efforts.
- **Cost**: Consider cloud storage and egress fees.

For a music recommendation engine:

A combination of DVC (for ML-specific data and model versioning) and Delta Lake (for big data versioning and processing) is effective. For AWS-heavy environments, pairing

S3 with versioning and MLflow might be advantageous for model management and experiments.

Delta file format

Delta file format is a storage layer that brings reliability, performance, and lifecycle management to data lakes. It stores data as Parquet files in blob storage but manages and orchestrates reads and writes in a more sophisticated manner. Here is a breakdown of how it operates:

- **ACID transactions**: Delta Lake uses ACID transactions to ensure that all data access is highly consistent. It enables simultaneous reads and writes, preventing data corruption.

- **Schema enforcement and evolution**
  - o It applies schema enforcement to prevent the insertion of bad records during write operations.
  - o It supports schema evolution, and you can add new columns and change the data type of a column.

- **Unified batch and streaming source and sink**
  - o Delta Lake can act as a source or sink for both batch and streaming data processing.

- **Time travel (data versioning)**
  - o Delta Lake provides snapshots of data, enabling developers to access and revert to earlier versions of data for audits, rollbacks, or to reproduce experiments.

The difference between Parquet and Delta is given in *Table 6.1*:

Aspect	Parquet	Delta
Type	Columnar storage file format.	Storage layer enhancing Apache Spark and big data workloads.
Optimized for	Read-heavy analytical workloads.	Both read and write-heavy analytical and transactional workloads.
Features	Immutable; data cannot be changed once written.	Supports CRUD operations, schema evolution, and full transactional support.
Use case	Ideal for large datasets with infrequent schema changes.	Fits well when frequent updates/deletes and transactional integrity are needed.
Integration	Native support with various data processing frameworks.	Built on top of Parquet; integrates with Spark for version control and data rollback.

Table 6.1: Comparison of Parquet and Delta file formats

Delta and Hadoop

Delta, compatible with Apache Spark and the Hadoop ecosystem, extends the capabilities of Parquet. By leveraging HDFS in Hadoop for storage, Delta enhances data operations within this framework. Its support through Spark means that within Hadoop, you can use Delta for version control, rollbacks, and performing **upserts** and deletes - functionalities not native to Parquet. Refer to the following statements:

```
# Using PySpark to read a Delta table stored in HDFS

df = spark.read.format("delta").load("hdfs://namenode:port/path/to/delta-table")
```

Delta Lake

Delta Lake, an open-source layer for Apache Spark, enhances big data workloads with ACID transactions, ensuring data reliability in data lakes. It is more efficient than standard Parquet, supporting data modifications and new additions.

The key features are as follows:

- **ACID transactions**: Guarantees data integrity and consistency.
- **Schema enforcement and evolution**: Maintains data consistency, handling schema changes over time.
- **Audit history (time travel)**: Offers access to historical data versions for audits and reproductions.
- **Scalable metadata handling**: Efficiently manages extensive metadata.
- **Unified batch and streaming source and sink**: Facilitates hybrid data workloads.
- **Support for existing data lakes**: Seamlessly converts Parquet and other formats to Delta.

Delta Lake works atop storage systems like HDFS, AWS S3, or Azure Data Lake Storage, and integrates with Apache Spark for reading/writing tables via Spark SQL.

Data versioning in Delta Lake

Through a transaction log, Delta Lake tracks and logs all data changes. This feature allows accessing previous data versions for debugging, auditing, or reproducing results, known as time-travel.

Example workflow in music recommendation engine is as follows:

- **Version 1**: Initial dataset of user interactions and music metadata.
- **Version 2**: Updated dataset after incorporating more user interactions.
- **Version 3**: Modified dataset with enhanced music metadata.

Data scientists can switch between these versions to train models, conduct experiments, or debug issues.

Implementing with Delta Lake:

```
from delta.tables import DeltaTable

from pyspark.sql import SparkSession


# Initialize Spark session

spark = SparkSession.builder.appName("DeltaLakeVersioning").config("spark.jars.packages", "io.delta:delta-core_2.12:1.0.0").getOrCreate()


# Initialize DeltaTable

delta_table = DeltaTable.forPath(spark, "/path/to/delta-table")


# Time-travel to version 1

df1 = spark.read.format("delta").option("versionAsOf", 1).load("/path/to/delta-table")


# Or via SQL

spark.sql("SELECT * FROM delta.`/path/to/delta-table@v1`")
```

The explanation of the code is as follows:

- This Python code is leveraging the Delta Lake to travel through different versions of the data.
- The **DeltaTable.forPath()** is used to point to the location of the Delta table.
- By setting the **versionAsOf** option, you can specify the version of the data that you want to access.
- The SQL variant allows you to access a specific version of the data using the **@v** syntax.

The benefits are as follows:

- **Reproducibility**: Facilitates reproducing results and comparisons between different versions.
- **Auditability**: Offers a transparent and auditable workflow by maintaining a history of data changes.
- **Debuggability**: Helps in identifying and rectifying issues or anomalies by analyzing previous states of data.

Refer to the following considerations:

- **Storage overhead**: Maintaining multiple versions of data can lead to increased storage requirements.
- **Management**: Proper mechanisms should be in place to manage and clean up old versions that are not required.

In the context of recommendation engine, the benefits of using Delta Lake for data versioning are multifold, especially in the rapidly evolving landscape of a recommendation engine where user interaction data and preferences are continually changing and evolving.

Delta Lake setup and usage

Delta Lake is a scalable and reliable storage layer that brings ACID transactions to Apache Spark and big data workloads. It has support for both batch and stream processing, making it versatile for a variety of use cases, including real-time analytics, ML, and ETL.

The setup is as follows:

- **Spark setup**: Delta Lake is built on top of Apache Spark, so you will need to have Spark set up in your environment.
- **Library inclusion**: Once Spark is ready, include Delta Lake's library in your Spark project by adding it to your build or including it in your notebook session.
- **Storage setup**: Set up the storage. Delta Lake can work with HDFS or cloud-based storage such as AWS S3, Azure Data Lake Storage, and so on. Refer to the following code:

```
pip install delta-spark
```

Setting up storage for Delta Lake involves selecting an appropriate storage system and configuring it for compatibility:

- **Storage system choices**
  - **On-premise/hybrid**: HDFS for local or mixed cloud setups.
  - **Cloud-native**: AWS S3, **Azure Data Lake Storage (ADLS)**, or **Google Cloud Storage (GCS)**.

The configuration steps are as follows:

1. **HDFS**: Proper setup and configuration of NameNode, DataNode, network, and firewall for Spark and HDFS communication.
2. **Cloud Storage**: Account setup with cloud provider, bucket/container creation, and configuring access keys and permissions for Spark interactions.
3. **Permissions and security**
   - Set user permissions and access controls on HDFS.
   - For cloud, configure bucket policies/access control lists.

4. **Storage path example**
   - HDFS: hdfs://namenode:port/path/to/delta-table
   - S3: s3a://bucket-name/path/to/delta-table
5. **Optimizing storage:** Select suitable storage types (for example, SSDs for speed).
6. **Partition data effectively**
7. **Manage file sizes to optimize read/write performance**

Testing

Ensure compatibility and seamless operation with Spark and Delta Lake, focusing on read/write functions before production deployment.

For example, Delta table on Hadoop:

```
from pyspark.sql import SparkSession


# Setup Spark Session for Delta Lake

spark = SparkSession.builder.appName("DeltaLakeStorageSetup").config("spark.
jars.packages", "io.delta:delta-core_2.12:1.0.0").getOrCreate()


# Writing Data to a Delta Table on HDFS

data = [("John", "Doe", 29), ("Jane", "Doe", 34)]

columns = ["first_name", "last_name", "age"]


df = spark.createDataFrame(data, columns)

df.write.format("delta").mode("overwrite").save("hdfs://namenode:port/path/
to/delta-table")
```

Delta table on AWS S3

```
from pyspark.sql import SparkSession


# Set up Spark session for Delta Lake

spark   =   SparkSession.builder.appName("DeltaLakeOnS3").config("spark.jars.
packages", "io.delta:delta-core_2.12:1.0.0").getOrCreate()


# Define the data and schema

data = [("John", "Doe", 29), ("Jane", "Doe", 34)]
```

```
columns = ["first_name", "last_name", "age"]

# Create a DataFrame
df = spark.createDataFrame(data, columns)

# Write the DataFrame to a Delta table on S3
df.write.format("delta").mode("overwrite").save("s3a://your-bucket-name/
path/to/delta-table")
```

Refer to the following considerations:

- Choose the storage solution based on your organization's infrastructure, preference, and the cloud provider being used.
- The configuration of access permissions is crucial in all environments to secure the data.
- The costs associated with cloud-based storage solutions need to be considered.

Lineage tracking

Lineage tracking is essential for understanding and visualizing the journey of data from its source, through transformations, to its final destination. It is useful for debugging, audit trails, compliance, and data quality assurance.

A lineage tracking tool is Apache Atlas. It provides governance services on Hadoop, including metadata management and data asset cataloging and governance.

The implementation steps are as follows:

1. Integrate Apache Atlas with your Hadoop/Spark setup.
2. **Metadata definition**: Define metadata for each data entity (schema, transformations, data source).
3. **Cataloging**: Track and catalog each data transformation and movement in the system using Atlas.
4. **Visualization**: Employ Atlas's UI or API to map out and understand data asset lineage.

Refer to the following code:

```
from pyspark.sql import SparkSession

# Initialize Spark session
spark = SparkSession.builder.appName("AtlasIntegration").getOrCreate()
```

```
# Assume `df` is a DataFrame representing your data.

# df = ...


def my_transformation_function(df):

    # Perform some transformations on `df`.

    # ...

    return transformed_df


# Perform some transformations on `df`.

transformed_df = my_transformation_function(df)


# Now, you can use Apache Atlas APIs to log this transformation.

# You would need to interact with the Apache Atlas APIs to log the transformation.


# The specifics would depend on the exact requirements and the Apache Atlas
API.
```

Conceptual flow

The conceptual flow is as follows:

- **Creating entities**: Entity creation involves two key steps:
  a. **For DataFrames**: When you work with DataFrames, create Apache Atlas entities for both the original and the transformed DataFrames.
  b. **Metadata**: Include metadata like schema, source, and transformations.
- **Creating relationships**: Establish relationships in Atlas to show lineage. For example, link DataFrame A to DataFrame B if B is derived from A.
- **Cataloging and visualization**: Apache Atlas then enables visualization of these relationships and the data journey, aiding in understanding data transformations.

Integration with Apache Atlas APIs:

Prerequisites: Ensure Apache Atlas is configured and its REST API is accessible.

The integration steps are as follows:

1. **Define Atlas entity**: Specify the entity type and attributes to reflect the metadata.
2. **Create Entity via API**: Utilize the Atlas REST API to add entities.
3. **Create relationships**: Also use the API to establish relationships between entities.

Below is a basic example of how you might use Python to interact with the Apache Atlas REST API to create an entity and a relationship:

```python
import requests

atlas_url = "http://atlas.apache.org:21000/api/atlas/v2"

headers = {"Content-Type": "application/json", "Accept": "application/json"}


def create_entity(entity_definition):

    url = f"{atlas_url}/entity/bulk"

    response = requests.post(url, json=entity_definition, headers=headers)

    # Handle response

    return response.json()


def create_relationship(relationship_definition):

    url = f"{atlas_url}/relationship"

    response = requests.post(url, json=relationship_definition,
    headers=headers)

    # Handle response

    return response.json()


# Define your entity and relationship according to your metadata and
transformation

entity_definition = {

    "entities": [

        {

            "typeName": "your_type",

            "attributes": {

                "name": "entity_name",

                # Other attributes

            }

        }
```

```
    ]
}


relationship_definition = {

    "typeName": "your_relationship_type",

    "end1": {"guid": "guid_of_entity1"},

    "end2": {"guid": "guid_of_entity2"},

    "attributes": {"attribute": "value"}

}


# Creating Entity and Relationship

create_entity(entity_definition)

create_relationship(relationship_definition)
```

Batch and real-time data processing for ML applications

When it comes to ML applications, especially in the context of a music recommendation engine, the process of data processing is crucial as it can significantly impact the accuracy and reliability of the models and, subsequently, the recommendations provided by the system.

Batch processing

Batch processing is a method of data processing where data is collected, processed in batches, and then the results are produced. This technique is opposed to real-time processing, where data is processed as it arrives. In the context of ML applications like a music recommendation engine, batch processing is particularly beneficial where you have a large volume of data that is not required to be processed in real time.

The characteristics of batch processing are as follows:

- **High latency**: The results are not produced in real-time, hence there is a delay (or latency).
- **High throughput**: Processes large volumes of data at once.
- **Comprehensive analysis**: Provides an opportunity for a detailed and thorough analysis of data.

In the realm of music recommendation, batch processing can be deployed to:

- Process historical user interaction data and update recommendation models periodically.

- Generate recommendation lists for users at scheduled intervals.

- Analyze user behavior patterns, preferences, and other analytical measures that do not require real-time processing.

Apache Spark

Apache Spark is a fast, in-memory data processing engine with elegant and expressive development APIs which enable data workers to efficiently execute streaming, ML or SQL workloads. It is designed to be highly accessible, offering simple APIs in Python, Java, Scala, and R.

The key components of Apache Spark are as follows:

- **Spark core**: It is the underlying general execution engine for the Spark platform that all other functionalities are built upon. It provides in-memory computing capabilities to deliver speed.

- **Spark SQL**: It enables users to run SQL and HQL queries seamlessly on top of Spark, providing support for various data sources, including Hive, Avro, Parquet, ORC, JSON, and JDBC.

- **Spark streaming**: Allows for processing real-time streaming data. It is scalable and can handle high-throughput.

- **MLlib**: It is Spark's scalable ML library consisting of common learning algorithms and utilities, including classification, regression, clustering, collaborative filtering, and so on.

- **GraphX**: For graph processing, providing various graph computation algorithms.

For instance, if you are developing a music recommendation engine, you could use Apache Spark to process user interaction data and train recommendation models. Example in Python (PySpark) is as follows:

```
from pyspark.sql import SparkSession

from pyspark.ml.recommendation import ALS


# Initialize Spark Session

spark = SparkSession.builder.appName("MusicRecommendationEngine").
getOrCreate()
```

```
# Read Data

data = spark.read.csv("path_to_your_data", header=True, inferSchema=True)


# Initialize Model

als = ALS(maxIter=5, regParam=0.01, userCol="userId", itemCol="musicId",
ratingCol="rating")


# Fit Model

model = als.fit(data)


# Generate Recommendations

recommendations = model.recommendForAllUsers(10)

recommendations.show()
```

The advantages are as follows:

- **Speed**
  - o Offers fast in-memory processing.
  - o Optimized engine that supports general execution graphs.
- **Ease of use**
  - o Provides high-level APIs in Java, Scala, Python, and R.
  - o Supports SQL queries for structured data processing.
- **Modularity**
  - o Contains libraries for diverse tasks ranging from SQL to streaming and ML, making it a versatile tool.
- **Scalability and fault tolerance**
  - o Scales from a single machine to thousands of servers.
  - o Offers fault tolerance through lineage information to compute lost data.

Refer to the following considerations:

- **Resource intensive**: It may require significant resources for in-memory computation, especially for large datasets.
- **Learning curve**: For users not familiar with Scala or Python, there might be a learning curve involved in understanding and utilizing Spark effectively.

Usage of Apache Spark in batch processing

In batch processing, Apache Spark processes data that has been previously stored and does not have the requirement for real-time processing. It is especially suitable for tasks like ETL jobs, data analysis, and ML model training where latency is not a critical factor. Here are the essential steps for leveraging Apache Spark in batch processing tasks:

1. **Initializing Spark session**: A Spark session is a unified entry point for reading data in Spark, and it is the first thing you create when developing a Spark application. Refer to the following code:

```
from pyspark.sql import SparkSession

spark = SparkSession.builder.
appName("MusicRecommendationEngineBatch").getOrCreate()
```

2. **Loading data**: Read data from various sources like HDFS, S3, databases, and so on.

```
df = spark.read.format("parquet").load("hdfs://namenode:port/path/to/
data"
```

3. **Data processing and transformation**

   o   Clean and preprocess the data: Handle missing values, outliers, and so on.

   o   Perform transformations, feature engineering.

   Refer to the following code:

```
from pyspark.sql.functions import col

cleaned_df = df.filter(col("user_id").isNotNull())

transformed_df = cleaned_df.withColumn("new_feature", col("existing_
feature") * 2)
```

4. **ML model training**

   o   Train models using the processed data.

   o   Perform model evaluation and parameter tuning.

```
from pyspark.ml.regression import LinearRegression

lr = LinearRegression(featuresCol='features', labelCol='label')

model = lr.fit(transformed_df)
```

5. **Data output/storage**: Write the processed data or model output to a storage system. Refer to the following code:

```
model.save("hdfs://namenode:port/path/to/model")
```

6. **Scheduling**

   o   Jobs can be scheduled to run at specific intervals using tools like Apache Airflow.

   o   Manage resource allocation and job priorities.

Music recommendation engine

This section highlights the application of Apache Spark in batch processing and showcases its ability to efficiently manage large-scale data tasks, emphasizing its critical role in developing dynamic and responsive recommendation platforms. The following key areas illustrate this impact:

- **Data ingestion**: Ingest user interaction data, music metadata, user profiles from various sources.

- **Data processing and transformation**: Preprocess the ingested data to handle inconsistencies, missing values, and derive new features.

- **Model training**: Train recommendation models using collaborative filtering, matrix factorization, and so on, based on the processed data.

- **Data output/storage**: Store the generated recommendations, trained models, or any other output for subsequent use or analysis.

- **Scheduling**: Set up the pipeline to run at scheduled intervals, for example, daily or weekly, to update the models and recommendations based on the new data.

In developing and refining Apache Spark data pipelines, three core principles guide our approach to ensuring they meet the demands of large-scale data processing tasks efficiently:

- **Scalability**: Our design philosophy prioritizes adaptability to fluctuating data volumes, emphasizing the importance of a scalable architecture that can dynamically accommodate growth without compromising performance.

- **Robustness**: Recognizing the inevitability of operational challenges, we implement comprehensive error handling and logging mechanisms. These practices are fundamental to diagnosing and addressing issues promptly, thereby maintaining the pipeline's integrity and reliability.

- **Optimization**: Continuous improvement is at the heart of our optimization strategy. By regularly evaluating and refining Spark jobs, we aim to enhance both their efficiency and resource utilization. This proactive approach ensures that our data processing workflows remain both effective and cost-efficient over time.

This Apache Spark-based batch processing pipeline would allow for the efficient handling, processing, and analysis of data, and is crucial for building a robust music recommendation engine, managing large volumes of data, and generating reliable outputs or models.

Real-time data processing

Real-time data processing involves the continuous input, processing, and output of data, allowing organizations to derive insights and act on them immediately or within a very short time frame. This is crucial in scenarios like fraud detection, monitoring system health, and delivering personalized content.

The characteristics are as follows:

- **Low latency**: Processes data quickly, usually in milliseconds, enabling immediate insights and actions.

- **Scalability**: Can handle large volumes of data and scale as the volume increases.

- **Fault tolerance**: Can recover and continue processing in the case of failure.

- **Statefulness**: Keeps track of the current state to make decisions based on it.

The components are as follows:

- **Event sources**: Where the real-time data originates, like sensors, logs, user interactions.

- **Stream processing engines**: Such as Apache Flink or Apache Storm, for processing the real-time data.

- **Data storage**: Stores processed data, for example, databases, data lakes, or data warehouses.

- **Analytical tools**: Tools or applications that analyze the processed data to derive insights.

Apache Kafka

Apache Kafka is a highly scalable, durable, and distributed streaming platform used extensively for building real-time data processing pipelines and streaming applications. It is designed to allow systems to process and re-process streamed data as needed.

The core components are as follows:

- **Producer**
  - o Send messages to topics.
  - o Responsible for choosing which record to assign to which partition within the topic.

- **Consumer**
  - o Read messages from topics.
  - o Keeps track of messages it has consumed by storing the offset of messages.

- **Broker**
  - o Kafka servers that store data and serve client requests.
  - o A Kafka cluster consists of multiple brokers.

- **Topic**
  - o A category to which records are published.
  - o Topics in Kafka are always multi-subscriber.

- **Partition**
  - o   Kafka topics are divided into a number of partitions.
  - o   Partitions allow Kafka to parallelize processing as different consumers can read different partitions at the same time.

- **Zookeeper**
  - o   It is used to coordinate and manage the Kafka brokers.
  - o   Maintains the list of brokers that are functioning at any given point in time.

Workflow

The Apache Kafka workflow encompasses several key stages:
- **Data ingestion**: Producers push records to topics.
- **Data storage**
  - o   Once data is ingested through topics, it is stored in partitions.
  - o   Data is immutable once written, providing a durable record of the stream.
- **Data processing**: Consumers subscribe to topics and read records from them to perform real-time or batch processing.

The key features are as follows:
- **High throughput**: Capable of handling a high number of reads and writes per second, and transferring substantial amounts of data.
- **Scalability**: Designed to scale out with the addition of more machines without downtime.
- **Durability and reliability**: Ensures that data is stored durably and is resilient to node failures.
- **Fault tolerance**: Supports replication to prevent data loss.
- **Stream processing**: Supports stream processing applications allowing for the processing of data in real-time.

Usage of Apache Kafka and Apache Spark in real-time processing

Below is a hypothetical scenario depicting the usage of Apache Kafka as a producer-consumer broker and Apache Spark for real-time processing in a music recommendation system.

In this system, user interactions with different songs are sent as events/messages to Kafka topics. These interactions could be plays, likes, skips, and so on. Spark Structured Streaming consumes these events in real-time from Kafka, processes them to update user profiles and recommendation models, and then provides updated song recommendations to users. The workflow of integrating Apache Kafka with Apache Spark for real-time processing unfolds as follows:

Workflow overview:

- **User interaction service (Producer)**: Sends user interaction events to the Kafka topic.
- **Apache Spark Structured Streaming (Consumer and processor)**:
  - o   Read the Kafka topic.
  - o   Deserializes and processes the interaction events in real time.
  - o   Updates the recommendation model based on user interactions.
  - o   The updated model then computes new recommendations for users.
- **Recommendation service**: Provides real-time music recommendations to users based on the updated model.

To elaborate on the workflow overview, the process is detailed as follows:

1. **Producer**: Here, the interaction service acts as a producer, publishing user interaction events to a Kafka topic. Refer to the following codes:

```
from kafka import KafkaProducer
import json

producer = KafkaProducer(
    bootstrap_servers='localhost:9092',
    value_serializer=lambda v: json.dumps(v).encode('utf-8')
)

# Suppose a user interacts with a song
interaction = {
    'userID': 'user123',
    'songID': 'songXYZ',
    'interactionType': 'like'
}

producer.send('user_interactions', value=interaction)
producer.close()
```

2. **Consumer and processing**: Apache Spark acts as a consumer, processing the real-time interaction data and updating the recommendation model. Refer to the following codes:

```python
from pyspark.sql import SparkSession
from pyspark.sql.functions import *
from pyspark.sql.types import StructType, StructField, StringType


# Initialize Spark Session
spark = SparkSession.builder.appName("MusicRecommendationStream").
getOrCreate()


# Define the Schema
schema = StructType([
    StructField("userID", StringType(), True),
    StructField("songID", StringType(), True),
    StructField("interactionType", StringType(), True)
])


# Read the Kafka Stream
raw_stream = spark \
    .readStream \
    .format("kafka") \
    .option("kafka.bootstrap.servers", "localhost:9092") \
    .option("subscribe", "user_interactions") \
    .load()


# Deserialize the JSON data
json_stream = raw_stream \
    .selectExpr("CAST(value AS STRING)") \
    .select(from_json("value", schema).alias("data")) \
    .select("data.*")


# Perform some transformation to update recommendation model
# Here, we are just counting the interaction types for each song
interaction_count = json_stream.groupBy("songID", "interactionType").
count()
```

```
# For demonstration, writing the stream output to the console
query = interaction_count \
    .writeStream \
    .outputMode("complete") \
    .format("console") \
    .start()

query.awaitTermination()
```

Conclusion

This chapter thoroughly examines data management in ML microservices, using a music recommendation engine as a case study. It covers the complexities of handling various data sources, ingestion methods, and storage, highlighting the use of Apache Parquet and Hadoop for efficient distributed storage. Key topics include data versioning and lineage tracking through tools like Delta Lake and Apache Atlas, ensuring data integrity and transparency.

The chapter also delves into batch and real-time processing, emphasizing the importance of Apache Kafka and Apache Spark in processing real-time data for the recommendation engine. Offering both theory and practical insights, this chapter aims to equip professionals and enthusiasts with the knowledge to build robust, scalable ML microservices, fostering innovative data handling and ML solution development.

Building on the foundational knowledge from this chapter, the next will explore scaling and load balancing for ML microservices, focusing on their application within AI-driven solutions. We will examine the intricacies of managing ML workloads, including discussions on horizontal versus vertical scaling, the role of stateless microservices, and the implementation of load balancing techniques, all through practical examples and the perspective of a music recommendation engine.

Points to remember

- **Data sources and ingestion**: Understand various data sources and ingestion methods; crucial for diverse data inputs.
- **Storage solutions**: Emphasis on using Apache Parquet and Hadoop for efficient, distributed storage.
- **Data versioning**: Implement Delta Lake for managing versions, enabling rollback, and maintaining data integrity.
- **Lineage tracking**: Utilize Apache Atlas for tracking data transformations and ensuring compliance and quality.

- **Batch versus real-time processing**: Differentiate and apply batch and real-time processing techniques.
- **Technologies in use**
  o **Apache Kafka**: Essential for handling real-time data streams.
  o **Apache Spark**: Key for efficient data processing and integration with other tools like Hadoop and Delta Lake.
- **Practical implementation**: Insights into practical applications, particularly in a music recommendation engine.
- **Resilience and scalability**: Focus on building resilient and scalable ML microservices.
- **Innovation and application**: Encourage innovative approaches in data management and ML microservice development.

Assignment

Develop a simplified e-commerce product recommendation engine:

- Utilize concepts learned in this chapter.
- Ingest data from various sources in both batch and real-time.
- Store data efficiently using distributed storage and Parquet format.
- Implement data versioning using Delta Lake.
- Set up a basic batch processing pipeline using Apache Spark and a real-time processing pipeline integrating Apache Kafka with Spark.

Multiple choice questions

1. **Apache Parquet is favored for data storage in ML microservices due to its:**
   a. Flexibility with schema evolution
   b. Columnar storage format for efficient read operations
   c. Compatibility with real-time streaming data
   d. Both A and B
2. **Delta Lake enhances data management by offering:**
   a. Mutable datasets and ACID transactions
   b. Real-time processing capabilities
   c. Automated data cleaning features
   d. a and b

3. **Which of the following best describes the role of Apache Atlas in ML microservices?**

    a. Data transformation tool

    b. ML model trainer

    c. Metadata management and lineage tracking

    d. Real-time data ingestion service

4. **In the context of ML microservices, batch processing differs from real-time processing by its:**

    a. Lower latency

    b. Ability to handle streaming data

    c. Scheduled execution and high throughput

    d. Dependence on real-time user interaction data

5. **Apache Kafka is integral to real-time data processing in ML microservices because it:**

    a. Stores data in a distributed file system

    b. Acts as a message broker for real-time data streams

    c. Directly trains ML models

    d. Provides ACID transactions for data consistency

6. **The use of Hadoop in ML microservices is primarily for:**

    a. Real-time analytics

    b. Managing and processing large-scale datasets

    c. Immediate data ingestion from user interactions

    d. Automated ML model selection

7. **Why is lineage tracking crucial in ML microservices?**

    a. To optimize algorithms in real-time

    b. For understanding and visualizing data transformations and flow

    c. To increase the throughput of data ingestion

    d. To reduce the latency of data processing tasks

8. **What is a primary use of object storage in ML microservices?**

    a. Caching data temporarily

    b. Storing unstructured data like files and images

    c. Handling real-time user interaction events

    d. Performing complex data transformations

9. **How do Apache Spark and Kafka contribute to ML microservices?**

   a. By storing metadata efficiently

   b. Facilitating real-time processing of data streams to update models

   c. Supporting data versioning and schema evolution

   d. Managing metadata and governance

10. **Data versioning in ML microservices is essential for:**

    a. Providing immediate recommendations to users

    b. Tracking changes and maintaining model consistency over time

    c. Reducing the storage requirements for data

    d. Enhancing the real-time processing capabilities of the system

Answer key

1	d
2	a
3	c
4	c
5	b
6	b
7	b
8	b
9	b
10	b

Join our book's Discord space

Join the book's Discord Workspace for Latest updates, Offers, Tech happenings around the world, New Release and Sessions with the Authors:

https://discord.bpbonline.com

## CHAPTER 7

Scaling and Load Balancing Machine Learning Microservices

Introduction

Scalability in **Machine Learning** (**ML**) microservices is not just about handling more data or serving more users; it is about ensuring that as the demand grows, the system performance remains optimal, without causing exorbitant costs. An unscaled system can lead to bottlenecks, degraded user experiences, and, in certain situations, complete system failures. In the domain of ML, where models are data-intensive and computationally heavy, scalability becomes paramount.

Balancing the load for **Artificial Intelligence** (**AI**) and ML operations presents a unique set of challenges. Unlike traditional systems where the workload can be relatively predictable, ML workloads can be highly variable. Training a deep learning model, for instance, might require massive computational resources for a short period, while inference might be more continuous but less resource-intensive. Striking a balance to ensure that resources are optimally utilized and costs are minimized while maintaining performance is a complex task.

Our journey in this chapter will revolve around a specific use case: A music recommendation engine. This choice is not arbitrary. Music platforms experience spikes in user activity during album releases, music festivals, or even cultural events. In such scenarios, ensuring that the recommendation engine is responsive, accurate, and efficient becomes crucial. It offers an excellent backdrop to understand, explore, and implement the concepts of scalability and load balancing in real-world situations. As we traverse through the chapter, we will continually revisit this system to see how it can be enhanced and optimized using the principles we discuss.

Structure

This chapter emphasizes scaling ML microservices for optimal performance amid diverse workloads. As AI applications grow, effective scaling becomes crucial to meet user demands and operational requirements. By the end of the chapter, you will be prepared to develop responsive, scalable ML services, ensuring consistent performance in AI-driven applications.

We will be covering the following topics in this chapter:

- Horizontal versus vertical scaling strategies
- Stateless microservices for scalability
- Load balancing techniques for ML workloads
- Auto-scaling ML microservices
- Kubernetes and its role in scaling
- Challenges and considerations in scaling and load balancing

Objectives

In this chapter, we aim to provide a clear and comprehensive guide on scaling and load balancing for ML microservices. We will delve into the unique challenges presented by ML workloads and highlight specialized solutions. Through practical examples, centered on a music recommendation engine, readers will be equipped with the knowledge and tools to enhance the efficiency and robustness of their AI-driven applications. To achieve these goals, we will explore several key areas that are foundational to mastering scaling and load balancing in ML microservices.

Horizontal versus vertical scaling strategies

Scaling is fundamental to ensuring that applications can handle increased traffic or workloads without compromising on performance. Two prevalent strategies adopted in industries are *horizontal and vertical* scaling. Each has its advantages, limitations, and use cases. Here, we will delve deeper into these two strategies, focusing on their core principles and differentiation.

Horizontal versus vertical scaling

Horizontal scaling, often referred to as *scaling out*, involves adding more machines to a system or increasing the number of nodes in a cluster. It is similar to increasing the number of workers in an assembly line.

Following are the key characteristics of horizontal scaling:

- **Distributed system**: The primary principle behind horizontal scaling is to distribute the system's load across multiple servers or instances, ensuring that no single server is overwhelmed.

- **Elasticity**: Horizontal scaling provides elasticity to the system, allowing it to expand and shrink based on demand. This is especially useful for applications that experience varying loads at different times.

- **Load balancing**: When scaling out, there is typically a load balancer in place that distributes incoming requests to the various servers, ensuring that no single server is a bottleneck.

Following are the advantages of horizontal scaling:

- **Fault tolerance**: If one machine or node fails, the others can take over its tasks. This provides higher availability and ensures that a single machine failure does not bring down the entire system.

- **Flexibility**: You can add more machines to the system as needed, allowing for almost limitless scalability.

- **Cost-effective**: Often, adding more standard machines to a cluster is cheaper than upgrading a single machine to super high specifications.

- **Better utilization**: As each node typically has its own set of resources (CPU, memory, storage), there is less contention for resources.

Here are some commonly faced challenges with horizontal scaling:

- **Complexity**: Managing and maintaining a distributed system can be challenging. It requires tools and expertise to handle distributed data, failover mechanisms, and synchronization.

- **Consistency issues**: In a distributed environment, ensuring data consistency can be tricky, especially if data is replicated across nodes.

- **Network latency**: As requests might have to travel between different servers or data might need to be synchronized, network latency can become an issue if not managed well.

Vertical scaling, commonly referred to as *scaling up*, means enhancing the capabilities of an existing machine, such as adding more RAM, CPU, or storage. It is akin to replacing a worker in an assembly line with a more efficient one.

Following are the key characteristics of vertical scaling:

- **Single system enhancement**: Unlike horizontal scaling, which adds more machines, vertical scaling focuses on upgrading the existing machine's capabilities.

- **Immediate resource boost**: As soon as the machine is upgraded, the system benefits from the added resources, potentially leading to immediate performance improvements.

- **Simplified data management**: As there is a single machine or node, data management, synchronization, and consistency are typically simpler compared to distributed systems.

Following are the advantages of vertical scaling:

- **Simplicity**: As the scaling involves just one machine, there is less complexity in terms of setup, maintenance, and management.

- **Reduced latency**: Without the need to communicate across multiple machines, there is typically less network latency involved.

- **Consistency**: With a singular centralized system, data consistency is inherently maintained, eliminating challenges like data replication across nodes.

Here are some commonly faced challenges with vertical scaling:

- **Limitations on growth**: There is a limit to how much a single machine can be upgraded. Beyond a certain point, you might find that you cannot scale up any further.

- **Potential single point of failure**: If the single machine faces an issue or fails, it could lead to complete system downtime.

- **Costly hardware**: High-end hardware upgrades can be expensive, especially when looking at top-tier components.

- **Downtime**: Upgrading a machine might necessitate downtime unless specific high-availability strategies or redundant systems are in place.

Deciding factors: Scaling strategy choices

Choosing between horizontal and vertical scaling for ML microservices like a music recommendation system depends on various factors, such as:

- **Application needs**: Decide based on the application's specific requirements.

- **Workload predictability**: Use vertical scaling for stable workloads; opt for horizontal scaling for fluctuating, unpredictable demands.

- **Fault tolerance**: Horizontal scaling provides better fault tolerance, which is crucial for maintaining user engagement.

- **Cost versus scalability**: While vertical scaling can be initially cheaper, horizontal scaling is more cost-effective and scalable in the long term.

- **Operational complexity**: Horizontal scaling brings complexity but offers scalability. Vertical scaling is simpler.

- **Architecture suitability**: Distributed applications and microservices frameworks are more aligned with horizontal scaling.

- **Downtime tolerance**: Horizontal scaling allows for adjustments with minimal downtime, essential for services requiring high availability.

- **Latency and performance**: Vertical scaling typically offers lower latency; horizontal scaling effectively distributes load to manage concurrent requests.

Given these factors, ML services like a music recommendation system, likely to experience significant growth and requiring high availability, might benefit more from horizontal scaling. However, a hybrid approach, adapting to each microservice's unique needs, could be most effective.

Hybrid approach: Combining horizontal and vertical scaling

The hybrid approach to scaling uses the best aspects of *horizontal* and *vertical* scaling to create a flexible, efficient, and resilient system. By tailoring the scaling approach to the specific requirements and characteristics of each microservice, you can achieve a balanced and optimized system. To realize the advantages of a hybrid scaling approach, we focus on several critical aspects that ensure system efficiency and adaptability:

- **Service-specific scaling**: In a system composed of multiple microservices, each microservice may have its unique scaling requirements. Some microservices might benefit more from horizontal scaling due to their stateless nature and demand variability. Others, which are computationally intensive but do not face high variability, might be more suited to vertical scaling.

- **Flexibility**: A hybrid approach provides the flexibility to adjust the scaling strategy based on changing conditions or requirements.

- **Optimized costs**: By only investing in expensive hardware where necessary (vertical scaling) and distributing loads in other areas (horizontal scaling), costs can be optimized.

Following are the advantages of this hybrid approach:

- **Balanced performance**: By combining both strategies, a system can handle large quantities of requests and perform intense computational tasks without lag.

- **Resilience**: The distributed nature of horizontal scaling offers resilience against failures, while the increased capability from vertical scaling ensures the handling of heavy tasks.

- **Optimal resource utilization**: Resources can be allocated and utilized in a manner that gets the maximum output for each microservice, preventing wastage and ensuring efficiency.

Use case: Scaling the music recommendation engine for a sudden influx of users

Imagine that a popular artist releases a new album unexpectedly. As a result, there is a sudden surge of users flocking to the music recommendation platform to listen to it. This unexpected event triggers a massive increase in multiple services - from user authentication to fetching the album's metadata and, more importantly, recommending other songs based on the new album.

Following are the steps to handle the influx:

1. **Monitoring and alerts**: Firstly, the system should have real-time monitoring in place. Once the user activity crosses a specific threshold, alerts are sent to the system administrators or are automatically handled by scaling mechanisms.

2. **Horizontal scaling for user authentication service**: As more users try to log in or sign up, the authentication service should scale out. New instances of the authentication microservice are spawned to distribute the load and prevent any one instance from being overwhelmed.

3. **Database replication and scaling**: Given the demand, the database responsible for storing the new album's metadata and user activity will see heightened read and write operations. Using horizontal scaling, replicas of the database can be created to distribute read operations. Write operations can be streamlined with optimized database operations or using caching mechanisms.

4. **Scaling the recommendation service**:
   a. **Horizontal scaling**: New instances of the recommendation service are initiated to handle the increased number of requests. This ensures that each user gets their recommendations in a timely manner.
   b. **Vertical scaling**: Given the computational nature of generating recommendations, adding more resources (like CPU or memory) to existing instances can speed up the recommendation process.

5. **Caching mechanisms**: Implement caching for frequently accessed data, such as the details of the new album or popular songs from that album. This reduces the number of direct database queries, allowing the system to serve users faster.

6. **Load balancers**: As new instances of services are spun up due to horizontal scaling, load balancers distribute incoming traffic to ensure each instance receives an optimal number of requests. This prevents any single instance from becoming a bottleneck.

7. **Post-event scaling down**: Once the surge dies down, it is equally important to scale down resources. Excess instances spawned during the influx can be terminated to save costs. This is where *auto-scaling* strategies, both for scaling up and scaling down, become vital.

Handling a sudden influx of users, especially in a scenario like an unexpected album release, tests the robustness and scalability of the music recommendation engine. With a combination of horizontal and vertical scaling, coupled with other strategies like caching and load balancing, the system can effectively manage the surge, ensuring users have a seamless and responsive experience.

Stateless microservices for scalability

Microservices fall into two categories: Stateful and stateless, based on how they manage data and sessions.

In a stateless microservice, each client request is treated as a new interaction. It does not retain session data, ensuring no context is saved between requests.

Concept of stateless microservices

In microservices architecture, services are designed as independent, modular units capable of autonomous operation and evolution. Key to their functionality, especially concerning scalability and manageability, is the concept of state.

State in computing refers to information retained about an interaction over time. Stateless microservices, as the name implies, do not preserve any memory of prior interactions. Each request to a stateless service is solely based on the information within that request, devoid of any reliance on past context.

Following are the characteristics of stateless microservices:

- **Idempotence**: Stateless services exhibit idempotence, ensuring consistent responses to repeated client requests, promoting reliability.
- **Self-contained requests**: Every request must encompass all necessary information for processing, including authentication tokens, data payloads, and required metadata.
- **Ephemeral behavior**: Stateless services can be created or terminated without concern for user sessions or context loss. This behavior supports effortless scaling in and out based on demand.
- **No session affinity**: Unlike traditional systems, stateless services do not require directing user requests to specific server instances for session continuity. Any available instance can handle any request.

- **Simplicity in design and scalability**: Stateless service design simplifies application logic. There is no need for session data management, handling session timeouts, or complex synchronization across instances. This simplicity directly facilitates scalability by simplifying the addition of new instances.

Benefits of stateless ML microservices

Statelessness in ML operations like music recommendation systems provides:

- **Scalability**: Enables easy scaling by handling each request independently with all necessary information, facilitating the distribution of operations.
- **Fault tolerance**: Minimizes disruption risk from failures, as failed requests can be rerouted without data loss.
- **Load balancing**: Improves load balancing, with requests distributed evenly since no user-specific data is tied to instances.
- **Resource utilization**: Optimizes resources, as each request is processed without retaining data, ensuring predictable memory use.
- **Maintenance ease**: Simplifies updates and system maintenance without the need to manage session data.
- **Consistent predictions**: Ensures reliable and consistent ML predictions, important for maintaining user trust in applications like music recommendations.
- **Deployment and iteration speed**: Allows for quick deployment and updates of ML models, supporting rapid adaptation to changes like shifts in user behavior during events.

Implementation with TensorFlow and PyTorch

Implementing stateless microservices with popular deep learning frameworks like *TensorFlow* and *PyTorch* can be relatively straightforward. This section discusses some simple examples to illustrate the concept.

Let us break down the implementation using TensorFlow, especially focusing on TensorFlow Serving, which is one of the primary methods for serving TensorFlow models as stateless microservices:

- **TensorFlow Serving**: TensorFlow Serving is a specialized, extensible serving system for ML models, designed for production environments. It can serve multiple models, or versions of models, simultaneously.

  The steps for TensorFlow Serving are:

  1. **Export the model in SavedModel format**: After training your TensorFlow model, it is essential to save it in the **SavedModel** format, as shown:

```
# Assume model is an instance of a trained TensorFlow Keras model
model.save("path_to_saved_model")
```

2. **Install TensorFlow Serving**: You can easily install TensorFlow Serving using Docker or apt-get. Here is the Docker method:

```
# Pulling the latest TensorFlow Serving Docker image
docker pull tensorflow/serving
```

3. **Serve the model**: Now, serve your model using the TensorFlow Serving Docker image:

```
docker    run    -p    8501:8501    --name=tf_model_serving    --mount
type=bind,source=/path/to/saved_model/,target=/models/model_name
-e MODEL_NAME=model_name -t tensorflow/serving
```

4. **Send requests**: Once your model server is up and running, you can send HTTP requests to get predictions. For instance, using Python:

```
import requests
import json


data = {
    "signature_name": "serving_default",
    "instances": [{"input_tensor_name": value}, ...]
}
headers = {"content-type": "application/json"}
json_response = requests.post('http://localhost:8501/v1/models/
model_name:predict', data=json.dumps(data), headers=headers)


predictions = json.loads(json_response.text)['predictions']
```

• **TensorFlow Lite**: TensorFlow Lite is suitable for mobile and embedded devices. A typical use case involves converting your trained TensorFlow model to the **.tflite** format, as shown:

```
# Convert a TensorFlow model to TensorFlow Lite format
converter = tf.lite.TFLiteConverter.from_saved_model("path_to_saved_
model")
tflite_model = converter.convert()
```

```
with open('model.tflite', 'wb') as f:
    f.write(tflite_model)
```

- **TFHub**: TensorFlow Hub facilitates the use of pre-trained models. For instance, to load a pre-trained image feature vector, you might use:

```
import tensorflow_hub as hub


feature_extractor_url = "https://tfhub.dev/google/tf2-preview/
mobilenet_v2/feature_vector/4"
feature_extractor_layer = hub.KerasLayer(feature_extractor_url)
```

- **Deploying on cloud with TF cloud:** TensorFlow Cloud enables training and deploying TensorFlow models on Google Cloud, requiring setup of a Google Cloud project, configuring the Google Cloud SDK, and using the **tf_cloud** Python package.

  Though these steps are briefly mentioned here, real-world implementations involve more complex decisions like preprocessing and versioning, aiming to integrate TensorFlow into stateless microservices effectively.

- **TorchServe**: TorchServe is a PyTorch model serving library developed in collaboration with AWS. It is designed to make it easy to deploy PyTorch models at scale without having to write custom code.

  The steps for TorchServe are:

  a. **Export the model in TorchScript format**: One of the initial steps to serve a PyTorch model is to convert it into TorchScript. TorchScript is a way to create serializable and optimizable models from PyTorch code, as shown:

```
# Assume model is an instance of a trained PyTorch model

scripted_model = torch.jit.script(model)

scripted_model.save("model.pt")
```

  b. **Install TorchServe**: You can install TorchServe using **pip**:

```
pip install torch torchtext torchvision sentencepiece

pip install torchserve torch-model-archiver
```

  c. **Package the model**: Before you serve the model, you need to package it with **torch-model-archiver**, as shown:

```
torch-model-archiver --model-name my_model --version 1.0 --model-
file model.py --serialized-file model.pt --handler image_classifier
```

d. **Serve the model**: Now, you can start the TorchServe:

```
torchserve --start --model-store model_store --models my_model=my_
model.mar
```

e. **Send requests**: Similar to TensorFlow Serving, once your model server is up, you can send requests to get predictions, as shown:

```
curl -X POST http://127.0.0.1:8080/predictions/my_model -T sample_
input.jpg
```

- **TorchScript in production**: TorchScript is not just for TorchServe. Once you have your model in TorchScript format (**model.pt**), you can load and run it in a variety of environments. This simple Python code uses the **torch.jit** module in PyTorch to load a saved TorchScript model from the specified path (**"model.pt"**):

```
import torch.jit


# Load the TorchScript model in Python
module = torch.jit.load("model.pt")
```

- **Open Neural Network Exchange (ONNX) export**: ONNX is an open standard format for representing ML models. PyTorch natively supports exporting models to the ONNX format, making it easier to interoperate with other deep learning frameworks, as shown:

```
# Exporting model to ONNX format
torch.onnx.export(model, dummy_input, "model.onnx")
```

Once in ONNX format, you can utilize a variety of runtime libraries like ONNX Runtime for efficient inference.

These examples showcase how PyTorch models, once trained, can be served in various ways to cater to different deployment scenarios. Whether you are deploying on a cloud server, edge device, or integrating with other frameworks, PyTorch offers flexibility and efficiency in model serving.

Load balancing techniques for ML workloads

Load balancing is an essential technique to distribute incoming network traffic or computational tasks across multiple servers, ensuring no single server is overwhelmed. With the intricacies and varying workloads of ML tasks, load balancing becomes crucial to ensure timely processing and efficient resource utilization. Let us explore this further.

Common load balancing techniques

Given the dynamic and intensive nature of ML workloads, combined with the demand for high availability and optimal performance, load balancing is not just an added benefit—it is a necessity. It provides a safety net, ensuring that ML systems remain operational, efficient, and user-centric, no matter the demand or challenges they face.

Load balancing techniques aim to distribute workloads across multiple servers or computing resources. Here are some widely used load balancing strategies:

- **Round robin**
  - o **Description**: Distributes client requests sequentially to each server in the list, starting again from the beginning.
  - o **Best use cases**: When servers have approximately equal processing power and resources, and there is not a significant discrepancy in server capabilities.

- **Least connections**
  - o **Description**: Directs traffic to the server with the fewest active connections, assuming that a server with fewer connections is less busy and can take on more work.
  - o **Best use cases**: When there is variability in server performance, and some servers are more powerful than others.

- **Least response time**
  - o **Description**: Selects the server with the lowest response time for a new connection, particularly effective when server response times are variable.
  - o **Best use cases**: For services where response time is crucial, such as real-time applications or high-concurrency services.

- **IP hash**
  - o **Description**: Uses a hash function based on the user's IP address to determine where to send a request, ensuring that the same IP is always directed to the same server.
  - o **Best use cases**: When there is a need for preserving session or user-specific data.

- **Weighted load balancing**
  - o **Description**: Assigns servers weights based on their processing capacity, allowing servers with higher weights to handle more requests.
  - o **Best use cases**: In environments with servers of differing capabilities.

- **Layer 7 load balancing**
  - o **Description**: Makes routing decisions based on attributes extracted from the application layer (Layer 7 of the OSI model), such as HTTP headers or specific content.
  - o **Best use cases**: When routing decisions need to be made based on content type, URL, or other message content, especially for HTTP/HTTPS traffic.
- **Sticky sessions**
  - o **Description**: Once a user establishes a session with a specific server, they continue to use that server for the duration of their session.
  - o **Best use cases**: Applications where user data is stored locally on the server during a session, like e-commerce shopping carts.

The choice of load balancing strategy often depends on the specific requirements of the application, the nature of the traffic, and the existing infrastructure. For ML workloads, considering their computational intensity and the need for real-time responses, techniques like *least connections* or *layer 7* load balancing might be more appropriate.

Implementing load balancing for the music recommendation engine

The **music recommendation engine (MRE)** must efficiently process real-time user interactions and provide customized music suggestions, demanding a scalable, robust infrastructure to handle peak loads. To ensure the music recommendation engine operates with optimal efficiency and reliability, we implement distinct load balancing strategies tailored to the unique requirements of each microservice involved. These strategies are designed to manage varying demands and ensure seamless service delivery:

- **User interaction microservice**: Manages user data like likes and skips, needing a round robin load balancer for equal request distribution and preventing server overload during sudden spikes.
- **Data processing microservice**: Transforms raw user data for the ML model, where a least connections load balancing strategy helps in quick, efficient data processing by directing tasks to less burdened servers.
- **ML model microservice**: Handles the recommendation algorithm, balancing quick inference tasks and resource-intensive model training with a weighted round robin strategy, assigning higher request weights to inference tasks.
- **Music delivery microservice**: Delivers song recommendations, employing session persistence load balancing to ensure a smooth, uninterrupted user experience by maintaining user-server connections for each session.

Effective load balancing across these microservices ensures timely recommendations, prevents server overload, and maximizes resource efficiency, with each microservice benefiting from a tailored strategy.

Auto-scaling ML microservices

Auto-scaling ML microservices ensures that ML applications dynamically adjust resources based on workload demands, optimizing performance and cost-effectiveness.

The dynamic nature of ML tasks

ML tasks are dynamic and evolving, contrasting with the more predictable behavior of traditional software:

- **Training versus inference**: Training involves learning from data and is computationally heavy, while inference makes predictions on new data and is generally faster but resource-intensive for deep models.
- **Model evolution**: Models must be periodically retrained or fine-tuned with new data, leading to variable computational demands.
- **Data variability**: Changes in data volume, variety, and velocity affect model training frequency and method.
- **Hyperparameter tuning**: Involves multiple training iterations under different settings, affecting computational load.
- **Batch versus online learning**: Batch learning requires considerable resources at once, whereas online learning updates models continually, causing fluctuating demands.
- **Distributed training**: Large datasets may require training across multiple machines or GPUs, adding complexity.
- **Complex pipelines**: ML workflows, including preprocessing, feature extraction, and validation, have varying and evolving resource needs.

ML's dynamic nature stems from changing data, model needs, and goals, requiring adaptable infrastructures for optimal performance.

Need for auto-scaling

Auto-scaling is crucial for ML microservices, adapting resources to meet changing demands in today's variable digital environment. The key benefits include:

- **Optimized resource utilization**: Auto-scaling ensures resources are neither wasted during low traffic periods nor overwhelmed during spikes, enhancing efficiency.
- **Cost efficiency**: It minimizes costs by allocating resources only as needed, avoiding unnecessary expenditure on idle capacity.

- **Improved availability and performance**: Auto-scaling prepares the system for traffic surges, maintaining consistent performance and avoiding outages or slowdowns.

- **Flexibility for uncertain demand**: It allows businesses to adapt to unpredictable traffic, ensuring reliable service.

- **Support for continuous learning**: Auto-scaling accommodates the varying computational demands of ML models, particularly in continuous learning scenarios.

In essence, auto-scaling ensures ML microservices remain resilient, cost-effective, and high-performing, regardless of demand fluctuations.

Kubernetes and its role in scaling

Kubernetes, a powerful container orchestration system, is revolutionizing the way applications, including ML microservices, are deployed, managed and scaled. Its dynamic resource allocation, coupled with its robust management features, ensures that systems can effortlessly adapt to changing loads, ensuring optimal performance and cost-efficiency in diverse operational scenarios.

Introduction to Kubernetes

Kubernetes (K8s) is an open-source platform for container orchestration, automating the deployment, scaling, and operation of application containers. Originating from Google's Borg system, it was handed to the *Cloud Native Computing Foundation* in 2015. The key concepts include:

- **Pods**: Basic deployment units in K8s, each pod runs a single application instance, which might be a single container or multiple containers sharing storage or network.

- **Nodes**: Worker machines hosting pods, managed by Kubelet.
  - o **Master node**: Manages the cluster and application distribution across nodes.
  - o **Worker node**: Executes the application instances.

- **Cluster**: A group of nodes managed by Kubernetes, ensuring applications run smoothly despite failures, and handling deployment and scaling.

- **Services**: An abstraction to expose applications on pods as a network service.
  - o `ClusterIP`: Only reachable within the cluster.
  - o `NodePort`: Accessible outside the cluster on each node's port.
  - o `LoadBalancer`: Creates an external load balancer with a fixed IP.
  - o `ExternalName`: Exposes services using an arbitrary name through a CNAME record.

Understanding these foundational elements is essential for deploying and managing apps with Kubernetes.

Kubernetes for ML microservices workloads

Kubernetes is a vital platform for deploying, managing, and scaling ML microservices, crucial for integrating machine learning in business operations. The key features include:

- **Isolation and reproducibility**: Containers in Kubernetes provide consistent environments, solving dependency issues and ensuring reproducibility.

- **Service discovery and load balancing**: Facilitates communication among different ML microservice components and distributes requests efficiently across pods.

- **Auto-scaling**: Dynamically adjusts microservice instances based on load, optimizing resource use and cost.

- **Rolling updates and rollbacks**: Enables zero-downtime updates and easy rollbacks for ML microservices.

- **Persistent storage**: Supports various storage backends for continuous data access, essential for services requiring persistent data like model weights.

- **Multi-cloud and on-prem flexibility**: Allows deployment across diverse environments, from multiple clouds to on-premises data centers, enhancing flexibility and preventing vendor lock-in.

- **Integrated monitoring and logging**: With tools like Prometheus and the ELK Stack, it provides real-time performance insights, aiding proactive management.

- **Security**: Ensures protection of ML microservices and sensitive data with features like RBAC, secrets management, and network policies.

Kubernetes thus offers a comprehensive solution for efficient, scalable, and secure management of ML-driven services.

Kubernetes auto-scaling: Standing out in scalability management

Kubernetes excels in dynamic workload management with its robust auto-scaling features, crucial for ML workloads and other applications.

The different types of auto-scaling are:

- **Horizontal Pod Autoscaler (HPA)**: Adjusts pod numbers based on CPU or custom metrics.

- **Vertical Pod Autoscaler (VPA)**: Optimizes pod CPU and memory limits.

- **Cluster autoscaler**: Resizes the cluster itself, focusing on overall resource demands.

- **Resource efficiency**: Aligns resources with demand, handling spikes and reducing costs by releasing unused resources.

- **Scaling approaches**
  - o **Reactive scaling**: Scales out in response to real-time metrics, like surging CPU usage.
  - o **Proactive scaling**: Predictively scales using custom and predefined metrics to prepare for upcoming demand.

- **Custom metrics**: Supports custom metrics for complex workloads, essential in ML for managing diverse factors like inference requests or model training times.

- **Seamless CNCF integration**: Integrates with CNCF tools like Prometheus, enhancing functionality with robust metrics and custom APIs.

- **User focus**
  - o **Developers**: Focus on application coding and logic.
  - o **Operators**: Ensure infrastructure scales automatically and appropriately.

- **Policy-driven autoscaling**: Uses policies to dictate scaling actions, maintaining operations within desired parameters.

Kubernetes auto-scaling, with its comprehensive, adaptable approach and integration with the CNCF ecosystem, is key for managing scalable, resilient, and efficient applications, particularly in complex environments like Machine Learning.

Implementing Kubernetes auto-scaling for the music recommendation engine on AWS requires the following steps:

1. **Initial deployment**: Setup an EKS Cluster: Use the `eksctl` command-line tool, which is the official CLI for Amazon EKS, as shown:

   ```
   # For EKS

   eksctl create cluster --name music-recommendation-cluster --region us-west-2 --nodegroup-name standard-workers --node-type t2.medium --nodes 3
   ```

2. **Deploy microservices**: Deploy the data preprocessing service as an example:

   ```
   # data-preprocessing-deployment.yaml

   apiVersion: apps/v1

   kind: Deployment

   metadata:
     name: data-preprocessing-deployment

   spec:
     replicas: 3
   ```

```
selector:
  matchLabels:
    app: data-preprocessor
template:
  metadata:
    labels:
      app: data-preprocessor
  spec:
    containers:
    - name: data-preprocessor
      image: music/data-preprocessor:v1
      ports:
      - containerPort: 8080
```

3. Apply the following configuration:

```
kubectl apply -f data-preprocessing-deployment.yaml
```

HPA configuration: Determine metrics and set up HPA:

```
kubectl autoscale deployment data-preprocessing-deployment --min=2
--max=10 --cpu-percent=80
```

VPA configuration

1. Enable VPA

```
# vpa-config.yaml
apiVersion: autoscaling.k8s.io/v1
kind: VerticalPodAutoscaler
metadata:
  name: data-preprocessing-vpa
spec:
  targetRef:
    apiVersion: "apps/v1"
    kind: Deployment
    name: data-preprocessing-deployment
  updatePolicy:
    updateMode: "Auto"
```

2. **Apply this configuration**:

```
kubectl apply -f vpa-config.yaml
```

3. **Cluster autoscaler configuration**: Amazon EKS provides its own auto-scaling groups which can be integrated with cluster autoscaler, as shown:

Define resource limits: Modify the deployment to include resource requests and limits.

```
spec:
  containers:
  - name: data-preprocessor
    image: music/data-preprocessor:v1
    resources:
      requests:
        memory: "64Mi"
        cpu: "250m"
      limits:
        memory: "128Mi"
        cpu: "500m"
```

4. **Monitor and optimize**: AWS provides its native monitoring solution, Amazon CloudWatch. However, for a more Kubernetes-native experience, you can use Helm to install Prometheus and Grafana:

```
helm install stable/prometheus --name prometheus
helm install stable/grafana --name grafana
```

5. **Handle special scenarios**: This would involve more monitoring, anticipation, and then adjusting the configurations based on predictions.

6. **Scaling data storage**: If you are using Amazon RDS or any other AWS database solution with Kubernetes, consider auto-scaling capabilities provided by AWS for that particular service.

Challenges and considerations in scaling and load balancing

Scaling is crucial but complex, involving more than just managing traffic. It requires careful planning and awareness of potential challenges:

- **Rapid over-scaling**: Avoids downtime but can lead to increased costs, resource waste, and management complexity.

- **Under-scaling**: Impairs user experience and strains the system.

- **Un-tested scale limits**: Can lead to unpredictable behavior and missed optimization chances.

- **Stateful components**: Complicate scaling due to replication issues, data inconsistencies, and recovery and scaling delays.

Following are the overhead costs in scaling:

- **Idle resources**: Causes wasted costs and environmental impacts.

- **Management complexity**: Requires advanced tools and potentially larger, specialized teams.

- **Data transfer costs**: Incur expenses related to bandwidth, data access, and redundancy.

Ensuring ML consistency across scales involves:

- **Model versioning**: Use tools like TensorFlow's ModelServer for consistent deployment.

- **Data consistency**: Tools like Apache Kafka ensure real-time data uniformity.

- **Hardware variances**: Kubernetes can manage deployments on similar hardware to avoid model performance discrepancies.

In summary, effective scaling and load balancing are key to maintaining performance and user trust, yet they pose challenges in cost, management complexity, and ensuring ML consistency.

Addressing these challenges in the MRE

To address the multifaceted challenges faced by the MRE and maintain its efficiency and reliability, strategic solutions are necessary. These encompass predictive scaling to preemptively manage user demand spikes, statelessness for operational consistency, cost monitoring to optimize expenses, a robust model management system for uniform recommendations, and regular benchmarking for system resilience. The following points outline how we tackle each challenge to ensure the MRE's performance and user satisfaction remain high:

- **Predictive scaling**: In the world of music, certain events like new album releases, award ceremonies, or music festivals can lead to predictable surges in user activity. Predictive scaling can be highly beneficial in such scenarios. Here are its features:

    o **Challenge**: Traditional scaling methods react to the immediate demand, which could be too late if thousands of users flock to the platform within a short span.

    o **Solution**: By analyzing historical data, patterns related to user activity during major events can be discerned. For instance, noticing a surge in activity every

Friday evening (typical album release time) can be a cue for the system. By predicting these surges in advance, resources can be allocated just before the surge, ensuring smooth user experience without abrupt over-scaling or delayed response times.

- **Statelessness**: The inherent distributed nature of a scalable music recommendation engine necessitates stateless operations for consistency and reliability.

  o **Challenge**: Retaining user session data, recent activity, or interim calculations during the recommendation process can lead to scalability bottlenecks and inconsistencies.

  o **Solution**: Designing each microservice in the recommendation engine to be stateless ensures that each request can be handled independently of others. Any required state, like user preferences or session details, can be stored in a centralized data store, like Amazon DynamoDB, which can be quickly accessed and updated.

- **Cost monitoring tools**: As the system scales, costs can escalate quickly, especially if resources are over-provisioned or left idle.

  o **Challenge**: Keeping track of the costs associated with each service, instance, or data transfer can become daunting as the infrastructure grows.

  o **Solution**: AWS provides tools like Cost Explorer, which offers a detailed breakdown of costs, trends, and forecasts. Regularly monitoring this can help in identifying unnecessary costs and optimizing the scaling strategy accordingly.

- **Model management system**: Consistency in recommendations is paramount for user trust and platform reliability.

  o **Challenge**: With multiple instances or nodes serving recommendations, ensuring all of them use the same model version and data can be challenging.

  o **Solution**: Implementing a model management system ensures that every time a model is updated, all instances are synchronized. Coupling this with a centralized data store or caching mechanism, like Redis, ensures that real-time data used for recommendations remains consistent across requests and nodes.

- **Regular benchmarking**: Ensuring the system's robustness against unexpected surges is crucial.

  o **Challenge**: Without stress tests or benchmarks, the system's potential breakpoints remain unknown, leading to vulnerabilities during real-world traffic surges.

  o **Solution**: Regularly simulating high-traffic scenarios using tools like Apache JMeter or AWS's own testing tools can provide insights into the system's performance under stress. This not only highlights potential weak points but also allows developers to optimize configurations, scale strategies, and resource allocations.

In summary, the dynamic nature of the music recommendation engine, coupled with the unpredictable world of music popularity, demands a proactive and informed approach to scaling. By anticipating challenges and implementing these solutions, the engine can remain resilient, efficient, and user centric.

Conclusion

This chapter explored the complex aspects of scaling and load balancing in ML systems. It began by comparing horizontal and vertical scaling, discussing their benefits and challenges, and what influences their use. It then highlighted the significance of stateless microservices, such as TensorFlow and PyTorch, in improving ML scalability. The chapter also examined load balancing, detailing traditional approaches and ML-specific methods like round robin and weighted least connections, and stressed the importance of auto-scaling in ML for adaptive, dynamic task management. Kubernetes was noted for its effectiveness not only in container orchestration but also in scaling ML workloads. The chapter acknowledged the challenges of scaling, such as rapid over-scaling and the necessity of maintaining consistent ML results across different scales. Using a music recommendation engine case study, it demonstrated practical scalability management during high-traffic events. Overall, the chapter provides a thorough guide on achieving a crucial balance in ML systems between scalability, efficiency, and consistency.

In the next chapter, we will dive into the critical aspect of security within the ML ecosystem. Highlighting the importance of safeguarding ML microservices, we will explore strategies for protecting against threats, prioritizing privacy through data anonymization, and securely deploying ML models.

Points to remember

- **Horizontal vs. vertical scaling**
  - o **Horizontal scaling**: Add more machines. Offers fault tolerance but introduces complexity.
  - o **Vertical scaling**: Increase a machine's capacity. May hit performance bottlenecks.
  - o Decision based on cost, architecture, traffic. Music recommendation engines might need horizontal scaling during peak influxes.
- **Stateless microservices**
  - o Stateless microservices do not retain client data between sessions.

o Enhances scalability and fault tolerance. Useful for ML like TensorFlow and PyTorch models.

o Music recommendation system benefits from statelessness for efficient processing.

- **Load balancing for ML**

o Distributes traffic across servers.

o ML-specific techniques needed. Methods include round robin, weighted least connections.

o Vital for the efficient functioning of the music recommendation system.

- **Auto-scaling ML microservices**

o ML tasks have variable computational demands.

o Auto-scaling monitors and adjusts resources based on demand.

o The music recommendation system should auto-scale with user activity patterns.

- **Kubernetes in scaling**

o **Kubernetes**: Container orchestration tool.

o Supports ML through specialized configurations. Provides dynamic auto-scaling.

o Helps the music recommendation system scale efficiently.

- **Challenges in scaling and load balancing**

o Watch for over-scaling, under-scaling, untested limits.

o Be aware of costs, wasted resources, and strain.

o Aim for consistent ML results. Address issues in the music system like data consistency and hardware variations.

- **Case study**

o See how the music system reacts to major events, for example, trending album releases.

o Demonstrates the practical use of statelessness, load balancing, and Kubernetes.

Mastering these key points ensures a sound understanding of ML system scaling and balancing nuances.

Assignment

Objective: To apply the principles of scaling and load balancing for ML systems.

Task:

- Design a scaled version of a hypothetical e-commerce platform.

- Make decisions on whether to implement horizontal or vertical scaling based on predicted user traffic for a major sales event (for example, Black Friday or Cyber Monday).

- Incorporate stateless microservices into your design. Choose a framework between TensorFlow and PyTorch and justify your choice for predictive analytics or personalized product recommendations.

- Implement a load balancing strategy suitable for your platform. Discuss why you chose this technique over others.

- Draft a plan for auto-scaling the microservices, keeping in mind the dynamic nature of ML tasks.

- Explore how Kubernetes would play a role in your platform's scaling strategy. Detail how you would use its auto-scaling feature.

- Identify potential challenges and considerations in your scaling and load balancing strategies and provide solutions to mitigate them.

- Conclude with a brief report summarizing your decisions, methodologies, and expected outcomes. Use visual aids (diagrams, flowcharts) where necessary.

Multiple choice questions

1. **What is the primary benefit of horizontal scaling for ML microservices?**

   a. Increased computational power of individual machines

   b. Fault tolerance and system availability

   c. Simplified data management

   d. Reduced network latency

2. **Vertical scaling is most suitable for applications that:**

   a. Require elasticity to handle variable loads

   b. Have a predictable workload

   c. Need to minimize network latency

   d. All of the above

3. **Which load balancing strategy is based on directing traffic to the server with the fewest active connections?**

    a. Round robin

    b. Least connections

    c. IP hash

    d. Weighted round robin

4. **What does a stateless microservice architecture imply?**

    a. The microservice requires continuous internet connectivity

    b. The microservice retains client state between sessions

    c. Each request to the microservice is treated as an independent transaction

    d. The microservice can only handle a single client at a time

5. **Kubernetes auto-scaling does NOT support which of the following features?**

    a. Horizontal Pod Autoscaler

    b. Vertical Pod Autoscaler

    c. Automatic model version updates

    d. Cluster Autoscaler

6. **In the context of ML microservices, predictive scaling is particularly useful for:**

    a. Reducing the cost of cloud resources

    b. Handling predictable surges in user activity

    c. Decreasing the time it takes to deploy new models

    d. Improving the accuracy of ML predictions

7. **Which of the following is not a commonly used Kubernetes object in scaling ML microservices?**

    a. Pods

    b. Nodes

    c. Clusters

    d. Firewalls

8. **The main challenge with stateful components in scaling ML microservices is:**

    a. Increased computational demands for inference

    b. High costs of storage

    c. Data inconsistencies and recovery issues

    d. Simplified rollback and version control

9. **Which load balancing technique uses a hash function based on the client's IP address?**

    a. Least response time

    b. Sticky sessions

    c. IP hash

    d. Weighted load balancing

10. **The use of auto-scaling in ML microservices ensures:**

    a. Manual intervention for scaling up during peak loads

    b. Uniform load distribution regardless of demand

    c. Resources are dynamically adjusted based on workload demands

    d. A fixed number of pods regardless of traffic

Answer key

1	b
2	d
3	b
4	c
5	c
6	b
7	d
8	c
9	c
10	c

Join our book's Discord space

Join the book's Discord Workspace for Latest updates, Offers, Tech happenings around the world, New Release and Sessions with the Authors:

https://discord.bpbonline.com

## CHAPTER 8

Securing Machine Learning Microservices

Introduction

In today's data-driven world, where sensitive data is a key asset, securing **Machine Learning (ML)** applications is critically important. ML systems, which learn and adapt from vast amounts of data, could have their core integrity compromised in a breach. Such breaches could have wide-reaching consequences, affecting everything from medical diagnoses to financial decisions.

Security in ML applications is, therefore, not just about protecting data but also about ensuring the reliability and accuracy of the decisions derived from this data. ML can significantly contribute to cybersecurity by detecting anomalies and automating responses. Yet, if left unsecured, these systems can become vulnerable points of failure.

In this chapter, we will delve into the crucial interplay between cybersecurity and ML, emphasizing the need to protect ML microservices not just for data confidentiality but to maintain the integrity and reliability of ML-driven decisions.

Structure

We will discuss the following topics in the chapter:

- Importance of securing ML microservice
- Best practices for secure communication

- Privacy concerns in ML and data anonymization
- Ensuring secure model deployment
- Use case: Music recommendation engine
- Recommendation service: Ensuring data privacy

Objectives

In this chapter, our focus is to enhance the security landscape of ML applications by addressing key areas crucial for maintaining the integrity and privacy of these systems. We aim to equip you with a deep understanding of the challenges and methodologies for protecting ML microservices against potential threats, emphasizing the importance of privacy through data anonymization techniques and highlighting strategies for the secure deployment of ML models. By integrating these objectives, we strive to ensure the operational efficiency and resilience of ML applications against unauthorized access and data breaches, thereby safeguarding the sanctity and reliability of our digital ecosystem.

Importance of securing ML microservices

ML microservices operate at the confluence of data processing, analytics, and predictive modeling. As such, the data they interact with and the models they generate become invaluable assets to organizations. This section talks about why ensuring the security of these ML microservices is not just beneficial but essential.

Sensitivity and value of ML data and models

ML models are as valuable as the data they are trained on. This segment addresses the dual emphasizing aspects of sensitivity and the intrinsic value associated with ML data and models, why their protection is paramount. To delve deeper into the significance of these aspects, consider the following key points that illuminate the multifaceted nature of ML data and models' sensitivity and value, highlighting the imperative for their rigorous protection:

- **Data sensitivity**: ML models often require large datasets, which can include sensitive information such as personal identifiers, financial records, or proprietary business insights. This sensitivity arises not only from the nature of the data itself but also from how it's used to derive meaningful patterns and predictions. A breach in this data can lead to privacy violations, legal consequences, and a breach of trust.

- **Intrinsic value of data**: In the ML context, data is not just a record; it is a foundational element that informs and shapes decision-making algorithms. The insights gleaned from data analyses drive strategic decisions, market predictions, and customer engagement strategies. Therefore, any compromise to the integrity or availability of this data can directly impact an organization's strategic direction and operational effectiveness.

- **Model integrity**: ML models represent a significant intellectual and strategic investment. They embody the learning derived from data and are tailored to specific operational goals. Compromise of these models through tampering or reverse engineering can result in intellectual property theft, strategic disadvantage, and potentially harmful decisions if these models are deployed for critical functions.

- **Commercial and competitive value**: ML models are often the competitive edge organizations have in understanding customer behaviors, optimizing operations, and innovating. Unauthorized access to these models can lead to loss of this competitive edge and can even empower competitors if proprietary methodologies and insights are leaked.

- **Regulatory compliance**: Many industries are bound by stringent regulations regarding data handling, privacy, and protection. Non-compliance due to poor security measures around ML data and models can result in severe penalties, legal actions, and damage to reputation.

By highlighting the sensitivity and value of ML data and models, this section underscores the critical need for stringent security measures in ML microservices. Protecting this data and the models ensures not only compliance and operational continuity but also safeguard the strategic assets of an organization.

Consequences of not securing ML services

Unsecured ML microservices can have far-reaching and severe consequences, which are as follows:

- **Data breaches**: Perhaps the most direct impact, data breaches can expose sensitive user data and proprietary information, leading to direct losses and undermining trust.

- **Regulatory non-compliance**: Violating data protection regulations such as **General Data Protection Regulation (GDPR)** or **Health Insurance Portability and Accountability Act (HIPAA)** can lead to hefty fines and legal complications.

- **Legal and financial liabilities**: Organizations may face lawsuits and further financial losses stemming from breaches, apart from regulatory fines.

- **Model tampering and manipulation**: Insecure services can be exploited to alter ML models, resulting in skewed predictions or decisions. This manipulation can be subtle, as seen in adversarial attacks, but has critical implications in sensitive applications.

- **Strategic disadvantages**: Tampered models can erode a company's competitive edge, especially if used for strategic decisions.

- **Reputation and trust**: Security breaches often result in long-lasting damage to an organization's reputation, eroding customer and stakeholder trust.
- **Operational disruption**: Attacks like **Distributed Denial of Service (DDoS)** can cause service downtimes, disrupt business operations, and lead to immediate revenue impacts.

Securing ML services goes beyond mere data protection; it is integral to maintain operational integrity, compliance, customer trust, and competitive advantage. This holistic view underlines the necessity of robust security measures in ML microservices.

Best practices for secure communication

In ML microservices, safeguarding the continuous data flow between services is critical. Secure communication is essential to balance accessibility with data protection. This section covers key security practices, focusing on:

- Encrypted communication through **Secure Sockets Layer/Transport Layer Security (SSL/TLS)** to protect data during transit.
- Using API key authentication and OAuth 2.0 for secure, controlled access.

Secure Socket Layer and Transport Layer Security

SSL is the original protocol for encrypting internet communication and ensuring data privacy and integrity between users and websites.

TLS is an advanced successor to SSL and provides enhanced security features. Developed due to vulnerabilities in SSL, it offers improved algorithms and key exchange methods, making it the preferred option today.

Exploring the foundational elements and advancements in securing digital communication, the following points describe the operational mechanics, certification processes, notable distinctions, and their pivotal role in safeguarding ML data integrity and confidentiality:

- **How they work**
  - o **Asymmetric PKI system**: SSL and TLS use a public key (shared openly) and a private key (kept secret). Data encrypted with one can only be decrypted with the other.
  - o **Handshake process**: Initiates a secure connection, where servers and clients exchange keys and agree on encryption methods and integrity checks.
- **Certificates and authorities**
  - o **Digital certificates**: Contain the server's public key and identity, assuring the user of the server's authenticity.
  - o **Certificate authorities**: Trusted entities that issue and manage these certificates.

- **Key differences**

  o **Algorithmic enhancements**: TLS versions (like TLS 1.2) incorporate better cryptographic techniques than SSL.

  o **Session resumption**: TLS can efficiently resume past sessions, speeding up repeated connections.

- **Importance in ML**

  o **Protecting data**: Crucial for securing sensitive ML data, including personal and proprietary information.

  o **Eavesdropping prevention**: Ensures data is encrypted during transit, protecting against leaks and tampering.

In summary, SSL and TLS are fundamental to secure online communication, particularly in ML, where data privacy and security are paramount.

API key authentication

API key authentication verifies the identity of applications accessing an API. It restricts API interaction to authorized users or applications. Delving into the mechanics and considerations of API key authentication, let us explore how this method ensures secure API access for applications, outlining its operation, strengths, limitations, and best practices:

- **How it works**

  o **Issuance**: Service providers generate a unique key for each client application, serving as pseudo-credentials for API access.

  o **Request**: Clients include this key in API call headers (or less securely, in URLs) to request access.

  o **Verification**: The server validates the key against its list of valid keys to grant or deny access.

- **Strengths and limitations**

  o **Simple use**: Easy to implement; suitable for tracking application usage rather than high-security needs.

  o **Rate limiting**: Useful for controlling application request frequencies.

  o **Security concerns**: Vulnerable to interceptions and exposure, API keys offer limited security.

  o **Static nature**: Being unchanging, compromised keys remain exploitable until revoked or updated.

- **Best practices**

  o **Secure transmission**: Use HTTPS to encrypt keys during transit.

  o **Key regeneration**: Rotate API keys periodically for better security.

  o **Secure storage**: Avoid exposing keys in client-side code or public areas.

  o **Access levels**: Employ distinct keys for different access privileges.

- **Relevance in ML**: In ML microservices, API keys often control access to prediction endpoints and data services. They must be used with extra security layers in sensitive or high-security contexts.

API key authentication is a practical access control method but requires careful security considerations, particularly in high-stakes environments like ML.

OAuth 2.0

OAuth 2.0 lets applications obtain user account access on HTTP services (for example, Facebook, GitHub) without exposing user passwords. It is used for authorization, not authentication. Let us discuss the OAuth 2.0 components and processes:

- **Components**

  o **Resource owner**: User who controls data access.

  o **Client**: Application wanting to access user data.

  o **Resource server**: Hosts user data, accessible with a valid access token.

  o **Authorization server**: Authenticates the user and issues tokens to the client after authorization.

- **Process**

  o **Authorization request**: Client asks for user's approval via the authorization server.

  o **User approval**: User logs in and grants permissions to the client.

  o **Authorization grant**: Server provides an authorization code to the client.

  o **Access token request**: Client exchanges the code for an access token.

  o **Access token issuance**: Server checks credentials and grants access token.

  o **Resource access**: Client uses a token to request data from the resource server.

- **Token types**

  o **Access token**: Short-lived, enables access to user data.

  o **Refresh token**: Long-lived, renews access tokens without user re-login.

- **Strengths**
  - o **Granular access**: Allows specific user permissions without sharing full credentials.
  - o **Short-lived tokens**: Reduces risk if tokens are intercepted.

- **Challenges**
  - o **Complex implementation**: Can be tricky for beginners.
  - o **Security risks**: Vulnerable to attacks if not carefully implemented.

- **ML relevance**: Ideal for ML microservices needing user data access (for example, a financial advisory tool requiring bank transaction data but not fund transfer permissions).

OAuth 2.0, crucial for web application security, enables granular data access authorization, although it requires careful, secure implementation.

Privacy concerns in ML and data anonymization

In ML, raw data often comprises personal and sensitive details. This section discusses the potential hazards of exposing such information and explores methodologies like data masking, pseudonymization, and differential privacy to protect individual identities while maintaining the data's utility. Safeguarding privacy is not just an ethical obligation; it is paramount for building trustworthy AI systems.

Risks of exposing personal information

ML models are only as good as the data they are trained on, and this often means utilizing vast datasets that may contain sensitive personal information. From names and addresses to health records or financial details, raw data presents various vulnerabilities. Highlighting key risks, the following points outline the potential dangers of exposing personal information through ML models:

- **Identity theft and fraud**: Exposure of personal information can lead to malicious actors stealing identities, leading to financial fraud, unauthorized transactions, and other malicious activities.

- **Model inference attacks**: If ML microservices are compromised, attackers might reverse-engineer the model to infer sensitive data about individuals, even if the data was not explicitly part of the training set.

- **Legal repercussions**: Many regulations, such as GDPR and **California Consumer Privacy Act** (**CCPA**), have strict guidelines on data privacy. Breaching these regulations by exposing personal information can result in significant penalties, fines, and legal actions against the organization.

- **Loss of consumer trust**: Once personal information is compromised, regaining user trust becomes immensely challenging. This can lead to a decline in user base and can adversely impact the business.

- **Bias amplification**: Unauthorized access and tampering can introduce biases into the ML models, leading to unfair or discriminative predictions, which can have grave societal implications.

- **Operational costs**: Post a data breach, organizations often have to spend heavily on damage control, from PR campaigns to compensate affected users, to restructuring their entire security framework.

- **Stakeholder relations**: Investors, partners, and other stakeholders might reconsider their association with a company that fails to protect personal data, affecting long-term business prospects.

For ML microservices, where data flow is continuous and often automated, the risk is compounded, emphasizing the need for robust security measures to guard against such exposures.

Data masking, pseudonymization, and differential privacy

Data masking, pseudonymization, and differential privacy are essential strategies in ML for protecting privacy while maintaining data utility.

Data masking and pseudonymization

Data masking alters original data (via scrambling, encrypting, obfuscating) to protect privacy, changing content but not structure.

Pseudonymization replaces personal identifiers with pseudonyms, preventing direct attribution to individuals without additional data.

Let us cover the following benefits, implementation strategies, and associated challenges:

- **Benefits**
  - o **Data usability**: Ensures data remains useful for ML despite alterations.
  - o **Regulatory compliance**: Meets privacy laws like GDPR.
  - o **Reduced breach impact**: Less actionable data in case of unauthorized access.

- **Implementation**
  - o **Dynamic masking**: Real-time masking during data requests, valuable in ML for immediate data access.

o **Static masking**: Pre-process masking in databases, securing data before ML use.

o **Tokenization**: Substitutes sensitive elements with non-sensitive equivalents.

- **Challenges**

    o **Data integrity**: Must retain effectiveness for ML tasks.

    o **Re-identification risks**: Preventing traceability back to original data.

Differential privacy

A mathematical approach that adds noise to data or queries, preserving privacy regardless of individual data inclusion.

The core principle of differential privacy and randomness in query results prevents deducing the presence of individual data.

Let us delve into their following benefits, implementation strategies, and associated challenges:

- **Benefits**

    o **Privacy protection**: Shields individual data points, even in summaries or aggregates.

    o **Regulatory adherence**: Complies with strict data protection laws.

    o **Trust building**: Increases user confidence in ML services.

- **Implementation**

    o **Noise addition**: Incorporates mechanisms like Laplace or Gaussian noise to obscure individual data points.

    o **Privacy budget**: Limits query numbers to safeguard long-term data privacy.

    o **Federated learning**: Applies differential privacy in decentralized ML training.

- **Challenges**

    o **Utility versus privacy**: Balancing noise level with data accuracy.

    o **Privacy parameter setting**: Requires expertise to ensure effective ML outcomes.

In ML microservices, these techniques offer robust solutions to harmonize data utility and privacy, which is crucial for fostering trust and adherence to privacy regulations.

Ensuring secure model deployment

As ML models drive critical decision-making processes across various industries, it is paramount to ensure their secure deployment. Ensuring this not only protects the intellectual property embedded within these models but also guarantees the accuracy and reliability of their predictions. Here is a closer look at some best practices:

Secure containers

Secure containers are pivotal in deploying ML microservices, providing consistent, isolated, and secure environments.

Some key aspects of containers in ML microservices are as follows:

- **Isolation**: Containers, like those provided by Docker, isolate ML services, limiting the impact of potential attacks on the contained environment.

- **Consistency**: Containers enable uniform execution across different environments, eliminating discrepancies that might lead to vulnerabilities.

- **Version control**: Containers support version tracking and easy rollback, enhancing security through better control over changes.

- **Minimal footprint**: Containers include only essential components, reducing potential attack surfaces.

- **Securing containers**: Enhancing container security involves several crucial practices as follows:

  o **Image verification**: Use trusted repositories and verify container image integrity.

  o **Read-only configuration**: Prevent modifications to container runtime environments after setup.

  o **Resource restrictions**: Set limits on container resources to guard against resource exhaustion attacks.

  o **Regular vulnerability scans**: Employ tools like *Clair* or *Trivy* for scanning container images.

  o **Network segmentation**: Restrict inter-container communication to prevent lateral movements in case of a breach.

- **Container orchestration**: Tools like Kubernetes are essential for managing, scaling, and securing multiple containers, further solidifying the security framework around ML microservices.

In summary, secure containers are essential for the robust and safe operation of ML microservices, ensuring integrity, consistency, and security in ML deployments.

Model encryption

Model encryption is crucial in protecting ML models from unauthorized access, theft, and tampering, enhancing security in various aspects:

- **Protection during transit**: Encrypting models prevents eavesdropping during their transfer, making intercepted data unusable to attackers.

- **Intellectual property safeguard**: As ML models represent valuable insights and business logic, encryption helps protect these proprietary assets.

- **Tamper resistance**: Encryption makes unauthorized alterations to a model difficult, maintaining its integrity and output reliability.

- **At-rest security**: Ensures models stored in databases or cloud solutions are safe from unauthorized access or theft.

- **Support for secure enclaves**: Enables the use of secure computation environments for ultra-secure inferencing without decrypting the data or model.

In summary, model encryption is a key strategy in securing ML microservices and guarding the confidentiality, integrity, and authenticity of ML models.

Access control

Access control in ML microservices involves managing and restricting access to ML models and data, playing a key role in secure deployments:

- **Authentication**: Verifying the identity of users or services using credentials like passwords or API keys.

- **Authorization**: Determining permitted actions for authenticated entities, often through **role-based access control (RBAC)**.

- **Auditing and monitoring**: Tracking access and actions to identify unauthorized or harmful activities.

- **Granular permissions**: Limiting access rights to the minimum necessary for specific tasks.

- **Temporal constraints**: Time-limiting access to enhance security.

- **Geographic and network restrictions**: Restricting access based on location or network for additional security layers.

- **Multi-factor authentication (MFA)**: Enhancing security by requiring multiple authentication methods for sensitive resources.

Effective access control ensures that ML resources are accessed only by authorized entities, safeguarding the system's integrity, confidentiality, and availability.

Use case: Music recommendation engine

Let us break down the use case for the music recommendation engine by examining a few services.

User service: OAuth 2.0 for secure user access

OAuth 2.0 is an authorization framework that provides applications the ability to access user accounts on an HTTP service, such as Facebook, GitHub, and so on. It works by delegating user authentication to the service that hosts the user account and authorizing third-party applications to access the user account. Implementing OAuth 2.0 within user services involves key steps to secure user access and data. The process unfolds through two main phases as follows:

1. **Setting up OAuth 2.0**: First, you will need to register your application with a service that offers OAuth 2.0 authentication (for example, Google, Facebook, or a custom provider). They will provide you with a *Client ID* and *Client Secret*.

2. **User login flow**: Here is a simplified flow of the OAuth 2.0 process:

    a. **Redirect to authorization server**: When a user wishes to log in, redirect them to the authorization server with the *Client ID*. Please find the implementation as follows:

    ```
    from flask import Flask, redirect, request, session
    import requests


    app = Flask(__name__)
    CLIENT_ID = 'YOUR_CLIENT_ID'
    REDIRECT_URI = 'http://localhost:5000/callback'
    AUTH_URL = 'https://authorization-server.com/oauth/authorize'


    @app.route('/login')
    def login():
        return redirect(f'{AUTH_URL}?client_id={CLIENT_ID}&redirect_
        uri={REDIRECT_URI}')
    ```

    b. **User grants/denies permission**: The user will then either grant or deny your application's request to access their data.

    c. **Obtain access token**: If the user grants permission, the authorization server will redirect to the provided **REDIRECT_URI** with a code. You will exchange this code for an access token.

    ```
    from flask import Flask, redirect, request, session, url_for
    import requests


    app = Flask(__name__)
    app.secret_key = 'YOUR_SECRET_KEY'  # Needed for session management
    ```

```
CLIENT_ID = 'YOUR_CLIENT_ID'
CLIENT_SECRET = 'YOUR_CLIENT_SECRET'
REDIRECT_URI = 'http://localhost:5000/callback'
AUTH_URL = 'https://authorization-server.com/oauth/authorize'
TOKEN_URL = 'https://authorization-server.com/oauth/token'

@app.route('/login')
def login():
    return redirect(f'{AUTH_URL}?client_id={CLIENT_ID}&redirect_
    uri={REDIRECT_URI}&response_type=code')

@app.route('/callback')
def callback():
    code = request.args.get('code')
    payload = {
        'grant_type': 'authorization_code',
        'client_id': CLIENT_ID,
        'client_secret': CLIENT_SECRET,
        'code': code,
        'redirect_uri': REDIRECT_URI
    }
    response = requests.post(TOKEN_URL, data=payload)
    token_info = response.json()
    session['token'] = token_info['access_token']
    return 'Logged in successfully!'
```

 # Additional routes and logic for using the access token to access user data can be added here.

This code snippet includes the callback route that handles the exchange of the authorization code for an access token. It incorporates the **CLIENT_SECRET** and makes a POST request to the token endpoint of the authorization server.

d. **Access user profile with token**: Now that you have the access token, you can use it to access the user's data from the resource server.

```
PROFILE_URL = 'https://authorization-server.com/user/profile'

@app.route('/profile')
def profile():
    headers = {
        'Authorization': f'Bearer {session["token"]}'
    }
    response = requests.get(PROFILE_URL, headers=headers)
    return response.json()
```

This is a simple example using flask in Python, but the logic remains largely consistent across different frameworks and languages.

Security tips:

- Always use HTTPS to ensure the confidentiality of the authorization code and tokens.
- Store **CLIENT_SECRET** securely and never expose it.
- Implement token expiration and handle token renewal with refresh tokens.
- Always validate the token before allowing access to user-specific resources.

Handling different grant types with OAuth 2.0

OAuth 2.0 specifies several grant types depending on the use case, including:

- **Authorization code**: As previously discussed.
- **Implicit**: For applications where the token is issued directly to the browser.
- **Password**: Used when users provide their credentials directly to the client.
- **Client credentials**: For server-to-server communication.
- **Refresh token**: Used to get a new access token without requiring user intervention.

For brevity, let us focus on the refresh token and password grant types.

Password grant type

This grant type is suitable for user agents that are absolutely trusted with the user's credentials, like a user's device.

```
PASSWORD_TOKEN_URL = 'https://authorization-server.com/oauth/token'

@app.route('/login_with_password', methods=['POST'])
def login_with_password():
```

```
    username = request.form.get('username')

    password = request.form.get('password')

    token_data = {

        'grant_type': 'password',

        'username': username,

        'password': password,

        'client_id': CLIENT_ID,

        'client_secret': CLIENT_SECRET

    }

    response = requests.post(PASSWORD_TOKEN_URL, data=token_data)

    token_info = response.json()

    session['token'] = token_info['access_token']

    session['refresh_token'] = token_info['refresh_token']

    return 'Logged in!'
```

Refreshing an access token

After an access token expires, instead of requiring the user to log in again, you can use a refresh token to obtain a new access token.

```
REFRESH_TOKEN_URL = 'https://authorization-server.com/oauth/token'


@app.route('/refresh_token')

def refresh_token():

    token_data = {

        'grant_type': 'refresh_token',

        'refresh_token': session['refresh_token'],

        'client_id': CLIENT_ID,

        'client_secret': CLIENT_SECRET

    }

    response = requests.post(REFRESH_TOKEN_URL, data=token_data)

    token_info = response.json()
```

```
session['token'] = token_info['access_token']

session['refresh_token'] = token_info['refresh_token']

return 'Token refreshed!'
```

Using libraries to simplify OAuth 2.0

While we have been showing raw implementations to highlight the process, libraries like OAuthLib (for Python) or Passport (for Node.js) abstract many of these steps.

For example, with Flask-OAuthlib, you can easily set up OAuth providers and protect routes. Here is a quick setup:

```python
from flask_oauthlib.client import OAuth


app = Flask(__name__)

oauth = OAuth(app)

authorization_server = oauth.remote_app(

    'AuthorizationServer',

    consumer_key=CLIENT_ID,

    consumer_secret=CLIENT_SECRET,

    request_token_params={'scope': 'user profile'},

    base_url='https://authorization-server.com/',

    request_token_url=None,

    access_token_method='POST',

    access_token_url=PASSWORD_TOKEN_URL,

    authorize_url=AUTH_URL,

)


@app.route('/login')

def login():

    return authorization_server.authorize(callback=REDIRECT_URI)
```

Using libraries can greatly speed up your development process and ensure adherence to best practices.

Always remember that while OAuth 2.0 offers various grant types, you should choose the one that best fits your specific use case. The Password grant type, for instance, should be used with caution and only in scenarios where the client can be fully trusted with user credentials.

Recommendation service: Ensuring data privacy

Let us deep-dive into ensuring data privacy in our recommendation service by leveraging more robust solutions and libraries. Here is a more comprehensive exploration.

This section includes inputs and outputs alongside code samples to provide a clear understanding of expected outcomes and the results of execution:

1. **Differential privacy using PySyft**: PySyft is a flexible library for encrypted, privacy-preserving ML. It extends PyTorch and TensorFlow to enable multi-party computations.

```
# You need to install pysyft: pip install syft[udacity]

import syft as sy
import torch

# Create a hook to PyTorch
hook = sy.TorchHook(torch)

def private_average(data, epsilon):
    """Compute a differentially private average using Laplace
    mechanism."""
    tensor_data = torch.tensor(data)
    average = tensor_data.float().mean()

    beta = 1.0 / epsilon
    noise = torch.tensor(np.random.laplace(0, beta, 1))

    return average + noise

# INPUT
ratings = [5, 4.5, 3.5, 5, 4]
epsilon = 0.1
```

```
# PROCESS
private_avg = private_average(ratings, epsilon)
```

```
# OUTPUT
print(private_avg)
```

The expected output is as follows:

```
tensor([4.5000])   # This will vary due to the added noise.
```

Differential privacy ensures that any individual's data contribution is indistinguishable from the output of a query. It achieves this by adding noise to the output. To ensure the privacy of individual contributions in our recommendation service, we employ differential privacy techniques. These methods add a layer of protection by introducing noise to the data, making it challenging to trace back to any individual. The following examples illustrate how we apply these principles to safeguard user data effectively:

- **User data**: Suppose we have a simple database with user ages. Our goal is to compute the average age without revealing individual ages. Refer to the following table:

UserId	Age
1	25
2	29
3	31
4	23

Table 8.1: User Ages

- **Differential privacy in action**: When computing the average age with differential privacy, noise (generated from a specific noise distribution, like Laplace of Gaussian) is added to the result.

  Without differential privacy:

  Average age = (25 + 29 + 31 + 23) / 4 = 27

  With differential privacy (assuming noise = +2 for illustration purposes):

  Private average age = 27 + 2 = 29

  The noise addition ensures that an adversary cannot determine the presence or absence of an individual in the dataset based on the result.

- **User identification**: Differential privacy protects the content of the query, not the identity of the user per se. To safeguard user identities, refer to the following table:

UserId	UserName	Password	AuthToken
1	Alice	hash1	token1
2	Bob	hash2	token2
3	Charlie	hash3	token3
4	David	hash4	token4

Table 8.2: Users

When a user logs in, they are authenticated and provided an AuthToken. This token and not their personal details, is used for subsequent interactions.

In systems employing differential privacy, the identity of the user making a query is separate from the privacy guarantee of the query's content. The system might know that *User with token1 asked for the average age,* but the differential privacy mechanism ensures that the answer does not compromise any individual's age.

2. **Data masking using faker library**: Data masking is about hiding certain data elements. For a recommendation service, we might mask certain parts of the data but still leave it useful. The Faker library allows generating fake data. It can be especially useful for masking data without losing its format.

```python
# Install faker: pip install faker
from faker import Faker

fake = Faker()

def mask_user_data(user_data):
    user_data['name'] = fake.name()
    user_data['address'] = fake.address()
    user_data['email'] = fake.email()
    return user_data

# INPUT
user = {
    "name": "Alice",
    "address": "1234 Real St, Imaginary City, IL 12345",
    "email": "alice@email.com"
}
```

```
# PROCESS
masked_user = mask_user_data(user)

# OUTPUT
print(masked_user)
```

The expected output (will vary since **faker** generates random data each time):

```
{
    'name': 'John Doe',
    'address': '5678 Fake St, Random Town, CA 67890',
    'email': 'john.doe@example.com'
}
```

Data masking, also known as **data obfuscation** or **data anonymization**, is the process of disguising original data to protect the data subject's privacy while maintaining the data's authenticity and usability.

Faker is a popular Python library that allows for the generation of a wide variety of fake data, from names and addresses to dates and other specialized types of data.

Let us use the Faker library for data masking, and we will employ a table design example to illustrate the process:

UserId	UserName	Address	Email
1	Alice	123 Apple St	alice@email.com
2	Bob	456 Berry Ln	bob@email.com
3	Charlie	789 Cherry Blvd	charlie@email.com
4	David	101 Pine Ave	david@email.com

Table 8.3: User profiles

Take a look at the following table:

UserId	UserName	Address	Email
1	John Doe	4567 Elm St	john.doe@email.com
2	Jane Smith	8910 Oak Ln	jane.smith@email.com
3	Steve Ray	1112 Maple Blvd	steve.ray@email.com
4	Ann Lee	1314 Spruce Ave	ann.lee@email.com

Table 8.4: Masked user profiles

To keep track of the actual users behind the masked data, a separate secure lookup table is maintained. This table, which links the UserID to the actual user, is kept confidential and access-restricted.

With this setup, the masked user profiles can be shared with external entities without exposing real user information. When necessary, the lookup table (which is maintained securely) can be used to map the masked profile back to the actual user.

Regulatory and legal repercussions

Regulatory frameworks like GDPR and CCPA enforce strict data privacy rules, critical for services like music recommendation systems. Compliance includes:

- **Data minimization**: Collect only necessary data for service functionality.
- **User rights**: Allow users to access and request deletion of their data.
- **Pseudonymization**: Use pseudonyms rather than personal identifiers, keeping actual identity data encrypted and separate.
- **Transparency**: Clearly communicate the purpose of data collection and usage.
- **Differential privacy**: Apply noise to data to protect individual identities, especially in analytics or shared research data.
- **Data portability**: Enable users to export their data in common formats like CSV or JSON.

Adhering to these principles not only enhances user trust but also ensures service accessibility globally. Keep systems and policies up-to-date with evolving regulations.

Conclusion

Securing ML microservices is crucial, involving stringent protocols from design to deployment. This includes protecting sensitive ML data and models against breaches. Some key practices include using SSL/TLS and OAuth 2.0 for safe data transmission and adopting data masking and differential privacy for compliance with regulations like GDPR and CCPA. For ML model deployment, using secure containers, model encryption, and tight access controls are essential. An example with music recommendation engine highlighted practical implementations of these security measures. Overall, security in ML microservices is a dynamic field, requiring continuous adaptation to new technologies and emerging threats.

In the next chapter, we will discuss the critical roles of monitoring and logging in maintaining the efficiency and security of AI-driven applications. We will explore strategies for implementing these practices within ML microservices, emphasizing their importance in early anomaly detection, system enhancement, and compliance with privacy regulations.

Points to remember

- **ML data and model security**
  - o Critical to secure large volumes of sensitive ML data.
  - o Unsecured ML models risk flawed outcomes.

- **Secure communication**
  - o Encrypt data transfers using SSL/TLS.
  - o Utilize API keys and OAuth 2.0 for secure user/system authentication.

- **ML data privacy**
  - o Protect against exposing sensitive personal data.
  - o Employ data masking and pseudonymization.
  - o Implement differential privacy to obscure individual data.

- **ML model deployment**
  - o Use containers (for example, Docker) for isolated and controlled model deployment.
  - o Encrypt models both during storage and transfer.
  - o Apply strict access control to limit model interactions.

- **Case: Music recommendation engine**
  - o Secure logins and profile access with OAuth 2.0.
  - o Enhance privacy in recommendations using data masking and differential privacy.
  - o Strengthen security through SSL/TLS and containerization for data handling and model deployment.

Assignment

The assignment is for the readers to develop a secure ML microservice for a movie recommendation engine

Objective: Create an ML microservice that recommends movies to users, ensuring that user data and model integrity are protected at every step.

- **Setup**
  - o Choose a simple movie dataset with user ratings. For example, the MovieLens dataset.

o Develop a basic movie recommendation model using a method of your choice (for example, collaborative filtering).

- **User authentication**

    o Implement OAuth 2.0 for user login and profile access. Make sure that the login and token retrieval processes are secure.

- **Recommendation service**

    o Ensure the privacy of user preferences.

    o Mask usernames and other personal details using the Faker library.

    o Implement differential privacy using PySyft or another tool to protect individual user's ratings when generating recommendations.

- **Secure communication**

    o Set up SSL/TLS for encrypted communication between the client and the server.

- **Deployment**

    o Use a secure container (for example, Docker) to deploy your recommendation service.

    o Implement basic access controls to ensure only authenticated users can request movie recommendations.

Multiple choice questions

1. **What is the primary reason for securing ML microservices?**

    a. Increase speed of data processing

    b. Ensure data confidentiality and integrity

    c. Reduce the cost of data storage

    d. Simplify ML algorithms

2. **Which protocol is considered the advanced successor to SSL for encrypting internet communication?**

    a. HTTP

    b. FTP

    c. TLS

    d. SSH

3. **What is a primary method to authenticate applications accessing an API?**

   a. OAuth 2.0

   b. API key authentication

   c. Password authentication

   d. Biometric authentication

4. **What does OAuth 2.0 primarily facilitate?**

   a. Encryption

   b. Authorization

   c. Data masking

   d. Compression

5. **Which of the following is a benefit of data masking?**

   a. Increases data storage requirements

   b. Enhances computational complexity

   c. Ensures data remains useful despite alterations

   d. Simplifies data access protocols

6. **What is the key challenge in implementing OAuth 2.0?**

   a. Simplifying user interface

   b. Reducing data transfer speeds

   c. Complex implementation

   d. Enhancing data visualization

7. **Which is not a component of OAuth 2.0?**

   a. Resource owner

   b. Client

   c. Resource server

   d. Data masker

8. **What is the primary purpose of SSL/TLS in ML microservices?**

   a. Data anonymization

   b. Protecting data during transit

   c. Increasing data processing speed

   d. Reducing data storage needs

9. **Which of the following best describes the concept of pseudonymization in data privacy?**

    a. Encrypting all user data

    b. Deleting sensitive information

    c. Replacing personal identifiers with pseudonyms

    d. Storing data in a decentralized manner

10. **Which approach is used to ensure the privacy of individual contributions in data sets or queries?**

    a. Tokenization

    b. SSL encryption

    c. Differential privacy

    d. Data minimization

Answer key

1	b
2	c
3	b
4	b
5	c
6	c
7	d
8	b
9	c
10	c

Join our book's Discord space

Join the book's Discord Workspace for Latest updates, Offers, Tech happenings around the world, New Release and Sessions with the Authors:

https://discord.bpbonline.com

CHAPTER 9

Monitoring and Logging in Machine Learning Microservices

Introduction

In **Machine Learning** (**ML**) microservices, where models transition from research prototypes to production-level applications, monitoring, and logging stand as two crucial pillars ensuring the reliability, efficiency, and robustness of deployed systems as ML-driven applications become increasingly entrenched in our daily lives, from online shopping assistants to music recommendation engines, the stakes for their uninterrupted, high-quality service rise substantially. Failures, inaccuracies, or minor inconsistencies can undermine user trust and satisfaction.

Monitoring offers a live pulse of the system, providing insights into its health, responsiveness, and overall performance. It alerts developers and operations teams about potential bottlenecks, service failures, or sub-optimal model predictions, allowing for timely interventions. On the other hand, logging offers a retrospective but detailed view of the system's operations. From user activities to system decisions and errors, logs are invaluable for debugging, auditing, and enhancing the system's efficacy.

As we navigate this chapter, we will delve deep into the intricacies of these two essential aspects within the context of ML microservices. Through the lens of our music recommendation engine, we will explore how to implement, optimize, and leverage monitoring and logging to drive unparalleled user experiences and ensure the consistent performance of AI-driven applications.

Structure

In this chapter, we will cover the following topics:

- Importance of securing ML microservices
- Implementing logging and metrics for ML services
- Troubleshooting and debugging ML microservices
- Use case: Recommendation engine diagnostics

Objectives

This chapter aims to underscore the pivotal role of monitoring and logging in fortifying the performance, reliability, and security of AI-driven applications, specifically within the domain of ML microservices. It is crafted to arm readers with the essential knowledge and practical tools required to implement robust monitoring and logging frameworks. By enhancing troubleshooting skills and applying these concepts to a real-world case study, the chapter seeks to foster intelligent decision-making and optimize user experiences, ultimately contributing to the resilience and operational efficiency of ML applications.

Importance of securing ML microservices

Monitoring in ML applications is pivotal to ensure that models perform optimally and adapt effectively to evolving data patterns. As these systems inherently possess a dynamic nature, regular oversight is crucial, unlike traditional software. Through consistent monitoring, anomalies are detected early, system reliability is maintained, and a foundation for proactive error resolution and optimization is established. This vigilance is the linchpin for maintaining the efficacy and reliability of AI-driven applications.

The uniqueness of monitoring in ML contexts

Traditional software applications are deterministic: given a specific input, they consistently produce the same output. Monitoring such applications typically involves tracking system health, resource utilization, and error rates. However, machine learning applications introduce an added layer of complexity due to their probabilistic and evolving nature. Here are the distinguishing aspects of monitoring in the ML context:

- **Model drift**: Over time, the data an ML model was trained on might differ from the real-world data it encounters. This drift can lead to a decline in model performance. Monitoring helps identify and address such drifts proactively.
- **Dynamic behavior**: ML models, especially those that learn continually, evolve. Their behavior might change as they encounter new data. Monitoring ensures that these changes do not introduce undesirable behaviors or outcomes.

- **Data quality**: Unlike traditional applications, where the focus might be on the volume and speed of incoming data, ML systems need to monitor the quality of incoming data. Anomalies or shifts in data quality can significantly affect model performance.

- **Resource consumption**: Training and inferencing in ML can be resource-intensive. Effective monitoring ensures system resources (like memory, CPU, and GPU usage) remain within acceptable thresholds.

- **Feedback loops**: Many ML systems benefit from feedback loops where predictions are validated and the model is updated. Monitoring these loops ensures they contribute positively to the model's learning.

- **Performance degradation**: Implement a mechanism to monitor and evaluate crucial performance metrics, such as prediction accuracy and response time, to swiftly identify and rectify any signs of model performance degradation. This ensures the model remains effective and reliable over time.

- **Model monitoring enhancements**: Augment monitoring systems to include real-time detection of anomalies and automatic adjustment mechanisms. By integrating predictive analytics and feedback loops, this approach ensures continuous adaptation and optimization of the model to dynamic data environments and operational demands.

Proactive error resolution and system optimization

Proactive error resolution is about anticipating issues before they become critical problems. This can mean the difference between a system running smoothly and one producing erroneous predictions in ML. Here is how monitoring plays a pivotal role:

- **Early anomaly detection**: Real-time monitoring can detect anomalies or spikes in metrics like prediction error rates, helping teams to intervene early before these escalate into more significant issues.

- **Capacity planning**: By observing trends in system usage, organizations can anticipate when they will need to scale resources up or down, optimizing costs and ensuring smooth operations.

- **Model retraining**: Monitoring can help identify when a model's performance is degrading. By observing this, teams can retrain models with fresh data, ensuring continued accuracy and relevance.

- **System health**: Beyond the model, the infrastructure that supports ML (like databases, APIs, or compute resources) also needs consistent monitoring. Ensuring these components are healthy guarantees the overall robustness of the ML application.

- **Optimization opportunities**: Continuous monitoring can uncover opportunities for optimization. This could be improving data preprocessing steps, tweaking model parameters, or streamlining post-processing.

In essence, proactive monitoring in ML systems is about preventing errors and continuously enhancing the system's efficiency, performance, and reliability. It is a proactive commitment to excellence and continuous improvement.

Tool spotlight: Prometheus and Grafana

In this section, we spotlight Prometheus and Grafana, two cornerstone tools in monitoring and visualization that have revolutionized the way we manage and interpret data in modern applications. Both tools offer unique strengths—Prometheus for its precise data collection and powerful querying capabilities, and Grafana for its extensive visualization and dashboarding features. Together, they provide a comprehensive solution for monitoring the performance and health of systems, including ML microservices, enabling developers and data scientists to gain actionable insights and drive operational excellence.

Prometheus: The open-source monitoring solution

Prometheus, a project hosted by the Cloud Native Computing Foundation, is a robust open-source monitoring solution widely adopted in modern infrastructures. Its main features are its multi-dimensional data model, flexible query language (PromQL), and lack of reliance on distributed storage.

The key features include:

- **Data collection**: Prometheus uses a pull model to regularly scrape and store time series data from instrumented targets.
- **PromQL**: A flexible and powerful query language that lets users select and aggregate time series data in real time.
- **Alerting**: Prometheus's Alertmanager handles alerts, allowing for deduplication, grouping, and routing. It integrates with most notification methods.
- **Service discovery**: It automatically discovers targets in many types of cloud environments.

The benefits in ML contexts are:

- Monitoring the health and performance of Machine Learning models.
- Tracking metrics related to model training, such as loss and accuracy over time.
- Observing system-level metrics to ensure resources are optimally used during heavy ML tasks.

Grafana: Visualizing your data

Grafana is an open-source platform for monitoring and observability, and it is often used in tandem with Prometheus to visualize the collected metrics. With Grafana, you can create, explore, and share dashboards representing data from many sources, not just Prometheus.

The key features include:

- **Rich visualizations**: Offers a range of visualization options from simple line charts to heatmaps, histograms, and geospatial support.
- **Flexible dashboards**: Users can create and customize dashboards based on their needs. These dashboards can be shared and even templated.
- **Alerting**: Grafana provides a robust alerting and rules engine, allowing users to define alert conditions and get notified through various channels.
- **Datasource integration**: Grafana supports a wide variety of data sources, from traditional databases like MySQL to time-series databases like InfluxDB and, of course, Prometheus.

The benefits in ML contexts are:

- Over time, visualize metrics related to ML model performance, like precision, recall, F1 score, and so on.
- Creating dashboards to track and visualize training processes, showcasing loss, accuracy, and other vital metrics over epochs.
- Monitoring the health and status of ML microservices, ensuring uptime, and observing response times.

Implementing logging and metrics for ML services

Distributed and modular microservices introduce complexity when tracking their activities and performance. Logging becomes essential in this context, providing a trail of events and actions occurring within each service. A centralized logging system can aggregate logs from all services, offering a holistic view of the entire application.

Key metrics to track in ML services

ML services, while sharing many characteristics with traditional software applications, possess unique intricacies due to the nature of ML. Monitoring these services requires a nuanced approach that considers both system and ML-specific metrics. Let us delve into some of the essential metrics to track:

- **Model performance metrics**

  o **Accuracy**: Represents the percentage of predictions the model got right. Especially important for classification problems.

  o **Precision and recall**: Precision measures the number of correct positive predictions made by the model, while recall measures the number of actual positives the model correctly captured.

  o **F1 Score**: The harmonic mean of precision and recall, giving a balanced measure of the model's performance.

  o **AUC-ROC curve**: Useful for binary classification problems, it provides an aggregate performance measure across all possible classification thresholds.

  o **Loss function**: Indicates how well the model predictions align with the true values. Common loss functions include mean squared error for regression problems and cross-entropy loss for classification.

- **System metrics**

  o **CPU usage**: Monitors the computational demands of your ML service. Spikes might indicate intense processes like model training or prediction.

  o **Memory consumption**: Track memory usage to ensure data loading, processing, or model inference does not overwhelm system resources.

  o **Disk I/O**: The rate data is read from or written to disks. High disk I/O can be a bottleneck, especially when dealing with large datasets.

  o **Network traffic**: Observing incoming and outgoing traffic can give insights into service interactions and potential bottlenecks.

- **Latency metrics**

  o **Response time**: Measures the time services take to respond to a request. High latency can degrade user experience, especially in real-time applications.

  o **Model inference time**: Specifically, for ML services, this tracks the time taken for a model to predict receiving input. Optimization here can be crucial for real-time ML applications.

- **Operational metrics**

  o **Error rate**: The rate at which errors (system or model-related) occur.

  o **Service uptime**: Measures the availability of the ML service. High uptime is crucial for ensuring a consistent user experience.

  o **Resource utilization**: A broader metric capturing how well resources (like compute and storage) are utilized, ensuring efficient operation.

- **Service-specific metrics**: For a system like our music recommendation engine, there might be several custom metrics:

  o **Recommendation frequency**: How often recommendations are provided to users.

  o **User feedback rate**: The rate at which users provide feedback on recommendations, offering insights into user engagement and satisfaction.

  o **Song play count**: Tracking the number of plays can indicate the popularity of songs and the efficacy of recommendations.

In the context of ML microservices, these metrics help maintain a pulse on the system. While traditional software might primarily focus on system metrics, the unique nature of ML demands a combined approach. Whether it is ensuring model accuracy, optimizing resources, or providing timely recommendations, tracking these metrics is integral to ML services' smooth operation and success.

Effective logging strategies and best practices

Logging, at its core, is the act of recording events or transactions that occur within a system. In the context of ML microservices, where complex operations such as data processing, model training, and inference occur, logging becomes even more vital. An effective logging strategy not only aids in debugging but also in understanding the behavior and performance of the system. Here are some of the key strategies and best practices for logging in ML services:

- **Log levels: Differentiate logs by their severity**

  o **DEBUG**: Fine-grained information primarily used for debugging. This can include details like intermediate outputs during data processing or specifics about model training iterations.

  o **INFO**: General operational messages indicating the normal functioning of the system, for example, *Model X started training*, or *Recommendation generated for User Y.*

  o **WARN**: Situations that do not cause errors but warrant caution. For instance, a sudden drop in model accuracy or nearing resource capacity.

  o **ERROR**: Explicit error situations where operations fail, for example, *Model failed to train due to insufficient memory.*

  o **FATAL**: Critical errors, such as data corruption or system-wide outages, may need immediate intervention.

- **Structured logging**: Instead of plain-text logs, generate logs in a structured format like JSON. This makes it easier to parse logs and extract necessary information, especially when logs become voluminous.

- **Context-rich logs**: Especially in the case of ML, logs should be rich in context. Instead of *Model training failed*, a log like *Model X training failed due to mismatched tensor dimensions at Layer Y* is more informative.

- **Include unique identifiers**: Especially in microservices architectures, where multiple services may communicate, attaching unique identifiers (like request IDs) to logs can help trace transactions or processes across services.

- **Rotation and retention**: Ensure logs are periodically rotated to prevent them from consuming all available storage. Determine retention policies based on the criticality and relevance of logs. For instance, DEBUG logs might be purged sooner than ERROR logs.

- **Centralized logging**: In distributed architectures like microservices, it is crucial to have a centralized logging system. Tools like the ELK Stack can aggregate logs from multiple services, offering a unified view and easing debugging.

- **Security**: Logs, especially in ML services, might contain sensitive information, user data or model details. Ensure logs are stored securely encrypted if necessary, and their access is strictly controlled.

- **Alerting mechanisms**: Integrate logs with monitoring tools to set up alerting mechanisms. For instance, if the error rate in an ML service spikes, an immediate alert can be triggered, allowing for rapid response.

- **Continuous review**: Regularly review and refine logging practices. As systems evolve, so do their logging needs. Ensure the logs are still relevant, comprehensive, and effective in aiding debugging and performance monitoring.

Effective logging is as much an art as it is a science. While tools and technologies aid in the process, understanding the nuances of your ML microservice, its potential pitfalls, and the most critical operations will guide the creation of informative, actionable logs.

Elasticsearch, Logstash, Kibana for centralized logging

Elasticsearch, Logstash, and Kibana (**ELK stack**) is a powerful combination of three open-source tools that provide an end-to-end logging solution. They offer a mechanism to collect, store, search, and visualize logs in real-time, making it indispensable for ML microservices looking for a robust logging solution:

- **Elasticsearch**
  - **Description**: Elasticsearch is a search and analytics engine for horizontal scalability, reliability, and real-time capabilities. It is built on top of Lucene and allows for complex search operations.
  - **Usage in ML microservices**: Elasticsearch acts as the storage layer in the ELK stack, storing logs sent to it. Given its powerful search capabilities, querying

logs, even in vast volumes, becomes efficient, helping developers quickly spot anomalies or gather insights.

- **Logstash**
  - o **Description**: Logstash is a server-side data processing pipeline that ingests, transforms, and sends data to a specified location, such as Elasticsearch. It supports numerous input and output plugins, making it highly versatile.
  - o **Usage in ML microservices**: Logstash is the workhorse that ingests logs from various sources. In the context of ML microservices, Logstash can take logs from application logs, server logs, or even metrics from model training processes, normalize and process them, and send them to Elasticsearch. It can handle structured or unstructured data perfectly for diverse logging needs.

- **Kibana**
  - o **Description**: Kibana is the visualization layer of the ELK stack. It provides a web interface to visualize and navigate the data stored in Elasticsearch. From dashboards to graphs and charts, Kibana provides powerful visualization tools.
  - o **Usage in ML microservices**: With Kibana, developers and operations teams can create dashboards that visualize logs and metrics from their ML microservices. This might include model performance metrics, error rates, or resource utilization, all displayed in an intuitive, easy-to-read manner.

- **Integrating ELK in ML microservices**
  - o **Data collection**: Utilize Logstash or other beats like Filebeat to collect logs from various parts of the ML microservice.
  - o **Processing**: Using Logstash's powerful transformation capabilities, process the logs. This can include operations like filtering, mutation, or enrichment.
  - o **Storage**: Send the processed logs to Elasticsearch. Given Elasticsearch's distributed nature, it can handle vast amounts of data, scaling as the logging needs grow.
  - o **Visualization**: Use Kibana to build visual representations of the logs. Create dashboards tailored to the needs of the ML microservice, highlighting crucial metrics and logs.

With its modular and scalable architecture, the ELK Stack is well-suited for ML microservices. It provides a mechanism to handle vast amounts of log data and offers tools to derive actionable insights from them. As ML microservices grow in complexity and scale, having a robust logging solution like ELK becomes indispensable.

TensorFlow's TensorBoard for ML-specific visualizations

TensorBoard is TensorFlow's visualization toolkit, offering an interactive suite of visualizations for inspecting and understanding Machine Learning models. Whether you are tuning hyperparameters, comparing runs, or tracking metrics, TensorBoard provides a comprehensive interface to aid researchers and developers in the model development phase. The key features include:

- **Scalars dashboard**

    o **Description**: Presents simple metrics like accuracy, loss, or learning rate as line graphs, enabling easy tracking of how these metrics evolve.

    o **Usage**: Helps in understanding how well the model is learning and if there are issues like overfitting or vanishing gradients.

- **Graphs visualization**

    o **Description**: Provides an interactive visual representation of the computational graph, showing TensorFlow operations and tensors.

    o **Usage**: Useful for understanding the flow of tensors and the structure of deep learning models and ensuring that the model has been built correctly.

- **Histograms and distributions**

    o **Description**: Displays the distribution of tensor values using histograms or even how the distributions evolve.

    o **Usage**: Helps diagnose issues related to weight initialization and spot irregularities in gradient distribution.

- **Projector**

    o **Description**: A tool for visualizing high-dimensional data embeddings using techniques like PCA or t-SNE.

    o **Usage**: Helps understand how different data points are grouped or clustered in the embedded space.

- **Image and audio visualizations**

    o **Description**: TensorBoard can render input images and audio, allowing users to inspect input data directly.

    o **Usage**: Useful for validating input datasets and understanding data augmentation effects.

- **Hyperparameter tuning**
  - o **Description**: Offers a dashboard to visualize the results of hyperparameter sweeps, enabling the easy comparison of runs.
  - o **Usage**: Simplifies the often arduous task of hyperparameter optimization, providing insights into which combinations yield better results.

- **Integration with ML microservices**
  - o **Model debugging**: Visualizing the computational graph can spot inconsistencies or issues in the model architecture, which is especially beneficial when deploying complex models as microservices.
  - o **Performance monitoring**: Scalar metrics can be used to monitor the performance of online training or fine-tuning in microservices, ensuring models maintain high accuracy during live operations.
  - o **Feature inspection**: Using the Projector or the histogram tools, one can validate and inspect the features being fed into the model in real-time, which is especially beneficial in systems where data constantly evolves.

While primarily designed for the model development phase, TensorBoard finds its utility even in deployed ML microservices. It bridges the gap between complex Machine Learning operations and tangible insights, ensuring that models are not just black boxes but understandable, debuggable, and optimizable entities. For anyone diving into TensorFlow-based applications, TensorBoard is an invaluable companion.

Troubleshooting and debugging ML microservices

While promising in scalability and modularity, ML microservices bring their unique challenges when it comes to debugging and troubleshooting. The intricate blend of software engineering and Machine Learning intricacies means that challenges can arise from various fronts - data flow, model performance, infrastructure, or even integration points.

Common challenges and pitfalls in ML microservices

Blending software engineering with data model dynamics in ML microservices presents unique challenges affecting reliability and performance. These issues stem from various factors, including the model, data, infrastructure, and system integrations:

- **Model drift**
    - o **Issue**: Changes in the statistical properties of the target variable lead to poor model performance over time.
    - o **Impact**: Increasingly inaccurate predictions affecting decisions and user experience.
    - o **Solution**: Regularly monitor and retrain models with new data.

- **Data issues**
    - o **Issue**: Problems like incorrect preprocessing, missing data, or quality changes.
    - o **Impact**: Low-quality input data leads to poor predictions.
    - o **Solution**: Implement data checks, monitor anomalies, and ensure consistent preprocessing.

- **Scalability concerns**
    - o **Issue**: Bottlenecks emerging under high request volumes.
    - o **Impact**: Slowdowns or outages during peak usage, affecting user experience.
    - o **Solution**: Perform load testing, monitor performance, and use scalable architectures (for example, Kubernetes).

- **Dependency failures**
    - o **Issue**: Reliance on other services that may fail or change.
    - o **Impact**: Disruptions in ML service functioning.
    - o **Solution**: Establish robust error-handling fallback mechanisms and monitor the health of dependent services.

- **Versioning issues**
    - o **Issue**: Challenges in managing updates to models, data, and preprocessing.
    - o **Impact**: Difficulty in rolling back during issues, leading to extended downtimes.
    - o **Solution**: Use ML-specific version control and maintain clear versioning for all components.

- **Communication overhead**
    - o **Issue**: Network overhead from service-to-service communication.
    - o **Impact**: Increased latency, particularly with poorly optimized or geographically distant services.
    - o **Solution**: Optimize inter-service communication, use service meshes, and strategically place services.

- **Operational complexity**
  - o **Issue**: Complexity in managing multiple services, especially with ML components.
  - o **Impact**: Higher risk of failures, misconfigurations, and security issues.
  - o **Solution**: Utilize microservices management tools and train teams in best practices.

- **Model reproducibility**
  - o **Issue**: Difficulty in replicating model results across different environments or over time, complicating debugging and validation efforts.
  - o **Impact**: Challenges in diagnosing issues, ensuring consistent model performance, and validating changes or updates across development, testing, and production environments.
  - o **Solution**: Use containerization for environment consistency, version control for all ML components, and document crucial settings.

Addressing these challenges is key to developing reliable, efficient ML microservices with robust design and optimization opportunities.

Approaches to identify and resolve the challenges

Let us delve into the approaches one can adopt to identify and subsequently resolve the challenges associated with ML microservices:

- **Automated testing**
  - o **Implementation**: Develop comprehensive test cases and leverage CI/CD pipelines to automate testing at every update or merge.
  - o **Benefits**: Detects issues early, ensures code quality, and validates that changes or updates do not introduce new issues.

- **Performance benchmarking**
  - o **Implementation**: Use tools like Apache JMeter or Locust.io to simulate user loads and assess the system's performance.
  - o **Benefits**: Quickly identify performance degradation or bottlenecks that could indicate underlying issues.

- **Real-time monitoring**
  - o **Implementation**: Use tools like Prometheus for metrics collection and Grafana for visualization. Set up alerting for unexpected behaviors.
  - o **Benefits**: Provides immediate insights into anomalies or unexpected behavior, allowing for swift responses.

- **Feedback loops**

  o **Implementation**: Integrate feedback buttons or forms within applications or dashboards. Monitor and analyze this feedback regularly.

  o **Benefits**: Helps in quickly identifying issues related to model outputs or user experience.

- **Root cause analysis (RCA)**

  o **Implementation**: Gather evidence using tools like logs, metrics, and tracing. Then, systematically diagnose to identify the root cause.

  o **Benefits**: Ensures that the underlying problem is addressed, preventing recurrence.

- **Rollback mechanisms**

  o **Implementation**: Use container orchestration systems like Kubernetes, which support rollback features. Maintain versioned backups of models and configurations.

  o **Benefits**: Minimizes downtime and user impact when issues arise.

- **Centralized logging**

  o **Implementation**: Use the ELK or similar tools to centralize, analyze, and visualize logs.

  o **Benefits**: Provides a holistic view of system behavior and simplifies debugging.

- **Continuous learning and adaptation**

  o **Implementation**: Set up systems that collect real-world outcomes, compare them to predictions, and use this data for periodic retraining.

  o **Benefits**: Counters model drift and ensures the model stays updated with current trends and patterns.

Addressing challenges in ML microservices requires a combination of proactive measures, real-time monitoring, and reactive strategies. By understanding potential pitfalls and implementing the above approaches, organizations can ensure that their ML microservices remain robust, responsive, and reliable in diverse operational scenarios.

Tool spotlight: Effective debugging and tracing tools

This section introduces essential debugging and tracing tools for ML microservices, highlighting pdb for in-depth Python code debugging and Jaeger for distributed system tracing. These tools are crucial for identifying and resolving issues, with pdb allowing detailed code inspection and Jaeger providing insights into service interactions for system optimization.

Python debugger for Python

Pdb is the built-in interactive debugger for the Python language. It provides an array of functionalities that make the process of debugging Python code much more straightforward:

- **Interactive debugging**
  - o **Description**: Pdb allows users to set breakpoints in the code at desired locations. Once the execution hits a breakpoint, it pauses, allowing the developer to inspect variables, evaluate expressions, or even change variable values.
  - o **Implementation**: Use the **break** or **b** command to set breakpoints and continue or **c** to resume execution.

- **Stepping through code**
  - o **Description**: With pdb, developers can step through the code one line at a time, diving deep into functions or jumping over them as needed.
  - o **Implementation**: Use commands like step or s to step into a function and next or n to move to the next line.

- **Inspecting variables**
  - o **Description**: Inspecting the current state of variables can provide invaluable insights into potential issues.
  - o **Implementation**: Use the list or l command to display lines of code around the current line and print or p to display the value of a variable.

- **Post-mortem debugging**
  - o **Description**: Even if a program crashes, pdb can be used to inspect its state during the crash, making it a potent tool for debugging exceptions.
  - o **Implementation**: Use the **post_mortem()** function of pdb to start the debugger after an unhandled exception.

- **Ease of integration**
  - o **Description:** Embedding pdb into scripts is straightforward, allowing for ad-hoc debugging sessions.
  - o **Implementation**: Insert **import pdb**; **pdb.set_trace()** in the code where you want the execution to pause.

Jaeger

Jaeger is a distributed tracing system that offers end-to-end request tracing, making it invaluable for microservices-based architectures:

- **End-to-end request tracing**
  - o **Description**: Jaeger can trace a request across multiple microservices, visualizing the path it takes and the time spent in each service.
  - o **Implementation**: Integrate Jaeger client libraries with your microservices to instrument incoming and outgoing requests automatically.

- **Performance optimization**
  - o **Description**: By visualizing request paths, developers can identify bottlenecks or areas of inefficiency in the system.
  - o **Implementation**: Analyze trace visualizations to identify services or processes that consume disproportionate amounts of time.

- **Service dependency analysis**
  - o **Description**: Jaeger provides a graph representing inter-service dependencies, highlighting the relationships and interactions between different microservices.
  - o **Implementation**: Use Jaeger's built-in UI to explore the service dependency graph and understand the data flow and dependencies.

- **Flexible storage backends**
  - o **Description**: Jaeger supports various storage backends, including Elasticsearch, Cassandra, and Kafka, catering to different scalability and performance needs.
  - o **Implementation**: Choose a storage backend based on your system's requirements and integrate it with Jaeger for trace storage.

- **Integration with metrics systems**
  - o **Description**: Jaeger can be integrated with monitoring tools like Prometheus, correlating traces with system metrics.
  - o **Implementation**: Use Jaeger's built-in support for Prometheus metrics to enable this integration.

Both pdb and Jaeger, though serving different purposes, are pivotal in diagnosing and addressing issues in an ML microservice ecosystem. While pdb focuses on granular code-level debugging, Jaeger provides a higher-level view of data flow across services, allowing for holistic system optimization and debugging.

Use case: Recommendation engine diagnostics

In the music recommendation engine use case, we explore the application of monitoring, logging, and debugging techniques to enhance system performance and user experience. By examining user activity, managing recommendation services, and implementing effective error handling, we illustrate how these practices contribute to a more reliable and efficient service.

The following practical examples demonstrate the integration of theoretical concepts into real-world scenarios, showcasing their impact on improving AI-driven applications:

1. **User service**

    a. **Monitoring user activity and tracking anomalies**: Observing user activity patterns is crucial. If there is a sudden drop in user activity or a spike, it might indicate system issues or popular trends.

    Python pseudo-code:

    ```
    if user_activity_today > avg_user_activity * 1.5:
        alert("Spike in user activity!")
    elif user_activity_today < avg_user_activity * 0.5:
        alert("Drop in user activity!")
    ```

    b. **Logging user queries, errors, and feedback**: Store all user queries to understand their needs better. Also, capture any system errors or feedback to enhance the system.

    Python pseudo-code:

    ```
    log.info(f"User query: {user_query}")
    log.error(f"Error encountered: {error_detail}")
    log.info(f"User feedback: {feedback}")
    ```

    The ELK Stack can be invaluable for collecting, analyzing, and visualizing user logs. This makes anomaly detection, error tracking, and user trend understanding more straightforward.

2. **Debugging with pdb**: To effectively address debugging challenges, pdb empowers developers with tools for interactive code investigation, facilitating a methodical approach to problem-solving:

    a. **Issue**: A problem where user queries are sometimes not logged.

    b. **Identifying the issue**: When going through the logs, some user queries are not logged, especially when the system is under heavy load.

c. **Using pdb for debugging**: First, you would want to set a breakpoint at the place in the code where user queries are processed.

Python pseudo-code:

```
import pdb

def process_user_query(query):
    # ... some logic here
    pdb.set_trace()  # This sets a breakpoint
    log.info(f"User query: {query}")
    # ... rest of the logic
```

Once the breakpoint is hit, pdb provides an interactive environment where you can inspect variables, evaluate expressions, and step through the code. By examining the state at the breakpoint, you might discover that the query variable is not being set correctly under certain conditions (like high load).

d. **Resolution**: After identifying the root cause, you could refactor the code to better handle high-load scenarios, ensuring all user queries are correctly logged.

3. **Recommendation service**

   a. **Metrics to track recommendation accuracy and efficiency**: Monitor how often users accept the given recommendation and how fast the recommendation is generated.

   Python pseudo-code:

```
if recommendation_accepted:
    increment_recommendation_acceptance_metric()
log_time_taken_to_generate_recommendation(time_taken)
```

   b. **Logging recommendation logic and outputs**: Store the reasoning or logic used for a recommendation and its resulting output for transparency and debuggability.

   Python pseudo-code:

```
log.info(f"Logic used: {recommendation_logic}")
log.info(f"Recommendation output: {recommended_song}")
```

   TensorBoard provides visual insights into the model's performance, helping understand areas of improvement or validate the model's efficiency.

4. **Tracing with Jaeger**: Leveraging Jaeger's tracing capabilities, we can elucidate the intricate interactions within microservices, pinpointing delays and inefficiencies to enhance overall system performance.

   a. **Issue**: Recommendations are taking longer than usual to be generated for certain users.

   b. **Identifying the issue**: Users report slow response times when requesting music recommendations. You need to determine where the bottleneck is occurring within the microservice architecture.

   c. **Instrumenting the code for Jaeger tracing**: To trace requests as they pass through various services, you would want to instrument your service code to send trace data to Jaeger.

   Python pseudo-code (using the jaeger-client library):

```python
from jaeger_client import Config

config = Config(
    config={
        'sampler': {
            'type': 'const',
            'param': 1,
        },
        'logging': True,
    },
    service_name='recommendation_service',
)
tracer = config.initialize_tracer()

def get_recommendations(user_id):
    with tracer.start_span('fetch_user_preferences') as span1:
        preferences = fetch_user_preferences(user_id)
    with tracer.start_span('generate_recommendations') as span2:
        recommendations = generate_based_on_preferences(preferences)
    return recommendations
```

   d. **Using Jaeger for inspection**: Once the traces are collected in Jaeger, you can view the traces for the **recommendation_service**. By examining the traces, you might discover that the `fetch_user_preferences` span is taking significantly longer than usual.

e. **Resolution**: Diving deeper using Jaeger's detailed trace view might reveal that a dependent service (perhaps the user service or a database) is the source of the delay. With this information, you can either optimize the slow service or adjust your recommendation service to handle such delays more gracefully.

Conclusion

The conclusion of this chapter underscores the essential roles of monitoring and logging in ensuring the efficiency and safety of AI-driven applications, highlighting their proactive role in anomaly detection, the importance of privacy, the impact of tools like Prometheus and Grafana, and the practical insights from a music recommendation engine case study.

Emphasizing customization for each ML microservice, it sets the stage for next chapter, which shifts focus to **continuous integration and deployment (CI/CD)** for ML microservices, introducing strategies for streamlining development and operations to enhance agility and reliability in deploying AI applications.

Points to remember

- **ML monitoring uniqueness**: Unlike traditional software, ML monitoring must address model drift and data dependency challenges.

- **Proactivity in monitoring**: Early error detection and system optimization are critical to minimize downtime and improve user experience.

- **Important tools**:
  o **Monitoring and visualization**: Use Prometheus and Grafana.
  o **Centralized logging**: Implement Logstash and ELK Stack.
  o **ML-specific visualization**: Apply TensorBoard for deeper insights.

- **Critical ML metrics**: Focus on model accuracy, prediction latency, and resource utilization.

- **Logging practices**: Maintain detailed, context-rich, and standardized logs across services.

- **Debugging ML microservices**: Understand common issues like data discrepancies and performance dips. Utilize pdb for Python and Jaeger for tracing in microservices.

- **Practical example**: The music recommendation engine illustrates the application of these concepts in a real-world scenario.

- **Data retention and security**: Comply with data retention policies and ensure secure storage.

- **Privacy considerations**: Anonymize sensitive log information and stay informed about data privacy regulations.

- **Real-time monitoring**: Set up instant alerts for anomalies, utilizing tools like Alertmanager with Prometheus for immediate notifications.

- **Continuous strategy updates**: Adapt monitoring and logging strategies regularly to meet evolving ML and microservice landscapes.

Remembering these points ensures the deployment of robust, secure, and efficient ML microservices.

Assignment

To understand and apply the concepts and best practices related to monitoring and logging in ML microservices discussed in the chapter.

Tasks:

- **Setup an ML microservice**: Deploy a simple ML model (for example, a linear regression or classification model) as a microservice using Flask or FastAPI.

- **Implement monitoring**: Integrate Prometheus with your ML microservice to monitor its performance. Focus on metrics like request rate, request duration, and error rate.

- **Visualization with Grafana**: Set up Grafana and create a dashboard to visualize the metrics collected from Prometheus.

- **Logging with the ELK stack**
  - o Install and configure the ELK Stack.
  - o Integrate your ML microservice with Logstash to centralize logs.
  - o Use Kibana to view and query your logs.

- **Debugging practice**
  - o Introduce a deliberate error in your microservice code.
  - o Use pdb for Python to debug and identify the error in the user service.
  - o For the Recommendation Service, set up Jaeger and trace a request to identify bottlenecks or failures.

- **Real-time alerts**: Using Alertmanager with Prometheus, set up a real-time alert for a specific condition (for example, the error rate goes above a certain threshold).

Multiple choice questions

1. **What is the primary purpose of monitoring in ML microservices?**

   a. To increase the system's computational power

   b. To detect anomalies and optimize system performance

   c. To reduce the amount of data stored

   d. To enhance the user interface design

2. **Which feature distinguishes Prometheus in the context of ML microservices?**

   a. Its reliance on distributed storage

   b. Its multi-dimensional data model and PromQL

   c. Its exclusive compatibility with non-cloud environments

   d. Its limited visualization capabilities

3. **What role does Grafana play when used alongside Prometheus?**

   a. Data encryption

   b. Data deletion

   c. Visualization of metrics

   d. Reduction of data storage needs

4. **Why is privacy compliance crucial in logging within ML microservices?**

   a. To enhance system performance

   b. For moral and legal reasons

   c. To reduce storage costs

   d. To improve user interface design

5. **What does the ELK Stack primarily provide for ML microservices?**

   a. Real-time gaming experience

   b. Centralized logging solution

   c. Direct messaging services

   d. Cloud storage solutions

6. **How does TensorBoard contribute to ML microservices?**

   a. By offering real-time chat functionality

   b. Through visualization of ML model metrics

   c. By decreasing database needs

   d. Through enhancing cybersecurity measures

7. **What advantage does automated testing offer for ML microservices?**

   a. Increases manual testing requirements

   b. Decreases code quality

   c. Detects issues early and ensures code quality

   d. Slows down the development process

8. **Why is proactive error resolution important in ML microservices?**

   a. It solely focuses on aesthetic improvements

   b. It prevents errors before they escalate

   c. It is only relevant for database management

   d. It reduces the effectiveness of the system

9. **Which of the following is a key practice for effective logging in ML microservices?**

   a. Avoiding log rotation

   b. Logging at varied severity levels

   c. Decreasing log detail for simplicity

   d. Using a single logging format for all applications

10. **What is the significance of model drift monitoring in ML microservices?**

    a. It is irrelevant to model performance

    b. It prevents the model from being updated

    c. It identifies changes affecting model accuracy over time

    d. It enhances the graphical design of the application

Answer key

1	b
2	b
3	c
4	b
5	b
6	b
7	c
8	b
9	b
10	c

Join our book's Discord space

Join the book's Discord Workspace for Latest updates, Offers, Tech happenings around the world, New Release and Sessions with the Authors:

https://discord.bpbonline.com

## CHAPTER 10

Deployment for Machine Learning Microservices

Introduction

In the rapidly evolving domain of **Machine Learning** (**ML**), delivering high-quality, robust, and scalable microservices has become imperative. The integration of **continuous integration** (**CI**) and **continuous deployment** (**CD**) practices in the ML workflow can be a watershed for organizations seeking agility and excellence in their AI-driven offerings. This chapter introduces the core concepts of CI/CD in the context of ML microservices, elucidating why they are not just beneficial but essential for contemporary ML operations.

Structure

As we navigate this chapter, we will unpack the methodologies and tools that have revolutionized the ML development lifecycle. Through this, we aim to equip readers with strategies to expedite their ML development processes, while ensuring precision and dependability:

- Fundamentals of CI/CD for Machine Learning
- Automation tools for ML CI/CD
- Continuous delivery and rollback capabilities
- Case study and best practices

Objectives

This chapter is designed to equip ML engineers and DevOps specialists with the knowledge and tools needed to efficiently deliver ML services, aiming to shorten the time-to-market and ensure robustness and performance in dynamic environments. It covers the importance of CI/CD principles, especially for ML microservices, and highlights the distinction between traditional software and ML workflows. Readers will gain insights into leveraging key technologies such as Jenkins, GitLab CI/CD, MLflow, and Kubeflow for automating ML development processes. Furthermore, it addresses the construction and management of complex ML CI/CD pipelines, including data validation, model training, evaluation, and deployment. The chapter also explores advanced CI/CD tactics like A/B testing and model versioning, alongside practical applications through a case study on a music recommendation system. By adopting best practices and understanding common pitfalls, practitioners will be better positioned to operationalize ML CI/CD effectively.

Fundamentals of CI/CD for Machine Learning

CI and CD are the backbone of modern software development practices, enabling teams to deliver code changes more frequently and reliably. CI involves automating the integration of code changes from multiple contributors into a single software project. This process often includes automatic testing to detect problems early. Meanwhile, CD automates the delivery of applications to selected infrastructure environments.

Differences between traditional CI/CD and ML CI/CD

While the principles of CI/CD apply to both traditional software and ML-based systems, several distinct differences emerge due to the nature of ML:

- **Data dependency**: Traditional CI/CD focuses primarily on the application's code, whereas ML CI/CD must also account for data quality, data validation, and data versioning.

- **Model training and evaluation**: ML CI/CD pipelines incorporate stages for model training, model evaluation, and possibly retraining, which are not present in traditional software pipelines.

- **Experimentation and versioning**: ML development involves a lot of experimentation, meaning the CI/CD process must support multiple parallel experiments and version both code and ML models.

- **Resource intensiveness**: Training ML models is resource intensive. The CI/CD system must manage computational resources efficiently and scale based on the workload.

- **Monitoring for model drift**: Once deployed, ML models require continuous monitoring for performance and accuracy, which might trigger automatic retraining and redeployment in the pipeline.

Key components and flow of ML CI/CD pipelines

The CI/CD pipeline for ML microservices generally includes the following components:

- **Version control system (VCS)**: Where all the code, model definitions, and sometimes data schemas are stored. It is the starting point for the CI/CD process.

- **CI server**: This component monitors the VCS for changes, runs tests, and triggers subsequent actions in the pipeline. Jenkins and GitLab CI are common examples.

- **Artifact repository**: A storage location for the artifacts generated during the CI process, including trained model binaries, datasets, and configuration files.

- **Testing frameworks:** These frameworks handle automated testing for code, data, and models. They ensure the integrity of the ML microservice before it is deployed.

- **Deployment mechanisms**: Tools that automate the deployment of the ML microservice to various environments, from staging to production.

- **Monitoring and logging tools**: Vital for observing the behavior of ML models in production, capturing model drift, and triggering alerts for potential issues.

The typical flow of an ML CI/CD pipeline might look as follows:

- **Code and model development**: Developers and data scientists write code and develop models, then push their changes to the VCS.

- **Automated testing**: The CI server automatically runs a series of tests, which may include unit tests, integration tests, and model validation tests.

- **Model training and evaluation**: If tests pass, the pipeline initiates training of the ML model with the latest data and evaluates its performance.

- **Deployment to staging**: A successful model is deployed to a staging environment where it can be tested in a setting that closely resembles production.

- **Deployment to production**: After thorough testing, the model is deployed to production, often using blue-green deployment or canary releases to minimize risk.

- **Monitoring and feedback**: The production model is closely monitored. Feedback from this stage can lead to model retraining and restarting the CI/CD cycle.

In this section, we have laid the groundwork for understanding how CI/CD for ML works and how it differs from traditional CI/CD practices. The subsequent sections will delve into each of these components and stages in detail, offering practical advice and insights on implementing an effective ML CI/CD pipeline.

Automation tools for ML CI/CD

In this section, we delve into the powerful suite of automation tools that underpin modern ML CI/CD pipelines. These tools facilitate the automation of complex workflows, enabling seamless integration, testing, deployment, and scaling of machine learning models. We explore their unique features, practical applications, and how they contribute to the robustness and efficiency of the ML lifecycle. From orchestrating model training to managing deployment, this section is the cornerstone for understanding how to leverage technology to streamline ML operations.

Introduction to Jenkins: Automating ML workflows

Jenkins is one of the most popular automation servers in use today. Its ability to integrate with a multitude of development, testing, and deployment technologies makes it an ideal choice for managing ML CI/CD workflows.

- **Jenkins for ML**: In the context of ML, Jenkins can be used to automate repetitive tasks like:
  - **Data validation**: Running scripts to check data integrity and quality before it's fed into a training pipeline.
  - **Model training**: Automatically initiating the training process when new data is available or when the codebase changes.
  - **Testing and evaluation**: Executing test suites to validate model accuracy, performance, and generalization on new data.
  - **Deployment**: Orchestrating the rollout of a model to a staging or production environment after passing specified benchmarks.

- **Jenkins Pipeline**: Below is an illustrative example (in **groovy**) of how a **Jenkinsfile** might look for an ML workflow. This file defines the pipeline and is checked into source control:

```groovy
pipeline {
    agent any  // This pipeline can be executed on any available agent

    stages {
        stage('Check Data Quality') {
            steps {
                // Run a data validation script
```

```
            sh 'python scripts/data_validation.py'
        }
    }
    stage('Train Model') {
        steps {
            // Train the ML model with the training script
            sh 'python scripts/train_model.py'
        }
    }
    stage('Test Model') {
        steps {
            // Test the ML model with the test dataset
            sh 'python scripts/test_model.py'
        }
    }
    stage('Deploy Model') {
        steps {
            // Deploy the model to a specified environment
            sh 'python scripts/deploy_model.py'
        }
    }
}
post {
    success {
        // Actions to take if the pipeline succeeds
        echo 'The pipeline succeeded!'
    }
    failure {
        // Actions to take if the pipeline fails
        echo 'The pipeline failed.'
    }
}
}
```

The key concepts in the above-mentioned code are:

- **Stages**: These are the sequential phases of the pipeline. Each stage contains steps that must be completed before moving on to the next stage.

- **Steps**: These are the actual commands executed within a stage. In the example, these are shell commands that run Python scripts.

- **Agent**: This specifies where the pipeline will run. Using agent any tells Jenkins to run the pipeline on any available agent.

- **Post**: This section defines the actions to take after the pipeline has run, whether it succeeds or fails.

Setting up Jenkins for ML:

To use Jenkins for ML workflows, you need to set up Jenkins with the necessary plugins and configure it to work with your ML tools and environments.

1. **Install Jenkins**: Download and install Jenkins from the official website or use a Docker image.

2. **Install plugins**: Install relevant plugins like the Git plugin for source control management and any other tools your ML workflow requires.

3. **Configure environment**: Set up your Jenkins environment with the necessary credentials and configurations to access data sources, ML environments, and deployment targets.

4. **Create Jenkinsfile**: Write a Jenkinsfile that defines your ML pipeline and check it into your repository.

5. **Create pipeline**: In Jenkins, create a new pipeline and link it to your repository where the Jenkinsfile resides.

6. **Run and monitor**: Run the pipeline manually or configure it to trigger automatically based on certain events, such as a push to a specific branch in your repository.

By using Jenkins, data scientists and ML engineers can collaborate more effectively, as the integration and deployment processes are standardized and automated. It provides a reliable environment where the ML lifecycle stages are clearly defined, and every change to the model or data can be tracked and managed in a controlled way.

GitLab CI/CD: A deep dive into ML pipelines with GitLab

GitLab CI/CD is an integrated part of the GitLab platform that automates the aspects of the development lifecycle. For ML workflows, GitLab CI/CD can be particularly beneficial due to its robust handling of pipeline execution, which includes automated testing, model training, and deployment.

Here are some theoretical foundations of using GitLab CI/CD for ML pipelines:

- **Pipeline configuration**: GitLab uses a file named **.gitlab-ci.yml** to define the pipeline's configuration, which GitLab's runner will interpret and execute.

- **Stages and jobs**: Pipelines are composed of stages, which are a series of jobs that run in sequential order. Each job can represent a part of the ML workflow, such as data preprocessing, model training, evaluation, and deployment.

- **Runners**: Runners are the agents that execute each job in the pipeline. They can be configured to run on various environments, which is ideal for ML jobs that may require specific computational resources.

- **Artifacts and caching**: To manage data and model persistence across stages, GitLab allows the definition of artifacts that can be passed between stages and cached data to speed up pipeline execution.

- **Review apps**: For ML, this can be used to deploy a version of the application using the newly trained model for testing and review.

To give a concrete example, let us consider a simple GitLab CI/CD pipeline for an ML project. Below is a snippet of **.gitlab-ci.yml** which outlines a basic ML pipeline:

```
stages:
  - validate
  - train
  - evaluate
  - deploy


validate_data:
  stage: validate
  script:
    - echo "Validating data..."
    - python validate_data.py
  artifacts:
    paths:
      - validated_data.pkl


train_model:
  stage: train
```

```
script:

  - echo "Training model..."

  - python train_model.py

artifacts:

  paths:

    - model.pkl


evaluate_model:

  stage: evaluate

  script:

    - echo "Evaluating model..."

    - python evaluate_model.py

  dependencies:

    - train_model

  artifacts:

    paths:

      - performance_report.txt


deploy_model:

  stage: deploy

  script:

    - echo "Deploying model..."

    - python deploy_model.py

  only:

    - main
```

In the above example:

- The pipeline is divided into four stages: Validate, train, evaluate, and deploy.
- Each stage consists of jobs such as **validate_data**, **train_model**, **evaluate_model**, and **deploy_model**.

- The **validate_data** job runs a script to validate the data, the results of which are then saved as an artifact.

- The **train_model** job trains the model and saves it as an artifact.

- The **evaluate_model** job depends on the **train_model** job and evaluates the model's performance, saving a report.

- The **deploy_model** job is set to run only when changes are made to the main branch.

This basic example shows how an ML workflow can be automated using GitLab CI/CD. Each project will have its own specific requirements and complexity that can be configured in the pipeline.

Leveraging MLflow for experiment tracking and model registry

MLflow is an open-source platform dedicated to the complete machine learning lifecycle. It encompasses four primary functions: Tracking experiments, packaging ML code, managing and deploying models, and providing a central model store. For CI/CD, MLflow's tracking, and model registry features are particularly critical.

- **Experiment tracking**

  o Experiment tracking with MLflow involves recording and querying experiments. Data scientists can log parameters, code versions, metrics, and output files, and later compare them across runs.

  o This tracking is key in a CI/CD pipeline as it enables the team to maintain a history of model training runs and their results, which facilitates the identification of the best models.

- **Model registry**

  o The model registry is a centralized repository for storing ML models. It allows you to version, annotate, and manage models in a collaborative environment.

  o In the context of CI/CD, the model registry functions as the storage location from which models are deployed to production. It supports stage transitions like from staging to production and handles versioning automatically.

  o **Integrating MLflow in CI/CD**: MLflow can be integrated into a CI/CD pipeline to automatically track experiments, register models, and handle transitions between different stages of the model lifecycle. The following steps are typically involved:

- **Data preprocessing and experimentation**

    o   As part of the CI/CD pipeline, data preprocessing scripts and ML experiments are run, with MLflow tracking each run.

    o   Parameters, metrics, and artifacts (for example, serialized models, plots) from each run are logged to an MLflow tracking server.

- **Model evaluation and selection**

    o   Models are evaluated based on performance metrics. The best-performing models are identified and flagged for deployment.

    o   MLflow's tracking server allows you to query and compare these metrics across runs.

- **Model registration**

    o   Selected models are registered in MLflow's Model Registry with a specific version number.

    o   Models can be annotated with descriptions and tagged for easier identification and management.

- **Model deployment**

    o   From the Model Registry, models can be transitioned to *Staging* for further testing or directly to *Production.*

    o   The registry allows rollback to previous model versions if needed, facilitating continuous delivery and easy rollbacks.

Code examples:

Integrating MLflow into a Python ML script typically involves importing the MLflow library and using its functions to log experiments. Here is an example:

```
import mlflow

from sklearn.ensemble import RandomForestClassifier

from sklearn import datasets

from sklearn.model_selection import train_test_split

from sklearn.metrics import accuracy_score


# Load dataset

iris = datasets.load_iris()
```

```
X, y = iris.data, iris.target

X_train, X_test, y_train, y_test = train_test_split(X, y, test_size=0.33,
random_state=42)


# MLflow Tracking

mlflow.set_experiment('iris_rf_experiment')


with mlflow.start_run():

    # Train model

    rf = RandomForestClassifier(n_estimators=100)

    rf.fit(X_train, y_train)


    # Predict

    predictions = rf.predict(X_test)


    # Log parameters, metrics, and model

    mlflow.log_param('n_estimators', 100)

    mlflow.log_metric('accuracy', accuracy_score(y_test, predictions))


    # Log model

    mlflow.sklearn.log_model(rf, "model")


# The model is now registered with MLflow and can be accessed or deployed from
the tracking server.
```

In this script, the **RandomForestClassifier** is used for training on the Iris dataset. MLflow logs the number of trees (**n_estimators**), the accuracy of the model, and the model itself.

The logged models appear in the MLflow UI, where they can be compared, managed, and deployed through the MLflow Model Registry. The CI/CD pipeline can automatically trigger these scripts upon new data arrival or code updates, ensuring that model training and tracking are part of the automated workflow.

Kubeflow: Orchestrating ML workflows on Kubernetes

Kubeflow is an open-source project that aims to make deployments of ML workflows on Kubernetes simple, portable, and scalable. It provides a straightforward way to deploy best-of-breed open-source systems for ML to diverse infrastructures. Kubeflow is designed to run everywhere Kubernetes runs, making it easy to orchestrate complex workflows that span multiple containers.

- **Kubeflow components**

    o **Kubeflow Pipelines**: A platform for building and deploying portable, scalable ML workflows based on Docker containers.

    o **Katib**: For hyperparameter tuning of ML models.

    o **KFServing**: Provides a serverless framework to deploy ML models to production environments.

- **Kubeflow pipelines**

    o A key feature of Kubeflow is the ability to create and manage complex ML pipelines. Pipelines consist of a sequence of steps, each of which is typically a container.

    o These pipelines can be set up to handle various tasks such as data preprocessing, model training, model evaluation, and serving.

- **Integrating Kubeflow in CI/CD**

    o Kubeflow can be incorporated into a CI/CD pipeline to ensure that every step of the ML workflow is reproducible, scalable, and manageable.

    o When new code is merged into a repository, the CI/CD pipeline can automatically trigger a Kubeflow pipeline run to test the changes.

    o Results and metrics from the run can be captured and used to make decisions about the deployment of models.

Code examples

Kubeflow uses YAML files to define the resources that will be created within Kubernetes. Below is an example of what a simple Kubeflow Pipeline might look like when defined as a YAML file:

```
apiVersion: kubeflow.org/v1

kind: Pipeline

metadata:
```

```
  name: sample-pipeline
spec:
  templates:
  - name: preprocess-data
    container:
      image: my-registry/preprocess:latest
      command: ["python", "/preprocess.py"]
  - name: train-model
    container:
      image: my-registry/train:latest
      command: ["python", "/train.py"]
      args: ["--data", "{{workflow.outputs.artifacts.preprocessed-data}}"]
  - name: deploy-model
    container:
      image: my-registry/deploy:latest
      command: ["python", "/deploy.py"]
      args: ["--model", "{{workflow.outputs.artifacts.trained-model}}"]

  entrypoint: sample-pipeline
  arguments:
    parameters:
    - name: data-path
      value: s3://my-bucket/raw-data
```

In practice, you would define your pipeline in Python using the Kubeflow Pipelines SDK, which allows for a more dynamic pipeline construction. Here is a simple Python example using the Kubeflow Pipelines SDK:

```
import kfp
from kfp import dsl


def preprocess_op():
```

```python
    return dsl.ContainerOp(
        name='Preprocess Data',
        image='my-registry/preprocess:latest',
        command=['python', '/preprocess.py'],
    )


def train_op(data):
    return dsl.ContainerOp(
        name='Train Model',
        image='my-registry/train:latest',
        command=['python', '/train.py'],
        arguments=['--data', data],
    )


@dsl.pipeline(
    name='Sample Pipeline',
    description='An example pipeline that trains and deploys a model.'
)
def sample_pipeline():
    preprocess_task = preprocess_op()
    train_task = train_op(preprocess_task.output)


# Compile the pipeline
pipeline_func = sample_pipeline
pipeline_filename = pipeline_func.__name__ + '.pipeline.zip'


kfp.compiler.Compiler().compile(pipeline_func, pipeline_filename)
```

This Python code defines a pipeline with two steps - preprocessing and training. Each step is implemented as a container operation (**ContainerOp**) using a specific Docker image. The **sample_pipeline** function orchestrates the order of operations.

The last part compiles the pipeline into a zip file which can then be uploaded to the Kubeflow pipelines UI or triggered via the Kubeflow pipelines API by a CI/CD system.

By using Kubeflow, teams can manage complex ML workflows with the same tools they use for managing other containerized applications, ensuring consistency, and simplifying operations across the board.

Jenkins or GitLab CI/CD integration with Kubeflow

Integrating Kubeflow with GitLab CI/CD or Jenkins allows for the creation of a robust CI/CD pipeline for ML projects. This pipeline would automatically test, build, and deploy ML models whenever changes are committed to your repository. Here is a conceptual overview of how this might work with both tools.

GitLab CI/CD integration with Kubeflow

In GitLab, you would define a **.gitlab-ci.yml** file to specify your CI/CD pipeline. This file instructs GitLab on what to do each time new code is pushed to the repository:

```
stages:
  - build
  - test
  - deploy


build_model:
  stage: build
  script:
    - echo "Build the Docker image for the ML model..."
    - docker build -t my-model:$CI_COMMIT_REF_SLUG .


test_model:
  stage: test
  script:
    - echo "Run tests on the built model..."
    - docker run my-model:$CI_COMMIT_REF_SLUG /bin/sh -c "python test.py"
```

```
deploy_to_kubeflow:

  stage: deploy

  script:

    - echo "Deploy the model to Kubeflow..."

    - python deploy_to_kubeflow.py $CI_COMMIT_REF_SLUG

  only:

    - main
```

The **deploy_to_kubeflow.py** script would interact with the Kubeflow Pipelines API to trigger a new pipeline run or update an existing service:

```python
import kfp

from kfp import Client


# Environment variables passed from the GitLab runner

model_image = f"my-model:{CI_COMMIT_REF_SLUG}"


# Kubeflow Pipelines client

client = Client(host='http://your-kubeflow-pipelines-endpoint')


# Find the pipeline by name

pipelines = client.list_pipelines(filter=f"name={pipeline_name}")

pipeline_id = pipelines.pipelines[0].id


# Run the pipeline

client.run_pipeline(pipeline_id, job_name, {"model-image": model_image})
```

Jenkins integration with Kubeflow

With Jenkins, you would define a **Jenkinsfile** (groovy) that outlines the stages of your CI/CD pipeline and uses the Kubeflow Pipelines SDK to trigger pipeline runs:

```
pipeline {
```

```
    agent any

    stages {

        stage('Build') {

            steps {

                echo 'Building the Docker image...'

                sh 'docker build -t my-model:$BUILD_NUMBER .'

            }

        }

        stage('Test') {

            steps {

                echo 'Testing the built model...'

                sh 'docker run my-model:$BUILD_NUMBER /bin/sh -c "python
                test.py"'

            }

        }

        stage('Deploy to Kubeflow') {

            when {

                branch 'main'

            }

            steps {

                echo 'Deploying to Kubeflow...'

                sh 'python deploy_to_kubeflow.py $BUILD_NUMBER'

            }

        }

    }

}
```

The **deploy_to_kubeflow.py** script would be similar to the GitLab version, using environment variables provided by Jenkins this time:

```
import kfp
```

```
from kfp import Client

import os


# Environment variables passed from Jenkins

model_image = f"my-model:{os.getenv('BUILD_NUMBER')}"


# Kubeflow Pipelines client

client = Client(host='http://your-kubeflow-pipelines-endpoint')


# Find the pipeline by name

pipelines = client.list_pipelines(filter=f"name={pipeline_name}")

pipeline_id = pipelines.pipelines[0].id


# Run the pipeline

client.run_pipeline(pipeline_id, f"deploy-{os.getenv('BUILD_NUMBER')}",
{"model-image": model_image})
```

Both the GitLab CI/CD and Jenkins configurations are simplified and will need to be adjusted for real-world projects. They assume the existence of Docker images for your model and a Kubernetes cluster running Kubeflow pipelines. The deploy scripts would interact with the Kubeflow API to create or update pipeline runs, passing in the Docker image built during the CI process as a parameter.

A/B testing in ML microservices

A/B testing, also known as **split testing,** in the context of ML microservices, refers to the practice of comparing two versions of an ML model to determine which one performs better in a real-world scenario. It involves routing a portion of traffic to the new model and comparing the results with the current production model.

- **Strategies for A/B testing**
  - o **Traffic splitting**: Divide incoming requests between the old and new model versions and measure performance.
  - o **Segmentation**: Route specific user segments to different models to test performance across diverse user bases.
  - o **Metrics focused**: Define clear performance metrics such as accuracy, click-through rate, or conversion rate to evaluate the success of the model.

- **Managing model versions and iterations**: Versioning models are just as crucial as versioning code. It involves keeping track of different iterations of models, their associated data sets, and the performance of each version.

    o **Version control**: Use tools like MLflow or **Data Version Control (DVC)** to track models and datasets.

    o **Registry**: Maintain a model registry to manage and serve different versions of models.

    o **Reproducibility**: Ensure that every model version can be traced back to its training data and training pipeline to reproduce results if needed.

- **Role of feature flags and canary deployments**

    o **Feature flags**: Use toggles to turn on or off certain features or models without deploying new code. This is useful for gradually introducing changes to a subset of users.

    o **Canary deployments**: Similar to A/B testing, canary deployments involve rolling out a change to a small subset of users before a full rollout. It is a phased approach to deploying new model versions.

    o **Monitoring and rollback**: Continuously monitor the performance of new models and have a rollback strategy in place if the new version underperforms.

- **Code example**: An example of feature flag usage in a Python microservice might look like this:

```python
from feature_flags import is_feature_active

def get_predictions(request):
    if is_feature_active('new_model'):
        # Use the new model
        predictions = new_model.predict(request.data)
    else:
        # Use the old model
        predictions = old_model.predict(request.data)

    return predictions
```

- **Code example**: Setting up a simple canary deployment in Kubernetes might involve:

```yaml
apiVersion: apps/v1
kind: Deployment
```

```
metadata:
  name: ml-model-canary
spec:
  replicas: 1 # a small portion of the traffic
  selector:
    matchLabels:
      app: ml-model
  template:
    metadata:
      labels:
        app: ml-model
        track: canary
    spec:
      containers:
      - name: ml-model
        image: ml-model:v2
        ports:
        - containerPort: 80
```

By implementing A/B testing and versioning strategies, organizations can ensure that they introduce new ML model updates to production in a controlled and measurable way. Feature flags and canary deployments add an extra layer of safety, allowing for quick rollbacks and minimal impact on the user experience if new models perform poorly. This section provides readers with the knowledge to confidently test and manage ML models in a production environment, leading to more robust and user-centric AI applications.

Continuous delivery and rollback capabilities

In the context of ML microservices, continuous delivery and rollback capabilities form the backbone of a resilient deployment strategy. This section of the chapter explores the methods and best practices to deploy ML models into production safely and how to revert changes if things go awry.

Continuous delivery for ML models

CD in ML involves automating the delivery of models from development to production environments. It ensures that models can be deployed at any time, promoting frequent and reliable releases.

- **Deployment strategies for ML models in production**

  o **Automated pipelines**: Create CD pipelines that take models from staging to production with minimal manual intervention.

  o **Containerization**: Utilize Docker or similar technologies to package models and their dependencies for consistent deployments.

- **Safe deployment techniques**

  o To mitigate risks associated with deployment, certain strategies are employed to ensure that new model versions do not adversely affect the production system.

- **Blue-green deployments**

  o This technique involves two identical production environments, blue and green. At any time, one of them is live.

  o When deploying a new model, it is released to the inactive environment (for example, green).

  o After testing and performance validation, traffic is gradually shifted from blue to green.

  o If any issues arise, traffic can be quickly reverted to Blue.

- **Rollbacks**

  o The ability to revert to a previous model version quickly is crucial if the new deployment fails or underperforms.

  o Rollbacks should be automated as part of the CD pipeline to ensure swift action when needed.

- **Monitoring and logging for CI/CD**: Monitoring and logging are critical in observing the model's performance once it is deployed and ensuring that any deviations from expected behavior are caught early.

- **Monitoring model performance**

  o Track performance metrics like accuracy, precision, recall, and response times.

  o Use tools like Prometheus, Grafana, or custom ML monitoring solutions for real-time insights.

- **Logging**
  - o Collect logs to provide insights into system behavior and model inference patterns.
  - o Use centralized logging solutions like ELK Stack (Elasticsearch, Logstash, Kibana) to manage logs from different services.

- **Code example**: Implementing a simple logging function (python) within an ML microservice could be as follows:

```python
import logging

def log_prediction(request_data, prediction):
    logging.info(f"Request data: {request_data}")
    logging.info(f"Model prediction: {prediction}")


# Later in the code, after making a prediction:
log_prediction(request_data, model_prediction)
```

- **Code example (YAML)**: A snippet to automate model rollback using a CI/CD tool (pseudo-code):

```yaml
rollback:
  script:
    - if [ "$MODEL_PERFORMANCE_METRIC" -lt "$ACCEPTANCE_THRESHOLD" ]; then
        echo "Rolling back to previous model version..."
        # Command to rollback to previous model version
    - rollback_model_version --to=previous
    fi
```

By establishing robust continuous delivery and rollback mechanisms, ML teams can ensure that their models are not only rapidly deployable but also maintain the highest levels of reliability and performance post-deployment. Monitoring and logging play a significant role in this process, providing the feedback loop necessary to make informed decisions about when to advance and when to retreat in the deployment cycle.

Case study and best practices

In this section, we delve into the practical application of CI/CD principles within a **music recommendation system** (**MRS**), showcasing the challenges and best practices. Through this case study, we highlight how advanced CI/CD techniques can significantly enhance the deployment and management of ML-driven services, providing insights into overcoming common pitfalls and implementing effective strategies for continuous improvement.

Case study: Music recommendation system

Suppose our MRS uses advanced CI/CD to manage its ML-driven recommendation services, such as Spotify's Discover Weekly. They deploy models in a sandbox environment to test the new algorithms on a fraction of the user base before full deployment. MRS also practices CI/CD by continuously integrating new music features and user feedback into their recommendation algorithms, deploying updates regularly to refine the user experience.

Music recommendation system pitfalls:

- **Overfitting to test data**: Continuously evaluating on the same test set may lead to overfitting during the CI/CD process. To avoid this, the MRS should use techniques like cross-validation and periodically refresh the test dataset.

- **Pipeline rigidity**: An ML pipeline that cannot handle data schema changes can break if the MRS introduces new user attributes. Implementing schema validation and evolution tools within the CI/CD process can prevent such issues.

Best practices with music recommendation system context:

- **Automated testing**: Implement comprehensive automated tests that cover data validation, model evaluation, and system integration to ensure that the MRS updates do not introduce bugs or performance issues.

- **Monitoring and rollback**: Use real-time monitoring tools to track the performance of deployed models. Have a rollback strategy to revert to the previous model version if an issue is detected post-deployment in the MRS.

- **Feature toggles**: Use feature toggles to gradually roll out new features in the MRS. This allows for canary releases and A/B testing to measure the impact of changes before they reach all users.

Consider a case where an MRS is part of a larger service like YouTube or Apple Music. They often need to deploy ML models that cater to diverse demographics and rapidly changing music trends. The CI/CD pipeline needs to be robust enough to handle frequent updates, each potentially affecting millions of users.

To maintain reliability, such services implement CI/CD pipelines that include:

- **Automated canary testing**: New model versions are tested on a small percentage of traffic to measure impact before full deployment.

- **Dark launches**: Features are deployed but not activated, allowing for extensive testing in the production environment without affecting users.

- **Data versioning**: Data versioning is crucial for the reproducibility of ML models. Services like DVC or MLflow are used to keep track of datasets and model versions.

Conclusion

The chapter has journeyed through the landscape of continuous integration and deployment, crystallizing its essence for ML microservices. We traversed the creation and refinement of CI/CD pipelines, ensuring each stage—from data validation to model training—is seamlessly integrated and reproducible. Our exploration of automation tools like Jenkins, GitLab, MLflow and Kubeflow revealed the breadth of options available for streamlining ML workflows. Advanced CI/CD concepts were unfurled, showcasing how automated training and rigorous testing strategies underpin robust ML systems. The art of A/B testing and the science of model versioning were demystified, highlighting their pivotal role in the evolutionary dance of Machine Learning. As we conclude, this chapter stands as a testament to the transformative power of CI/CD in the realm of AI, ensuring agility, quality, and resilience in the ever-evolving tapestry of ML microservices.

In the next chapter, we will explore real-world applications of ML microservices across various sectors, showcasing their transformative power in industries such as media, finance, healthcare, smart cities, agriculture, and energy management. Through detailed case studies, we'll examine success stories, learn from challenges encountered, and extract best practices to understand how ML microservices drive innovation, efficiency, and sustainability.

Points to remember

- CI/CD pipelines for ML microservices encompass data validation, model training, and automated testing, vital for delivering robust AI-driven applications.

- Jenkins automates ML workflows, enabling continuous integration and streamlined deployment processes.

- GitLab CI/CD provides a comprehensive platform for constructing ML pipelines, fostering collaboration and efficiency.

- MLflow tracks experiments and manages the model registry, enhancing the management of ML lifecycle stages.

- Kubeflow orchestrates ML workflows on Kubernetes, offering a scalable and flexible platform for deploying complex ML systems.

- Advanced CI/CD concepts integrate automated model training and evaluation, supporting continuous delivery and robust ML operations.

- Containers and microservices architecture are leveraged for scalable ML workflows, catering to the dynamic nature of ML applications.

- A/B testing and model versioning in ML microservices enable systematic testing and gradual feature rollouts, mitigating risks associated with new model deployments.

Assignment

Implementing CI/CD in ML microservices: Apply the principles and tools of CI/CD to construct and manage a continuous integration and deployment pipeline for a music recommendation ML microservice.

Tasks:

- **Create a simple ML microservice**
  - o Develop a basic ML model for music recommendation.
  - o Containerize your ML microservice using Docker.

- **Set up a CI/CD pipeline**
  - o Initialize a Git repository for version control of your ML microservice code.
  - o Use Jenkins to create a pipeline that triggers on every commit.
  - o Include steps for code checkout, build, and unit tests.
  - o Integrate your pipeline with GitLab CI/CD for automated model training and deployment upon successful testing.

- **Orchestrate workflows with Kubeflow**
  - o Deploy Kubeflow on a Kubernetes cluster.
  - o Create a workflow in Kubeflow to manage the lifecycle of the ML microservice from training to deployment.

- **Implement A/B testing**
  - o Introduce feature flags in your microservice for A/B testing new model versions.
  - o Use canary deployments to gradually roll out updates and monitor performance.

- **Version control and rollback**
  - o Manage model versions using MLflow.
  - o Prepare a rollback strategy in case of degraded performance or issues post-deployment.

Multiple choice questions

1. **What is the primary goal of integrating CI/CD in ML microservices?**
   a. To reduce the cost of cloud resources
   b. To enhance the security of ML models

    c. To streamline the ML service delivery process

    d. To increase the complexity of ML workflows

2. **Which of the following tools is NOT mentioned as a key technology for automating ML development processes?**

    a. Jenkins

    b. GitLab CI/CD

    c. TensorFlow

    d. MLflow

3. **What is the main difference between CI/CD in traditional software development and ML CI/CD?**

    a. ML CI/CD does not require automated testing

    b. Traditional CI/CD does not handle data validation

    c. ML CI/CD is less complex

    d. Traditional CI/CD focuses more on data quality

4. **Which CI/CD practice is crucial for avoiding overfitting in ML models?**

    a. Continuous deployment only

    b. Periodic refreshing of the test dataset

    c. Solely relying on automated tests

    d. Avoiding A/B testing

5. **What role does Jenkins play in ML CI/CD workflows?**

    a. Data storage

    b. Automating repetitive tasks

    c. Visualization of data

    d. Manual testing

6. **How do feature toggles contribute to ML CI/CD?**

    a. By reducing the need for data validation

    b. Allowing for gradual rollout of new features

    c. Eliminating the need for monitoring deployed models

    d. Increasing the speed of model training

7. **Which of the following is a recommended strategy for managing ML pipeline rigidity?**

    a. Ignoring schema changes

    b. Implementing schema validation tools

    c. Decreasing the frequency of deployments

    d. Using a single version of the model indefinitely

8. **What is a key benefit of automated canary testing in ML CI/CD pipelines?**

    a. Completely replacing A/B testing

    b. Testing new model versions on a small percentage of traffic

    c. Eliminating the need for rollback strategies

    d. Simplifying data preprocessing

9. **In the context of ML CI/CD, why is model versioning important?**

    a. To ensure that models can be deployed without testing

    b. To avoid using continuous integration practices

    c. To manage and track different iterations of models

    d. To reduce the use of automated testing frameworks

10. **What is the purpose of implementing rollback strategies in ML CI/CD?**

    a. To increase deployment frequency

    b. To ensure swift recovery in case of deployment failures

    c. To eliminate the need for monitoring tools

    d. To complicate the deployment process

Answer key

1	c
2	c
3	b
4	b
5	b
6	b
7	b
8	b
9	c
10	b

Join our book's Discord space

Join the book's Discord Workspace for Latest updates, Offers, Tech happenings around the world, New Release and Sessions with the Authors:

https://discord.bpbonline.com

CHAPTER 11
Real World Use Cases

Introduction

This chapter examines **Machine Learning (ML)** microservices, showcasing their transformative impact across various industry verticals. Here, we will dissect how ML microservices are not mere technological advancements but pivotal enablers of innovation, efficiency, and strategic breakthroughs. From the nuances of content personalization in media to the precision of predictive maintenance in manufacturing, ML microservices are at the heart of modern problem-solving and value creation. This chapter brings to life the stories of organizations that have harnessed these services to catapult their offerings, streamline operations, and carve out competitive advantages.

Structure

Armed with the diverse use cases, you will be better equipped to envision the potential of AI-driven solutions for your organizations, empowering them to embark on innovative projects that transform industries and improve lives.

This chapter will cover the following topics:

- Implementing ML microservices in various industries
- Success stories and lessons learned from real projects
- Enhancing media and entertainment with AI

- Financial services: Fraud detection
- Healthcare: Diagnostics and personalized treatment
- Smart cities: Urban management
- Agriculture: Advancements in precision farming
- Energy: Sustainable management and optimization
- Recommendation engine

Objectives

This chapter aims to provide a comprehensive view of the application of ML microservices across diverse industries, extracting pivotal insights from real-world implementations that underline the strategic and operational benefits of these technologies. It endeavors to showcase how ML microservices are meticulously engineered and deployed to tackle specific business challenges and opportunities, drawing from successful deployments to highlight best practices and common pitfalls. Through inspirational success stories, the chapter intends to demonstrate the tangible impact ML microservices have on business outcomes and customer experiences, ultimately empowering readers with practical knowledge applicable to envisioning and actualizing ML microservices within their own sectors.

Implementing ML microservices in various industries

In the evolving landscape of technology, ML microservices play a pivotal role in enabling real-time predictions and decision-making across a multitude of industries. These microservices are auxiliary components and at the heart of transforming operations into more efficient, intelligent, and data-driven ecosystems. By leveraging tailored ML algorithms, these microservices can process and analyze data in real-time, facilitating immediate and informed decisions.

For instance, in healthcare, ML microservices are crucial for predictive diagnostics, where real-time analysis of patient data can lead to timely and personalized treatment plans, significantly improving care outcomes. In the realm of financial services, they are indispensable for real-time fraud detection, analyzing transaction patterns instantly to pinpoint irregularities and potential fraud. Similarly, precision farming is revolutionized in agriculture by ML microservices that process satellite imagery and sensor data in real-time, optimizing crop yields and resource utilization.

The core of these applications lies in their ability to not only collect and analyze vast datasets but to do so with a speed and accuracy that allows for immediate action. This involves the integration of specialized ML algorithms and models that are designed for speed and efficiency, ensuring that predictions and decisions are made in a timely manner. The seamless integration of these services into broader operational infrastructures ultimately drives efficiency, reduces costs, and enhances overall decision-making capabilities.

Success stories and lessons learned from real projects

The chapter presents numerous examples of ML microservices across different sectors, demonstrating their transformative impact. In media and entertainment, personalization and moderation microservices have significantly enhanced user engagement and content relevance. Financial services have seen a paradigm shift in fraud detection, leveraging ML for real-time transaction analysis and anomaly detection. Healthcare showcases advancements in predictive diagnostics and personalized treatment, emphasizing the importance of data privacy and ethical considerations.

In smart cities, ML microservices have improved traffic management and public safety, underscoring the need for scalability and integration with existing infrastructure. Agriculture benefits from precision farming techniques, highlighting sustainability and the adaptation to climate change. The energy sector's focus on sustainable management and optimization illustrates the challenges of data integration and the potential for predictive analytics to improve energy efficiency.

Each industry's success story brings forward common lessons as follows:

- The critical role of data quality and availability for ML effectiveness.
- The importance of scalability and adaptability in ML solutions to meet evolving needs.
- Ethical considerations and privacy concerns are paramount, especially in handling sensitive data.
- Collaboration between technical experts and industry specialists is essential for successful implementation.

These examples and lessons provide a comprehensive view of the practical applications of ML microservices, offering valuable insights for organizations looking to implement similar technologies.

Having explored the transformative applications of ML microservices across various industries, and having distilled the success stories and critical lessons from real-world projects, we now proceed to delve deeper into the specifics. This exploration has set the stage for a comprehensive understanding of how ML microservices are not just technological advancements but pivotal enablers of strategic innovation and operational efficiency. As we transition into detailed examinations of industry-specific applications, from media personalization in entertainment to predictive diagnostics in healthcare, let us keep in mind the broader impacts and challenges these technologies address. This approach will guide us through the nuanced applications and the tangible benefits realized by organizations that have successfully integrated ML microservices into their operations.

Enhancing media and entertainment with AI

In the bustling arena of media and entertainment, the advent of ML microservices has revolutionized the way content is curated, delivered, and consumed. The relentless pursuit of personalization, coupled with the need for robust content moderation, has driven industry giants and nimble startups alike to adopt ML microservices as their standard. This shift is not simply a trend but a response to the consumer's growing demand for tailored experiences and the industry's need for scalable, responsive systems.

ML microservices in this domain are multifaceted. They learn from vast troves of user data to recommend content that resonates on a personal level and vigilantly monitor streams of user-generated content to uphold community standards. From streaming services that adapt to viewing habits to platforms that dynamically filter and flag inappropriate content, these microservices are the silent orchestrators of the user experience.

This section delves into how ML microservices are not just enhancing user engagement and satisfaction but also acting as gatekeepers of digital spaces, ensuring they remain conducive and safe. As we peel back the layers of their implementation, we witness a synergy of advanced algorithms, real-time data processing, and seamless integration—all working in concert to shape the future of media and entertainment.

Personalization techniques in media

The media landscape is witnessing an unprecedented personalization revolution, powered by sophisticated ML microservices. These services use a blend of collaborative filtering, content-based filtering, and hybrid methods to create a bespoke media experience that resonates with individual preferences and behaviors.

Collaborative filtering algorithms sift through mountains of user interaction data, identifying and predicting preferences based on patterns of similarity among users. They suggest content that others with similar tastes have enjoyed, weaving a social tapestry of recommendations. On the other hand, content-based filtering zeroes in on the attributes of the content itself—genres, artists, themes—and aligns suggestions with the user's past interactions and stated preferences.

The most potent personalization comes from hybrid models that combine both approaches, capitalizing on the strengths of each to mitigate their individual limitations. This synergy ensures a well-rounded recommendation system that not only understands what content a user might like but also why they might like it.

These personalization microservices are continually learning and adapting, employing advanced techniques like deep learning to parse through content and user data. They refine their recommendations over time, becoming more attuned to the subtle nuances of user preference.

Through these techniques, media platforms can offer a highly curated feed, ensuring that users are engaged and content consumption is maximized. It is a strategy that not only elevates user experience but also drives platform loyalty and content discoverability.

Personalization services architecture

At the heart of any media platform's personalization is a robust architecture that seamlessly blends user data with content intelligence. This architecture consists of several key services, each dedicated to a specific facet of the personalization process:

- **User profile service**: Central to personalization, this service aggregates user data such as demographics, preferences, viewing history, and engagement metrics. It is a dynamic repository that evolves with every interaction, providing a comprehensive view of the user's tastes and behaviors.

- **Content metadata service**: This service catalogs content characteristics, including genre, release date, cast, and director, as well as derived attributes through analysis like themes or mood. It acts as the content's digital DNA, enabling precise matching with user profiles.

- **Recommendation engine**: The engine employs ML algorithms to match user profiles with content metadata, generating personalized recommendations. It continuously learns from user feedback, improving its predictions over time.

- **Feedback loop**: User interactions with the recommendations feed back into the system, allowing the recommendation engine to validate and refine its algorithms, ensuring a self-improving system.

- **API gateway**: Serving as the entry point for the front end, the API gateway routes requests to appropriate services and consolidates responses into a cohesive user experience.

This architecture is typically cloud-native, leveraging scalable containerized microservices that respond dynamically to user demand. Services communicate via well-defined APIs, with data streaming through a message bus like Kafka to ensure real-time responsiveness.

By adopting this architecture, media platforms ensure that personalization is not just a one-time event but a continuous, evolving journey, creating a user experience that is both engaging and uniquely tailored to each individual.

Moderation methods overview

In the ever-evolving realm of media and entertainment, maintaining platform integrity and user safety is paramount. This is where ML microservices play a crucial role, employing sophisticated techniques to monitor, analyze, and moderate content.

- **Natural language processing (NLP)**: This branch of ML deals with understanding and interpreting human language. In content moderation, NLP services analyze text in comments, posts, and descriptions. They are trained to identify harmful language patterns, such as hate speech, explicit content, or cyberbullying. Utilizing models like BERT or GPT, these services can understand context, nuances, and even slang, making their filtering more accurate and less prone to false positives.

- **Image recognition models**: With the proliferation of visual content, image recognition models have become indispensable. These models, trained on vast datasets, can identify explicit or violent imagery, trademarks, or other restricted visual content. They use **convolutional neural networks (CNNs)** to detect patterns and anomalies in images and videos that may be inappropriate or harmful. This not only helps in automatic filtering but also aids in categorizing content for targeted audiences.

- **Anomaly detection**: This method is critical in identifying content that may not explicitly violate guidelines but is nonetheless unusual or potentially problematic. Anomaly detection models are trained to understand normal content patterns and flag deviations. This could include unusually high levels of user engagement (which might indicate spam or coordinated inauthentic behavior) or sudden changes in the nature of the content being posted. These flags can then be reviewed by human moderators for appropriate action.

In summary, these methods form a multifaceted defense, leveraging the power of AI to maintain a safe, respectful, and enjoyable media environment. They ensure that content is not only engaging and relevant but also adheres to the necessary ethical and legal standards. Through continuous learning and adaptation, ML moderation services are becoming increasingly sophisticated, providing platforms with the necessary tools to foster positive and safe online communities.

Moderation services and workflow integration

In the dynamic field of media and entertainment, content moderation is not just a feature but a necessity. It involves several key services, intricately interwoven, to ensure the content adheres to community standards and regulatory requirements. Here is a breakdown of the core services involved in the moderation workflow:

- **Content analysis service**: This is the frontline of the moderation workflow. Leveraging ML models, this service automatically screens incoming content—be it text, images, or videos—against predefined standards and guidelines. The service utilizes various AI techniques, such as text analysis for profanity or hate speech detection and image recognition for identifying inappropriate visuals. If content is flagged as potentially problematic, it is routed to the **moderation queue service** for further review.

- **Moderation queue service**: This service acts as a central hub for content flagged by the analysis service. It categorizes and prioritizes content based on the severity and type of potential violation. Human moderators access this queue to review flagged content, making it a critical junction where AI-generated recommendations meet human judgment. This service often includes tools to aid moderators in decision-making, such as highlighting specific aspects of the content that triggered the flag.

- **Enforcement service**: Once a piece of content has been reviewed and a decision has been made (be it clearing, editing, or removing the content), the enforcement service steps in. This service is responsible for implementing these decisions. For instance, it could involve removing a post, suspending an account, or sending a warning to the content creator. This service also logs actions taken for accountability and future reference.

The integration of these services into a cohesive workflow is key to an efficient moderation system. It ensures that content is screened rapidly and accurately, flagged content is reviewed systematically, and appropriate actions are consistently applied. This integrated approach not only upholds platform integrity but also scales effectively as the volume of content grows, crucial for the ever-expanding universe of media and entertainment.

Challenges and considerations in personalization and moderation

Implementing ML microservices in the media and entertainment industry, particularly for personalization and moderation, presents unique challenges and considerations:

- **Ethical use of data**: Central to the success of personalization is the ethical handling of user data. This involves transparent data collection practices and ensuring that personalization algorithms respect user privacy and data protection laws, such as GDPR. Offering users clear control over their data is not just a legal requirement but an ethical obligation.

- **Compliance with local regulations**: The global nature of the media and entertainment sector requires adherence to a mosaic of local regulations. This includes not only data protection laws but also content moderation standards that vary by jurisdiction. ML microservices must be designed to flexibly adjust to these variable standards, ensuring legal compliance across different regions.

- **Addressing bias**: The potential for ML algorithms to introduce or perpetuate bias poses a significant ethical challenge. In the context of entertainment, such biases can skew content visibility and recommendations, impacting user experience. It is crucial to actively identify and mitigate these biases to maintain fairness and uphold diverse representation.

- **Adaptability**: The fast-paced evolution of the media landscape, influenced by cultural shifts and emerging trends, demands that ML microservices remain agile. This not only pertains to technological adaptability but also to aligning with evolving industry standards and ethical norms, ensuring that personalization and moderation services stay relevant and effective.

Financial services: Fraud detection

In the dynamic and complex world of financial services, fraud detection stands as a bastion against the ever-evolving threats of financial crimes. Traditional methods of fraud detection, which often rely on static rules or simple anomaly detection algorithms, are increasingly proving to be inadequate in the face of sophisticated and constantly changing fraudulent techniques. As financial transactions grow in volume and complexity, the need for more advanced, adaptable, and robust systems becomes paramount. This is where ML microservices step into the spotlight.

The integration of ML microservices in fraud detection represents a significant leap in financial security. These services bring the power of advanced analytics, pattern recognition, and predictive modeling to the table, allowing financial institutions to not only identify known fraud patterns but also predict and adapt to new fraudulent behaviors. ML microservices can process vast amounts of transactional data in real-time, flagging anomalies, and unusual patterns that could indicate fraudulent activities.

Moreover, the use of ML in fraud detection aligns closely with the growing emphasis on customer trust and experience in financial services. By accurately identifying and preventing fraud, financial institutions can protect their customers from potential losses and maintain their trust. This is particularly crucial in an era where digital transactions are the norm, and customers expect high standards of security and convenience.

Additionally, the integration of ML microservices in fraud detection aligns with regulatory compliance needs. Financial institutions are under constant scrutiny from regulatory bodies to ensure that they are doing everything in their power to prevent fraud. ML-driven systems can provide a more robust and effective defense against financial crimes, meeting and often exceeding regulatory requirements.

In essence, the application of ML microservices in fraud detection is more than a technological upgrade; it is a strategic necessity for financial institutions aiming to safeguard their operations, customers, and reputation in a digitally-driven and risk-laden financial landscape.

Understanding banking fraud detection systems

Banking fraud detection systems are designed to identify and prevent a wide range of fraudulent activities, each with its unique modus operandi and challenges:

- **Types of fraud**
    - o **Transaction fraud**: Involves unauthorized transactions made by individuals other than the account holders. This type of fraud can range from small unauthorized online purchases to large-scale illegal funds transfers.
    - o **Identity theft**: Here, fraudsters impersonate individuals to gain access to their banking details, loans, and credit facilities. They often use stolen personal information like social security numbers and addresses.

o **Card skimming**: This occurs when devices are illegally installed on ATMs and card machines to capture card information, which is then used for fraudulent transactions.

o **Phishing attacks**: These are deceptive tactics used to trick customers into revealing sensitive information, such as bank account details and passwords.

o **Loan fraud**: Involves the use of false information to obtain loans or credit lines from financial institutions.

- **Challenges in detection**

o **Evolving fraud patterns**: Fraudsters continuously develop new techniques to evade detection, making it challenging for traditional rule-based systems to keep up.

o **Real-time analysis**: Financial transactions occur around the clock, necessitating systems that can analyze and flag fraudulent activity in real-time.

o **High false positive rates**: Overly sensitive fraud detection systems can flag legitimate transactions as fraudulent, leading to customer frustration and reduced trust.

o **Data silos**: Banks often have data stored in disparate systems, making it difficult to have a unified view essential for effective fraud detection.

o **Balancing security and customer experience**: Implementing rigorous security checks can sometimes impede transaction speed or convenience, negatively affecting the customer experience.

o **Regulatory compliance**: Financial institutions must navigate complex regulatory landscapes while innovating in fraud detection methods.

o **Maintaining customer privacy**: Ensuring the privacy and security of customer data while using it for fraud detection is a crucial balancing act.

In summary, banking fraud detection systems face a multifaceted challenge: evolving fraud strategies, the need for real-time processing, managing false positives, data integration, regulatory compliance, and preserving customer experience and privacy. These systems must be agile, comprehensive, and robust to effectively counter the sophisticated and varied nature of banking fraud.

ML microservices for real-time transaction analysis

In the financial services industry, the deployment of ML microservices for real-time transaction analysis is crucial for fraud detection, leveraging sophisticated ML algorithms and comprehensive data integration and processing techniques. These solutions offer a nuanced approach to identifying anomalies in real-time, ensuring financial integrity. Let us begin by understanding the foundational aspects of data integration and processing, which enable these advanced analytical capabilities:

- **Data integration and processing**

  o **Data aggregation**: Data from various sources, such as transaction databases, customer profiles, and external databases, are aggregated. This comprehensive data view is crucial for accurate fraud detection.

  o **Preprocessing**: The raw data is cleaned, normalized, and transformed to be fed into ML models. This might involve handling missing values, encoding categorical variables, and scaling numerical inputs.

  o **Feature engineering**: Essential in ML, this involves creating new features from raw data that better represent the underlying patterns related to fraudulent transactions.

  o **Real-time data stream processing**: Technologies like Apache Kafka or AWS Kinesis are used to process and analyze data streams in real time, ensuring immediate response to potential fraud activities.

Following the establishment of a robust data foundation, we can explore the specific ML services that directly contribute to real-time transaction analysis:

- **Transaction monitoring service**: Continuously monitors transactions for signs of fraudulent activity, evaluating them against factors such as amount, location, and frequency.

- **Pattern recognition algorithms**: Employs models like neural networks and decision trees trained on historical data to recognize legitimate and fraudulent transaction patterns.

- **Predictive analysis**: Analyzes transaction trends to forecast potential fraud, allowing for preemptive measures.

In conclusion, the integration of sophisticated ML algorithms with agile data processing techniques forms the backbone of ML microservices for real-time transaction analysis in the financial services industry, instrumental in staying ahead in the battle against fraud.

Architecture of fraud detection ML microservices

The architecture for fraud detection in financial services utilizes a service-oriented approach, integrating multiple specialized microservices. This modular structure enhances scalability, flexibility, and the overall efficiency of the fraud detection system. Below, we delve into the modular structure that underscores the scalability, flexibility, and efficiency of these systems:

- **Service-oriented structure**

  o **Data ingestion service**: The primary entry point for transactional data, gathering information from various sources like ATM transactions, online banking activities, and point-of-sale systems.

  o **Data processing and preprocessing service**: Responsible for cleaning, normalizing, and transforming the data into a suitable format for analysis. This service ensures data quality and prepares datasets for subsequent ML processes.

  o **Model training service**: Utilizes historical data to train and update ML models. It employs various algorithms to identify patterns and characteristics of fraudulent activities.

  o **Real-time analysis service**: This crucial service deploys trained ML models to analyze incoming transactions in real-time. It identifies potential fraud by comparing current transactions against known fraud patterns and behaviors.

  o **Alert generation and notification service**: When a potential fraud is detected, this service triggers alerts and notifies the relevant parties, such as internal security teams, account managers, or directly to customers, depending on the protocol.

- **Workflow**

  o **Data collection**: Data from multiple sources enters the system through the data ingestion service.

  o **Data preparation**: The collected data is processed and prepared for analysis. This step includes tasks like normalization, feature extraction, and handling missing values.

  o **Model training and updating**: ML models are trained with historical data to identify and understand patterns of fraudulent transactions. These models are continuously updated with new data to adapt to evolving fraud techniques.

  o **Real-time transaction analysis**: Each transaction is analyzed in real-time against the trained models. The system looks for anomalies or signs of fraud, comparing transaction details against historical fraud patterns.

  o **Fraud detection and alerting**: On detecting a transaction that fits the criteria for potential fraud, an alert is generated. This alert can trigger further investigation or direct actions like transaction blocking or customer notification.

  o **Feedback and improvement**: The system incorporates feedback from the results of its fraud predictions to refine and improve the models and overall process.

The architecture of fraud detection ML microservices in financial services exemplifies a sophisticated amalgamation of data processing, ML, and real-time analytics. It is a testament to how ML can be harnessed to protect financial assets and maintain consumer trust in an increasingly digital world.

Challenges and best practices

Implementing fraud detection services in the financial sector is fraught with challenges. However, navigating these with strategic best practices ensures the effective identification and prevention of fraudulent activities. It is equally crucial to adhere to industry-specific ethical standards, which play a pivotal role in shaping these practices. The following points offer a comprehensive look at overcoming obstacles with proven methodologies, while also emphasizing the importance of ethical considerations:

- **Scalability and performance**
    - o **Challenge**: The service must handle high volumes of transactions without lag, ensuring real-time analysis.
    - o **Best practice**: Utilize scalable cloud services and robust infrastructure, along with efficient data processing algorithms, to manage volume without compromising performance.

- **Accuracy and false positives**
    - o **Challenge**: Balancing accurately detecting fraudulent transactions with minimizing false positives is essential. Excessive false positives can lead to customer dissatisfaction and operational inefficiencies.
    - o **Best practice**: Employ advanced ML algorithms and continuously refine them with updated data. Implementing a feedback loop for analyzing false positives and tuning models can significantly reduce errors.

- **Regulatory compliance and ethical standards**
    - o **Challenge**: The financial services sector is governed by stringent regulatory requirements, including data security and privacy laws, alongside ethical standards that dictate fair and equitable treatment of customer data.
    - o **Best practice**: Ensure strict adherence to regulatory standards such as GDPR, PCI DSS, and industry-specific ethical guidelines. Regular audits, encryption, and other data security measures are essential to safeguard customer data, maintain compliance, and uphold the highest ethical standards. Engaging in transparent communication with customers about how their data is used and ensuring fairness in fraud detection practices reinforces trust and integrity in financial services.

By focusing on these areas and integrating ethical standards into best practices, financial institutions can develop robust, efficient, and compliant fraud detection services. This not only safeguards the interests of the institutions and their customers but also contributes to the broader goal of maintaining ethical integrity in financial operations.

Healthcare: Diagnostics and personalized treatment

ML has revolutionized modern healthcare, emerging as a key technological catalyst in transforming patient care and medical research. In an era where precision and efficiency are paramount, ML stands at the forefront, driving significant advancements in various healthcare sectors. From streamlining diagnostic procedures to tailoring patient-specific treatments, the integration of ML has enabled a more nuanced approach to medicine.

Predictive diagnostics, one of the prime applications of ML, leverages algorithms to forecast potential health risks and disease progression. This proactive methodology empowers healthcare professionals to intervene earlier, improving patient outcomes substantially. Furthermore, personalized treatment, another critical domain, has been immensely enhanced by ML's capability to analyze vast datasets. Here, ML algorithms synthesize information from patient genetics, lifestyle, and previous health records to formulate customized treatment plans, marking a shift from the one-size-fits-all approach to a more individualized healthcare strategy.

This segment of healthcare, driven by ML, is not just a technological leap but a paradigm shift towards more predictive, preventive, and personalized care, paving the way for a future where healthcare is more responsive, effective, and aligned with individual patient needs.

Predictive diagnostics in healthcare

Predictive diagnostics represents a transformational approach in healthcare, leveraging advanced analytics to forecast potential health risks and outcomes. This proactive strategy is pivotal in early disease detection, patient risk assessment, and tailoring preventive measures, significantly enhancing patient care and outcomes.

The cornerstone of predictive diagnostics is its reliance on ML to analyze complex medical data. ML's strength lies in its ability to process and interpret vast arrays of diverse data – from genetic information and lab results to patient histories and demographic details. By sifting through this data, ML models can identify patterns and correlations often imperceptible to human analysis, predicting disease onset, progression, and patient response to various treatments.

Common ML models used in diagnostics include:

- **Decision trees**: Simple yet effective, these models mimic human decision-making processes, making them useful for straightforward diagnostic criteria.

- **Neural networks**: Particularly deep learning models, excel in handling unstructured data like medical imaging, enabling nuanced interpretations in diagnostics.

- **Support vector machines (SVM)**: With their robust classification capabilities, SVMs are instrumental in categorizing patients into high-risk or low-risk categories based on their medical profiles.

- **Random forests**: An ensemble learning method that aggregates decisions from multiple trees, providing more accurate predictions and reducing the risk of overfitting.

- **Regression analysis**: Used for predicting continuous outcomes, such as the likelihood of disease development or its progression rate.

- **XGBoost**: Known for its performance in classification and regression, XGBoost handles complex datasets efficiently. It also offers model explainability through SHAP values, crucial for understanding predictive influences in healthcare.

Incorporating these ML models into diagnostic processes has led to remarkable advancements. For example, algorithms analyzing retinal images can predict cardiovascular risks, while others examining histopathology slides can detect early signs of cancer with remarkable accuracy. Predictive diagnostics, thus, stands as a testament to the power of ML in transforming healthcare, offering a more nuanced, data-driven approach to early disease detection and patient care.

Personalized treatment and patient data analytics

The advent of ML in healthcare has ushered in a new era of personalized treatment, revolutionizing how care is delivered to patients. At the heart of this transformation is the ability of ML to dissect and interpret vast amounts of patient data, paving the way for tailored treatment strategies that cater to individual health profiles and needs.

Personalized treatment, also known as precision medicine, hinges on the integration of various patient data points - genetic profiles, lifestyle factors, environmental exposures, and medical histories. ML algorithms excel in sifting through these data layers, uncovering patterns and insights that can inform treatment decisions. For example, oncology has witnessed a significant shift with ML models identifying specific cancer subtypes and predicting which chemotherapy or immunotherapy regime would be most effective for a particular patient.

The process involves several steps:

1. **Data aggregation**: Collecting comprehensive patient data from **electronic health records** (**EHRs**), genomic sequencing, diagnostic tests, and wearable health devices.

2. **Predictive modeling**: Using ML models to analyze the data, predict disease progression, and identify potential response to treatments.

3. **Treatment customization**: Based on the predictive analysis, clinicians can devise treatment plans that are highly tailored to individual patients, increasing the efficacy and reducing potential side effects.

However, this powerful tool comes with significant ethical considerations and privacy concerns. The handling of sensitive patient data mandates strict adherence to data protection laws like **Health Insurance Portability and Accountability Act (HIPAA)** in the US and **General Data Protection Regulation (GDPR)** in the EU. Furthermore, there is a moral responsibility to ensure that the data analytics does not lead to discrimination or biases in treatment availability and quality.

In essence, personalized treatment facilitated by ML and patient data analytics represents a significant leap forward in healthcare. It offers hope for more effective, efficient, and patient-centric care. However, this must be balanced with stringent ethical practices and robust data privacy measures to protect patient rights and ensure equitable access to these advanced healthcare solutions.

Architecture of ML services in healthcare

The architecture of ML services in healthcare is structured to efficiently handle vast and varied data sets, apply sophisticated analytical models, and provide actionable insights. This architecture is generally composed of multiple interconnected services and components, each playing a crucial role in the overall system. Below, we detail the essential service components that together create a seamless, interconnected system, each contributing significantly to the holistic application of ML in enhancing patient care and outcomes:

- **Data ingestion service**: At the base lies the data ingestion layer, responsible for collecting a wide array of data from various sources such as EHRs, medical imaging, genomics data, and patient-generated data (like wearables). This layer ensures that data is systematically gathered and stored for processing.

- **Data preprocessing and normalization**: Data from various sources is often in different formats and may contain inconsistencies. This service standardizes and cleanses the data, preparing it for effective analysis. Tasks like normalizing lab values, standardizing image formats, and handling missing data fall under this service.

- **Data validation**: A critical step following data ingestion and preprocessing, ensuring that the data meets quality and consistency standards before model training. Validation checks can include verifying the accuracy of patient information, ensuring the completeness of datasets, and identifying any anomalies that could impact model performance.

- **Model training and validation service**: This core service involves the development of ML models. Using the prepared data, models are trained to detect patterns, predict outcomes, or provide recommendations. This process involves selecting algorithms, training models on historical data, and validating their performance through techniques like cross-validation.

- **Patient data analysis service**: This service applies the trained models to new patient data to provide diagnostic support, predict outcomes, or recommend personalized treatment plans. For instance, applying a trained model to new radiology images to detect signs of disease.

- **Feedback loop**: An often overlooked but crucial component is the feedback loop. As healthcare professionals use the system, their inputs and the outcomes of the predictions (like treatment success or failure) are fed back into the system. This data is used to continuously improve and refine the models, ensuring they adapt to new information and remain accurate over time.

- **User interface**: Finally, the results of the ML analysis are presented to healthcare professionals through user-friendly interfaces. These interfaces provide actionable insights, alerts, and recommendations, aiding clinicians in decision-making.

This architecture represents a holistic approach to integrating ML into healthcare. It emphasizes not just on the technical aspects of data handling and model development but also on the practical application of these models in a clinical setting, ensuring that they provide real value to healthcare providers and patients.

Challenges and future directions in healthcare ML

Healthcare ML faces unique challenges that must be navigated to unlock its full potential:

- **Scalability**: As data volumes grow exponentially, scaling ML solutions to handle this influx while maintaining performance is crucial. Future advancements must focus on more efficient data processing and model training methods.

- **Accuracy and reliability**: The accuracy of ML predictions is vital, especially when they directly impact patient care. Ongoing research is required to enhance model accuracy and reduce errors, particularly in complex cases.

- **Ethical considerations**: The use of patient data raises significant ethical questions, especially concerning privacy and consent. Future directions must prioritize ethical data usage, ensuring that patient confidentiality is maintained and that data is used responsibly.

Looking ahead, ML in healthcare is poised for transformative advancements:

- **Integrative data analysis**: Future trends include the integration of diverse data types (genomic, imaging, lifestyle) for a more holistic view of patient health, potentially revolutionizing personalized medicine.

- **Advanced predictive models**: The development of more sophisticated models, perhaps leveraging techniques like deep learning, could significantly improve diagnostic accuracy and treatment efficacy.
- **Ethical AI frameworks**: There is a growing emphasis on developing ethical AI frameworks to guide the responsible use of ML in healthcare, balancing innovation with moral considerations.

In conclusion, while challenges persist, the future of ML in healthcare is bright, with immense potential to enhance patient care and revolutionize medical practices.

Smart cities: Urban management

Smart cities represent the pinnacle of urban planning and technology integration, aimed at enhancing the quality of life for residents through improved efficiency and services. These cities leverage advanced technologies like **Internet of Things (IoT)**, AI, and big data to optimize resources, reduce costs, and improve connectivity among urban systems. They transform urban landscapes into dynamic entities that adapt and respond intelligently to everyday challenges, from traffic congestion to energy distribution.

Enhancing urban management with ML microservices

The core of a smart city's functionality lies in its ability to process vast amounts of data and use it to make informed decisions. This is where ML microservices come into play. By breaking down complex ML tasks into smaller, more manageable services, these microservices enable cities to analyze and interpret diverse data streams in real-time. They facilitate predictive analytics for traffic flow, energy use, public safety, and more, turning data into actionable insights.

ML microservices' modular nature allows for rapid development and deployment, fostering a more agile and responsive urban management system. They enable cities to evolve into living ecosystems that continuously learn from their environment and enhance the urban experience, making smart cities not just a concept, but a reality of improved urban life.

Tackling urban traffic challenges

Traffic congestion in urban areas is a perennial challenge, affecting everything from air quality to economic productivity. Traditional traffic management systems often fall short in addressing the dynamic nature of urban traffic, leading to inefficiencies and frustrations.

Real-time traffic analysis with ML

ML microservices is a game-changer in urban traffic management. ML algorithms excel at processing vast amounts of data from various sources, such as traffic cameras, sensors, and GPS devices in real-time. By analyzing this data, ML models can identify patterns, predict traffic congestions, and suggest optimal traffic flows. This can lead to adaptive traffic signal control, dynamic route planning for public transport, and even real-time traffic advisories for commuters.

Predictive modeling for smoother traffic

The predictive capabilities of ML extend beyond immediate traffic analysis. They can forecast potential bottlenecks due to events, weather changes, or roadworks, enabling proactive traffic management. Cities can optimize public transport schedules, adjust traffic light sequences, and plan infrastructural improvements based on these predictions.

Case studies of success

Numerous cities worldwide have started integrating ML into their traffic systems with remarkable results. For instance, Singapore uses ML-powered traffic models to optimize public bus routes and schedules, significantly reducing waiting times and congestion. Another example is Los Angeles, where an ML-based traffic management system synchronizes traffic lights across the city, resulting in smoother traffic flow and reduced travel times.

These case studies demonstrate how ML microservices not only make traffic management more efficient but also enhance the overall quality of urban life. With continuous advancements in ML and data analytics, the potential for smarter, more responsive traffic systems in cities is vast and promising.

Public safety and ML-driven insights

In the intricate tapestry of urban planning, public safety emerges as a paramount thread. Ensuring a safe environment is not just about preventing crime; it is about fostering a community where residents can live, work, and thrive without fear. This is where ML steps in, offering a transformative approach to enhancing public safety in urban landscapes.

Predictive policing with ML

One of the most significant applications of ML in public safety is predictive policing. By analyzing historical crime data, ML models can identify patterns and predict potential hotspots of criminal activity. Police departments can then allocate resources more effectively, increasing patrols in high-risk areas at times when crimes are more likely to occur. For example, the *Chicago Police Department* uses an ML-based system to predict the likelihood of specific individuals being involved in a shooting, either as a victim or perpetrator, allowing for proactive intervention.

Optimizing emergency response

ML microservices also revolutionize emergency response strategies. By integrating data from various sources like 911 calls, traffic patterns, and hospital availability, ML models can optimize the routing of emergency vehicles, reducing response times significantly. For instance, in New York City, an ML-driven system analyzes emergency call data in real-time to dispatch fire department units faster and more accurately.

Integrating public surveillance with ML

The rise of smart surveillance systems, equipped with ML capabilities, marks another stride in urban public safety. These systems can monitor public spaces in real time, recognizing suspicious behaviors or unattended packages, and alerting authorities promptly. In cities like London, ML-enhanced CCTV networks are becoming an invaluable tool in maintaining public security and aiding crime investigations.

Emergency services and ML insights

Beyond crime prevention, ML microservices are instrumental in disaster management. They can predict natural disaster patterns, like floods or earthquakes, enabling cities to prepare and respond effectively. ML models can also analyze social media and other public communication channels during a disaster to provide real-time updates and guidance to both residents and responders.

In summary, the integration of ML in public safety is a testament to the potential of technology in creating safer, more responsive urban environments. By harnessing the power of data and predictive analytics, cities are not only addressing the challenges of today but are also preparing for a more secure tomorrow.

Challenges and future prospects in smart cities

Smart cities, powered by ML microservices, face a unique set of challenges that require careful navigation:

- **Scalability**: As urban populations rise, the scalability of ML systems becomes crucial. Managing increasing data volumes and maintaining system performance demands robust, scalable architectures.
- **Data privacy**: With the vast amount of personal data processed, privacy concerns are paramount. Ensuring data security and compliance with privacy laws is essential to maintain public trust.

- **Integration complexities**: Integrating ML microservices with existing urban infrastructures and systems presents a technical challenge, requiring seamless interoperability and collaboration among various stakeholders.

Peering into the future

Looking ahead, the future of smart cities seems poised for transformative growth:

- **Advanced predictive analytics**: Future smart cities might employ more sophisticated ML algorithms for predictive analytics, enhancing everything from traffic management to public health.

- **IoT and ML convergence**: The integration of IoT with ML microservices will further amplify the capabilities of smart cities, leading to more efficient resource management and better quality of life.

- **Sustainable urban development**: ML will play a pivotal role in driving sustainable urban development, optimizing energy use, reducing waste, and contributing to a greener environment.

- **Proactive edge computing**: Enhances city planning by processing data in real-time at the source with IoT devices, reducing latency and improving responsiveness to urban challenges like traffic and public safety.

In essence, while challenges persist, the prospects of smart cities are boundlessly promising, heralding an era of urban spaces that are not only intelligent but also sustainable, secure, and adaptable to the needs of their ever-evolving populace.

Agriculture: Advancements in precision farming

Precision farming represents a pivotal shift in agricultural practices, where farmers use information technology and a range of items such as GPS, soil scanning, data management, and IoT to optimize crop yields and reduce waste. This approach focuses on ensuring efficiency, reducing costs, and minimizing environmental impact.

The integration of ML microservices into precision farming is revolutionizing this sector. ML microservices analyze vast amounts of data from various sources such as, satellite imagery, sensor data, weather forecasts, and more, to make informed decisions about planting, fertilizing, and harvesting crops. These services can predict optimal planting times, potential pest issues, and even forecast yield, enabling farmers to make more precise and profitable decisions.

Moreover, ML microservices offer scalability and flexibility, adapting to different farm sizes and types. This adaptability ensures that even small-scale farmers can leverage the benefits of advanced analytics, leading to more democratized access to technology in agriculture. As a result, precision farming facilitated by ML is not just a tool for increasing productivity; it is a means to ensure sustainability and food security in an increasingly unpredictable world.

In summary, ML microservices are not just enhancing precision farming; they are reshaping the future of agriculture. They provide a path to a more efficient, sustainable, and productive farming industry, aligning with the global goals of reducing hunger and promoting environmental stewardship.

Machine Learning in yield prediction

Predicting crop yield is a complex task influenced by numerous variables, including weather patterns, soil conditions, pest infestations, and farming practices. Traditional methods often rely on historical data and farmers' experience, which may not always accurately reflect the dynamic nature of these factors.

Application of ML microservices for accurate yield forecasting

ML microservices have revolutionized agriculture in several ways. By leveraging data from various sources - satellite images, IoT sensors in the field, weather stations, and historical yield data, these services can analyze patterns and correlations that are invisible to the naked eye. ML algorithms, particularly those focusing on predictive analytics and pattern recognition, process this data to forecast yields with greater accuracy.

For example, an ML model can analyze satellite imagery to assess plant health, use sensor data to monitor soil moisture levels, and incorporate weather forecasts to predict how these factors might affect the final yield. This holistic approach enables farmers to anticipate potential issues and make informed decisions to maximize their yields.

Case study: Yield prediction using ML

A notable instance is the adoption of ML microservices by a midwestern farm in the United States. The farm, spanning several hundred acres, integrated an ML-based yield prediction system. The system utilized data from field sensors, weather reports, and satellite imagery to forecast yields for different crops, including corn and soybeans. The results were remarkable: The farm reported a 15% increase in yield accuracy compared to traditional prediction methods. This improvement translated into better resource allocation, optimized harvest schedules, and increased profitability. It also helped in environmental conservation efforts by reducing unnecessary water and fertilizer usage.

The success of this case illustrates how ML microservices are not merely technological upgrades but essential tools in modern agriculture's shift towards more data-driven and precise farming practices.

Case study: Implementing ML for enhanced farming practices

In the heart of California's agricultural belt, a progressive farming cooperative embarked on a mission to integrate ML into its operations. The cooperative, encompassing multiple farms, primarily focused on fruit orchards and vegetable cultivation. The initiative was to implement ML microservices for enhanced farming practices, encompassing aspects from irrigation management to pest control.

ML integration and solutions

The cooperative introduced a series of ML-based applications, including:

- **Predictive irrigation systems**: Utilizing soil moisture data from field sensors and weather forecasts, the ML models provided precise irrigation schedules, optimizing water usage.

- **Disease prediction models**: By analyzing historical data and current weather patterns, the system could predict potential outbreaks of pests and diseases, enabling preemptive measures.

- **Yield optimization algorithms**: These algorithms analyzed various data points, such as plant growth rates, weather conditions, and soil health, to predict optimal harvest times and maximize yields.

Impact and results

The impact of integrating ML into the cooperative's farming practices was substantial:

- **Resource optimization**: Water usage was reduced by 25%, thanks to the predictive irrigation system, while maintaining crop health and yields.

- **Increased productivity**: Early disease detection and yield optimization strategies led to a 20% increase in overall productivity across the farms.

- **Environmental sustainability**: Reduced pesticide usage and better resource management contributed to more sustainable farming practices.

- **Economic benefits**: The cooperative saw a significant return on investment, with increased yields and reduced costs leading to higher profitability.

This case study exemplifies how ML microservices can transform traditional farming into precision agriculture. By leveraging data and intelligent algorithms, farms can optimize their operations, reduce environmental impact, and significantly enhance productivity and profitability. It marks a paradigm shift in agriculture, where data-driven decisions pave the way for more efficient and sustainable farming practices.

Some challenges and future directions in agricultural ML are:

- **Data availability and quality**: One of the primary challenges in agricultural ML is the availability of high-quality, diverse datasets. Accurate predictions and analysis heavily depend on detailed, comprehensive data, which can be difficult to gather, especially in remote or under-resourced farming areas.
- **Climate change impacts**: With the unpredictable nature of climate change, ML models face the challenge of adapting to rapidly changing environmental conditions. This includes extreme weather events and shifting pest and disease patterns that can significantly affect crop yields.
- **Technological adoption barriers**: The integration of ML in agriculture often faces resistance due to the high initial investment and the skill gap in technology usage among farmers. There is a need for more user-friendly, cost-effective ML solutions and better training for farmers and agricultural workers.

Future trends and advancements:

- **Focus on sustainability**: Future advancements in agricultural ML will likely emphasize sustainable farming practices. This includes optimizing resource use (like water and soil nutrients) and minimizing environmental impacts, aligning with global sustainability goals.
- **Climate resilience**: ML models are expected to become more sophisticated in predicting and mitigating the impacts of climate change on agriculture. This could involve advanced forecasting models that guide farmers in adapting their practices to changing weather patterns.
- **Enhanced accessibility and automation**: Advances in IoT and drone technology, coupled with ML, will make precision farming more accessible and widespread. Automation in monitoring and data collection will provide farmers with actionable insights without the need for extensive technological know-how.

In conclusion, while challenges remain, the potential for ML in agriculture is vast, with future trends indicating a move towards more sustainable, resilient, and accessible farming practices. As ML technology advances, it holds the promise of revolutionizing agriculture, making it more efficient and better equipped to face the challenges of the future.

Energy: Sustainable management and optimization

Sustainable energy management embodies a comprehensive approach to producing and consuming energy in ways that meet the needs of the present without compromising the future. It is a delicate balance between environmental protection, economic development, and societal welfare. In an era increasingly aware of climate change impacts, sustainable energy management becomes not just a choice, but an imperative for a healthier planet.

Crucially, this field is witnessing a paradigm shift, driven by ML microservices. These advanced, data-driven technologies are revolutionizing how we understand and optimize energy use. By harnessing vast amounts of data—from weather patterns affecting renewable energy sources to consumer energy usage behaviors—ML microservices are enabling smarter, more efficient energy systems.

They offer predictive insights for demand and supply, optimize grid operations, and facilitate the integration of renewable resources. This innovation leap is paving the way for more resilient energy infrastructures that are both efficient and eco-friendly. As we advance, ML microservices stand at the forefront of this transformative journey, making sustainable energy management a tangible reality in the quest for a sustainable future.

ML microservices in energy consumption prediction

Predicting energy consumption accurately is a challenge fraught with complexities. The variability in weather, consumer behaviors, and the unpredictability of renewable energy sources make energy demand forecasting intricate. This is where ML microservices come into play, transforming how we approach energy consumption prediction.

Some challenges in energy consumption prediction are:

- **Variability and uncertainty**: Energy demands fluctuate with seasons, weather conditions, and socio-economic factors. This variability makes accurate forecasting challenging.
- **Integration of renewable sources**: With the rise of renewable energy, the traditional energy grid faces the challenge of integrating unpredictable sources like solar and wind.
- **Diverse consumer patterns**: Energy usage patterns differ significantly across residential, commercial, and industrial sectors, adding another layer of complexity to prediction models.

ML solutions for energy consumption prediction

ML microservices address these challenges by offering sophisticated, data-driven approaches such as:

- **Algorithmic approaches**: Utilizing algorithms such as time series analysis, regression models, and neural networks to analyze historical data and predict future consumption patterns.
- **Real-time data analytics**: Leveraging IoT devices and smart meters, ML microservices can process real-time data for immediate insights, enhancing prediction accuracy.

- **Adaptive learning**: Continuously learning from new data, ML models adapt to changes in consumption patterns, improving their predictive capabilities over time.

- **Climate-informed predictions**: Integrates long-term climate trends and changing weather patterns into predictive models, anticipating shifts in energy needs and optimizing for future sustainability and resilience.

Real-world impact of ML in energy prediction

The deployment of ML in energy consumption prediction has shown promising results:

- **Case study 1**: A European city implemented ML algorithms to predict residential energy usage. The system analyzed data from smart meters, weather patterns, and user behaviors, resulting in a 20% reduction in energy wastage.

- **Case study 2**: A renewable energy company utilized ML to forecast wind energy output. By analyzing historical wind patterns and real-time data from sensors, the ML model enhanced the efficiency of energy distribution, aligning supply with anticipated demand peaks.

In conclusion, ML microservices are revolutionizing energy consumption prediction. They not only offer precise forecasting but also pave the way for a more sustainable, efficient, and adaptable energy management system, aligning with global sustainability goals.

Case study: ML-driven sustainable energy

The case study revolves around GreenTech Energy, a multinational company specializing in sustainable energy solutions. GreenTech embarked on an ambitious project to optimize energy consumption in industrial sectors using ML microservices, aiming to reduce carbon emissions and lower energy costs.

Delving into the strategies and outcomes below, we highlight the innovative use of predictive analytics, anomaly detection, and automated systems that have led to significant advancements in energy efficiency and sustainability:

- **Solutions implemented**
  - **Predictive analytics for energy usage**: GreenTech developed an ML microservice that utilized predictive analytics to forecast energy consumption patterns in industrial facilities. The service used historical data and real-time inputs from IoT sensors to predict energy needs accurately.
  - **Anomaly detection for energy waste reduction**: By implementing anomaly detection algorithms, the system identified unusual energy usage patterns, indicating potential inefficiencies or equipment malfunctions.
  - **Automated demand-response systems**: The ML service integrated with automated demand-response systems, dynamically adjusting energy

consumption in response to real-time grid conditions and renewable energy availability.

o **User engagement interface**: An interactive dashboard was developed for facility managers, providing insights into energy consumption trends, predictions, and actionable recommendations for optimizing energy use.

- **Outcomes**

    o **Reduced energy consumption**: Within the first year, GreenTech's ML microservices helped participating industrial facilities reduce their energy consumption by an average of 25%, translating into significant cost savings.

    o **Enhanced use of renewable energy**: The predictive analytics service improved the integration of renewable energy sources, increasing their utilization by 40%. This shift reduced reliance on fossil fuels and lowered carbon emissions.

    o **Operational efficiency**: Anomaly detection led to early identification and resolution of energy wastage issues, enhancing overall operational efficiency.

    o **User empowerment**: Facility managers used the insights from the dashboard to make informed decisions, leading to more conscious energy use and behavioral changes towards sustainability.

    GreenTech Energy's application of ML microservices in the energy sector demonstrates a successful intersection of technology and sustainability. This case study exemplifies how ML-driven initiatives can significantly contribute to energy conservation and environmental stewardship while yielding economic benefits.

    The challenges and future directions in the energy sector are:

    o **Data integration**: A major challenge is integrating disparate data sources, including IoT devices, weather data, and user patterns. Ensuring seamless data flow and processing is key to effective ML application.

    o **Real-time processing**: The dynamic nature of the energy sector demands real-time data analysis for quick decision-making. Scaling up ML microservices to process and analyze data in real time remains a hurdle.

    o **Scalability challenges**: As the demand for energy evolves, scaling ML solutions to accommodate growing datasets and complex predictive models is critical yet challenging.

- **Future trends**

    o **Advanced predictive analytics**: Future advancements in predictive modeling will likely offer more accurate and granular predictions, enhancing energy management strategies.

o **Integration of renewable energy sources**: ML will play a crucial role in better integrating renewable energy sources into the grid, optimizing their usage based on predictive demand and supply patterns.

o **Smart grid optimization**: The evolution of smart grids with enhanced ML capabilities can lead to more efficient energy distribution and management, reducing waste and improving sustainability.

o **AI-driven sustainability models**: Upcoming ML technologies will focus on creating models that not only predict and manage energy consumption but also prioritize sustainability, reducing the carbon footprint.

o **Personalized energy solutions**: Tailored energy solutions based on individual or organizational consumption patterns, enabled by ML, can optimize energy usage and contribute significantly to sustainability efforts.

Recommendation engine

Recommendation engines are sophisticated ML tools designed to enhance user experience by personalizing content and product suggestions across various industries. They analyze user behavior, preferences, and interaction data to deliver tailored recommendations, significantly improving engagement and conversion rates. In the retail sector, these engines suggest products to customers based on their browsing history and purchase patterns, leading to increased sales and customer loyalty. In the media and entertainment industry, recommendation engines curate personalized content playlists, keeping viewers engaged and reducing churn. These engines embody the intersection of AI and user experience, showcasing the power of data-driven insights in creating compelling, customized user journeys.

A notable case study in the use of recommendation engines is Netflix's approach to content personalization. Netflix uses complex algorithms to analyze viewer data, including viewing history, search queries, and even the time spent on selections. This data-driven approach allows Netflix to recommend shows and movies with remarkable accuracy, significantly enhancing user satisfaction and engagement. The success of Netflix's recommendation engine is evident in its ability to keep users engaged for longer periods, contributing to its high retention rates and substantial growth in subscriber numbers. This case study exemplifies how recommendation engines can transform user experience and business outcomes in the media and entertainment industry.

Amazon utilizes recommendation engines to enhance shopping experiences by suggesting products based on user activities, such as previous purchases, search history, and item ratings. This personalization not only improves customer satisfaction but also significantly increases cross-selling and upselling opportunities. By leveraging vast amounts of user data and sophisticated ML algorithms, Amazon's recommendation system provides highly relevant product suggestions, driving sales growth and fostering customer loyalty.

This use case illustrates the transformative impact of recommendation engines in retail, showcasing their role in driving personalized marketing strategies and business success.

Beyond Netflix and Amazon, recommendation engines are making significant impacts in other sectors as well. Spotify, a leader in the music streaming industry, offers another compelling case study. Spotify's recommendation engine personalizes the listening experience by suggesting songs, artists, and playlists based on individual listening habits, search history, and even the playlists of users with similar tastes. By analyzing billions of data points daily, Spotify's algorithms manage to not only keep existing users engaged but also to attract new subscribers by offering a uniquely personalized experience. This approach has been instrumental in Spotify's growth, showcasing the power of recommendation engines in enhancing user engagement and fostering loyalty in the highly competitive music streaming market.

Conclusion

This chapter has explored the transformative role of ML microservices across industries, from enhancing media personalization to advancing healthcare diagnostics and enabling smart agriculture. We have seen how these technologies not only solve real-world problems but also open new avenues for innovation and efficiency. Including the discussion on recommendation engines, we illustrated their pivotal role in retail and media, enhancing user experiences through personalized suggestions.

As we move forward, the next chapter will delve into the integration challenges and opportunities of ML within microservices architecture, focusing on practical solutions for data handling, system coordination, and leveraging AI for sustainable and intelligent application development. This progression ensures a comprehensive understanding of ML's current applications and future potential in driving industry advancements.

Points to remember

- **Media and entertainment**
  - o ML microservices drive personalized content and effective moderation systems.
  - o Challenges: Balancing personalization with privacy and combating algorithmic bias.

- **Financial services**
  - o Fraud detection in banking is enhanced by ML microservices.
  - o Focus on real-time transaction analysis and pattern recognition for security.

- **Healthcare**
  - o ML contributes to predictive diagnostics and personalized treatment.

- o   Ethical considerations and data privacy are paramount in data handling of patients.
- **Smart cities**
  - o   ML microservices improve urban management, particularly in traffic control and public safety.
  - o   Challenges include scalability and integration with existing urban infrastructure.
- **Agriculture**
  - o   Precision farming leveraged through ML for yield prediction and crop management.
  - o   Future trends focus on sustainability and adapting to climate change.
- **Energy sector**
  - o   Sustainable management and optimization in energy consumption are key ML applications.
  - o   Challenges include data integration and scaling for real-time processing.
- **Key lessons**
  - o   The importance of scalability and accuracy in ML microservices.
  - o   Ethical considerations and regulatory compliance are critical in all sectors.
  - o   Continuous innovation and adaptability are needed to address evolving challenges.

Assignment

To gain hands-on experience by implementing an ML microservice inspired by one of the use cases discussed in this chapter. This project will enhance your understanding of how ML microservices are integrated into different industries.

Select one of the following use cases based on your interest:
- Media and entertainment (Content personalization)
- Financial services (Fraud detection)
- Healthcare (Predictive diagnostics)
- Smart cities (Traffic management)
- Agriculture (Yield prediction)
- Energy sector (Energy consumption prediction)

Tasks

- **Research and planning**
  - o Conduct brief research on your chosen use case.
  - o Outline the basic requirements and functionalities of the ML microservice.

- **Data collection and preparation**
  - o Gather relevant datasets (you can use publicly available datasets or simulated data).
  - o Clean and preprocess the data suitable for ML processing.

- **Model development**
  - o Develop an ML model relevant to your use case (for example, classification model for fraud detection, regression model for yield prediction).
  - o Train and evaluate the model using your prepared dataset.

- **Microservice development**
  - o Implement your ML model in a microservice using a framework like Flask or FastAPI.
  - o Ensure the microservice can receive input data, process it using the ML model, and return the output.

- **Integration and testing**
  - o Integrate your microservice into a mock environment mimicking real-world application (for example, a web app for the media recommendation system).
  - o Test the end-to-end functionality of the microservice.

- **Deployment (Optional)**
  - o Deploy your microservice on a cloud platform or local server.
  - o Document the deployment process and any challenges faced.

Multiple choice questions

1. **What is the primary goal of implementing ML microservices in various industries?**
   a. To reduce operational costs only
   b. To enhance user experience and operational efficiency
   c. To replace human workers
   d. To increase data storage needs

2. **Which of the following best describes the concept of a recommendation engine in ML microservices?**

   a. A tool for data encryption

   b. A service for personalized content or product suggestions

   c. A database management system

   d. A protocol for secure communication

3. **In ML microservices architecture, what role does the data ingestion service play?**

   a. It encrypts sensitive information

   b. It collects and stores data from various sources for processing

   c. It directly interacts with the user interface

   d. It trains ML models on real-time data

4. **What is a significant challenge when deploying ML microservices for real-time analysis in financial services?**

   a. Decreasing the volume of transactions

   b. Handling high volumes of transactions without lag

   c. Completely avoiding the use of cloud services

   d. Reducing the accuracy of predictions

5. **Why is scalability considered a crucial aspect of ML microservices?**

   a. It ensures that services can handle reduced workloads efficiently

   b. It is only relevant for large enterprises

   c. It allows the system to manage increasing workloads without performance loss

   d. It decreases the system's flexibility

6. **Which best practice is essential for managing false positives in fraud detection systems?**

   a. Ignoring user feedback

   b. Employing basic ML algorithms

   c. Utilizing advanced ML algorithms and continuous model refinement

   d. Decreasing the amount of training data

7. **In the context of ML microservices, what does a feedback loop primarily accomplish?**

   a. Reduces the need for user interfaces

   b. Increases data storage requirements

c. Improves and refines models over time with new data

d. Eliminates the need for data preprocessing

8. **What is a key benefit of employing ML microservices in smart cities?**

a. To reduce the cultural diversity

b. To increase traffic congestion

c. To improve public safety and traffic management

d. To promote the use of non-renewable energy resources

9. **How do recommendation engines in media and entertainment enhance user experience?**

a. By limiting content variety

b. Through personalized content suggestions based on user behavior

c. By increasing subscription costs

d. Through uniform content distribution to all users

10. **What signifies the successful integration of ML microservices in healthcare?**

a. Decrease in EHR usage

b. Reduced personalization in treatment plans

c. Enhanced predictive diagnostics and personalized treatment plans

d. Increased use of manual processes

Answer key

1	b
2	b
3	b
4	b
5	c
6	c
7	c
8	c
9	b
10	c

## CHAPTER 12

Challenges and Future Trends

Introduction

Machine Learning (ML) microservices is at a fascinating intersection of cutting-edge technology and practical, scalable applications. As we delve into this chapter, we will cover ML microservices, which stands as the backbone of modern **Artificial Intelligence (AI)** driven solutions, offering modularity, scalability, and the agility needed to adapt to rapid technological advancements.

Our exploration is framed around the pivotal integration of ML microservices with transformative technologies such as sustainable AI, edge computing, quantum computing, and generative AI. These integrations are not mere enhancements; they represent a paradigm shift, enabling unprecedented levels of efficiency, innovation, and capability in various industry sectors. The discussion extends to emerging trends that are shaping the future landscape, highlighting how these services are evolving to meet the demands of tomorrow's tech-driven ecosystem.

Structure

This chapter intricately connects the core challenges in ML microservices with the emerging trends that offer promising solutions. By understanding these challenges through the lens of future technological advancements, we can explore innovative approaches to overcoming them. The structure is designed to highlight how the latest trends in technology can address the existing and forthcoming obstacles in ML microservices.

We will cover the following topics:

- Core challenges in ML microservices
- Emerging trends in ML microservices

Objectives

The objectives of this chapter are structured to guide you through a comprehensive understanding of ML microservices, emphasizing the integration of emerging technologies and addressing the core challenges. The chapter aims to enhance your grasp of how current trends and innovations can be leveraged to solve existing problems in ML microservices, ensuring they are well-equipped to navigate AI technology. It seeks to provide insights into the transformative potential of these technologies, illustrating their practical applications and the future prospects they hold. By the end of this chapter, you should be prepared to apply this knowledge in advancing the field of ML microservices, driving innovation, and contributing to the development of sustainable, efficient, and cutting-edge AI solutions.

Core challenges in ML microservices

In the rapidly evolving domain of ML microservices, practitioners are increasingly confronted with a set of core challenges that can impede progress and diminish the efficacy of AI-driven solutions. This section delves into the pivotal hurdles inherent in the deployment and scaling of ML microservices, spotlighting the crucial areas of scalability and efficiency, interoperability and integration, as well as security and privacy. By unpacking these challenges, we pave the way for a nuanced understanding and exploration of innovative solutions.

Scalability and efficiency

Scalability and efficiency are pivotal when deploying ML microservices, as they directly impact the system's ability to adapt to varying loads and maintain high performance under different conditions. Scalability refers to the capacity of the system to handle a growing amount of work by adding resources, either horizontally (more machines) or vertically (more powerful machines). This is crucial for ML microservices, which must efficiently manage increased demands without degrading the quality of service.

Efficiency relates to the system's ability to maximize output while minimizing wasted resources. In ML microservices, this means ensuring that the services utilize computational resources judiciously, maintain low latency, and provide high throughput, even as the volume of requests or the complexity of the tasks increases.

Addressing scalability with edge computing

Edge computing can significantly enhance scalability by distributing processing closer to the data source, reducing the latency and network congestion often associated with centralized cloud computing. It allows ML microservices to perform data processing locally, enabling faster responses and the ability to scale out services geographically to meet demand without overloading the core infrastructure.

Enhancing efficiency with quantum computing

Quantum computing offers transformative potential for efficiency in ML microservices by providing computational capabilities far beyond traditional computing paradigms. Its ability to process complex datasets and perform computations exponentially faster than classical computers can dramatically reduce the time required for data processing and model training, leading to more efficient and scalable ML microservices.

By integrating these technologies, organizations can overcome the scalability and efficiency challenges inherent in traditional ML microservices, paving the way for more responsive, agile, and capable AI-driven systems. The next sections will delve into how these technologies not only resolve current issues but also set the stage for future advancements in ML microservices architecture.

Interoperability and integration

Interoperability and integration stand as significant challenges in the realm of ML microservices, especially as the diversity and complexity of systems increase. These challenges revolve around the need for different services, often developed with varied technologies and standards, to work together seamlessly, sharing data and functionality without friction.

Interoperability challenges

Interoperability refers to the ability of different systems or components to exchange and make use of information. In ML microservices, this is crucial for creating cohesive, efficient systems where each service can effectively communicate and operate with others, regardless of their underlying technologies or architectures. The challenge lies in achieving this seamless interaction without introducing latency or data bottlenecks, ensuring that services can dynamically interact and scale.

Integration challenges

Integration involves combining different computing systems and software applications physically or functionally, to act as a coordinated whole. The complexity arises when these integrated services need to maintain consistent performance, reliability, and accuracy, especially when they are subject to continual updates and improvements. Ensuring that these disparate services can not only communicate but also effectively work together to deliver a unified service or result is a significant undertaking.

Streamlining with generative AI and AI advancements

Generative AI can play a transformative role in enhancing interoperability and integration. By generating data, simulations, or even code, generative AI can help bridge the gaps between disparate systems, providing a common ground for interaction. It can automate the creation of interfaces or adaptors between different services, reducing the manual overhead and accelerating the integration process.

Moreover, advancements in AI can facilitate smarter, more adaptive integration strategies. They can enable services to dynamically adjust their operations based on the available data, context, and service requirements, leading to more fluid and efficient system behavior. AI-driven tools can also predict and mitigate integration issues before they impact the system, ensuring smoother, more reliable inter-service operations.

Incorporating these AI technologies helps tackle the integration and interoperability challenges by automating and optimizing the processes involved, leading to more robust, scalable, and efficient ML microservices architectures. The subsequent discussion will further delve into specific technologies and methodologies that enhance these aspects, illustrating their practical applications and benefits.

Security and privacy

In the context of ML microservices, security and privacy are paramount, given the sensitive nature of the data they often process and the distributed nature of their architecture. The challenges here involve safeguarding the data transmitted between services, ensuring the integrity of the ML models, and maintaining the confidentiality of personal and sensitive information.

Evolving security threats

As ML microservices frequently interact with various endpoints, they are exposed to a broad spectrum of security vulnerabilities and potential attack vectors. Ensuring the security of these services requires robust encryption, secure data transmission protocols, and stringent access controls to protect against unauthorized access and data breaches.

Privacy concerns

With increasing regulations like **General Data Protection Regulation (GDPR)** and **California Consumer Privacy Act (CCPA)**, there is a heightened focus on user privacy. ML microservices must be designed to comply with these regulations, ensuring that personal data is processed and stored securely, and that privacy is maintained throughout the data lifecycle.

Role of blockchain technology

Blockchain can significantly enhance the security framework of ML microservices. Its inherent characteristics, such as decentralization, immutability, and transparency, provide a robust layer of security and trust. Blockchain can be used to create secure, unalterable logs of data transactions, ensuring traceability and integrity. Additionally, smart contracts can automate and enforce security policies, while the decentralized nature of blockchain helps in mitigating risks associated with centralized data storage, thus enhancing data privacy.

Integrating blockchain into ML microservices can lead to a more secure and privacy-preserving ecosystem, enabling secure data exchanges, enhancing trust in AI decisions, and ensuring compliance with data protection regulations. The subsequent sections will explore practical applications and the implications of adopting blockchain and other technologies to bolster security and privacy in the ML microservices landscape.

Data management and quality

Effective data management and maintaining high data quality are essential challenges in ML microservices, especially given the distributed nature of these systems and the reliance on data for making accurate predictions.

- **Data consistency**: Ensuring consistency across different microservices, which might use various data formats or sources, can be challenging. Inconsistent data can lead to inaccurate ML predictions and unreliable service behavior.
- **Data quality**: High-quality data is vital for the training and operation of ML models. Poor data quality, such as incomplete datasets, incorrect information, or bias, can significantly impact the performance and fairness of ML applications.
- **Data governance**: Establishing robust data governance protocols is critical to address issues related to data privacy, compliance, and ethical use of AI. It involves setting clear policies for data access, usage, and sharing to ensure that data is handled responsibly across all microservices.

Incorporating a discussion on data management and quality could provide a more rounded perspective on the challenges in ML microservices, emphasizing the importance of good data practices for the success of AI-driven systems. This addition would enrich the chapter without overextending the content, ensuring it remains focused and valuable to the readers.

The challenge of data management and quality in ML microservices can be addressed by leveraging future trends such as edge computing, quantum computing, and generative AI in the following ways:

- **Edge computing**: By processing data closer to where it is generated, edge computing ensures real-time data analysis and decision-making, enhancing the relevance and timeliness of the data used by ML models. This proximity can also improve the quality of data by reducing transmission errors and latency.
- **Quantum computing**: Quantum computing can revolutionize data analytics by enabling the processing of vast datasets much faster than traditional computers,

potentially uncovering new insights and improving the quality of data through advanced algorithms that can detect patterns and anomalies beyond the scope of classical computing.

- **Generative AI**: This technology can enhance data quality by generating synthetic data that helps overcome issues of data scarcity, bias, or privacy. It can provide diverse, high-quality datasets for training ML models, ensuring robustness and reducing the risk of overfitting on limited data samples.

Integrating these technologies can significantly mitigate the challenges of data management and quality in ML microservices, ensuring that the data is accurate, consistent, and of high quality, which is crucial for the effective functioning of AI-driven systems.

Service orchestration

Service orchestration in ML microservices encompasses coordinating numerous services to work together seamlessly, ensuring they collectively fulfill complex business functions. This process faces several challenges as follows:

- **Complex coordination**: As the number of microservices increases, orchestrating them becomes more complex, requiring sophisticated coordination logic to manage the interdependencies, data flow, and consistent execution of services.

- **Dynamic scalability**: Ensuring that the orchestration layer can dynamically scale in response to varying loads, while maintaining high availability and reliability, is a significant challenge, especially in distributed environments.

- **Real-time monitoring and adaptation**: Continuously monitoring the health, performance, and interactions of microservices in real-time, and adapting the orchestration logic dynamically to handle failures, changes, or updates without disrupting the overall system.

Future trends offering solutions

Emerging technologies can address these orchestration challenges by providing more intelligent, flexible, and resilient solutions:

- **AI-Enhanced orchestration**: Leveraging AI and ML algorithms can help predict optimal orchestration patterns, automate decision-making, and enhance the system's ability to self-heal, adapt to changes, and optimize resource utilization in real-time.

- **Blockchain for trust and transparency**: Incorporating blockchain can ensure a secure, transparent, and tamper-proof orchestration process, facilitating trust among different services, especially in decentralized environments.

By addressing the challenges in service orchestration with these future trends, ML microservices can achieve more efficient, reliable, and autonomous operations, significantly enhancing the system's overall performance and scalability.

Monitoring and maintenance

Effective monitoring and maintenance are crucial in ensuring the robustness and reliability of ML microservices. They encompass a wide array of practices aimed at observing the system's performance, foreseeing potential issues, and ensuring the system's health over time. Let's delve into the specific challenges that make monitoring and maintenance a pivotal aspect of managing ML microservices.

- **Continuous monitoring**: Ensuring real-time, continuous monitoring of numerous microservices can be complex, requiring sophisticated tools to track performance, detect anomalies, and trigger alerts for potential issues.
- **Proactive maintenance**: Transitioning from reactive to proactive maintenance is challenging, as it necessitates predictive capabilities to foresee potential failures or performance degradations before they impact the system.
- **Automated healing**: Developing systems capable of self-diagnosis and self-healing, automatically resolving issues without human intervention, is a significant challenge, especially in complex, dynamic environments.

Future trends offering solutions

Emerging technologies are poised to transform how we approach the monitoring and maintenance of ML microservices, offering innovative solutions that promise enhanced efficiency, predictive capabilities, and autonomous system healing. These advancements are not just about detecting problems but proactively managing the system to maintain optimal performance consistently.

- **AI and ML**: Advanced AI and ML algorithms can enhance monitoring by predicting system failures, automating root cause analysis, and facilitating proactive maintenance strategies, thereby reducing downtime and improving system reliability.
- **Autonomic computing**: Inspired by the human body's autonomic nervous system, this computing paradigm focuses on creating self-managing computing systems capable of self-healing, self-optimizing, and adaptive functioning, which can significantly improve the maintenance of ML microservices.

Addressing monitoring and maintenance is essential for the long-term sustainability and efficiency of ML microservices. Incorporating these considerations ensures the system's resilience, adaptability, and continuous optimization, aligning with the overarching goal of creating robust, scalable, and intelligent microservice architectures.

Emerging trends in ML microservices

This section dives into the latest advancements and emerging trends in the field of ML microservices, highlighting how new technologies and methodologies are shaping the future landscape of AI-driven applications:

- **Innovations at the forefront**: We explore cutting-edge developments, from advancements in AI algorithms to novel architectural patterns, and how they are being integrated into ML microservices to drive efficiency, scalability, and enhanced capabilities.

- **Towards a transformative future**: The focus is on the potential impact of these trends, not only on the technology itself but also on how businesses and industries can leverage them for groundbreaking applications and solutions.

Automation and AI-driven development

Embarking on a transformative journey, the advent of AI in the development and deployment of microservices heralds a new era in software engineering. This section will explore how AI acts as a catalyst for automation, enhancing every stage of microservice development—from design through to deployment. We will discuss the role of AI in customizing development strategies, facilitating predictive operations, and shaping the future landscape of software development, underscoring its potential to revolutionize the creation and management of software solutions as follows:

- **Advent of AI in development**: The integration of AI into the development and deployment of microservices marks a significant shift in how we approach software engineering. This convergence of AI and development processes is not just streamlining operations but also opening new vistas in software creation and management.

- **AI as a catalyst for automation**: AI algorithms are increasingly employed to automate various stages of microservice development, from initial design to deployment. These AI-driven tools can analyze vast amounts of data from past projects to make informed decisions, predict potential issues, and suggest optimizations. This automation extends to continuous integration and deployment processes, where AI algorithms can manage and streamline workflows, leading to more efficient and error-free outcomes.

- **Customized development at scale**: One of the most exciting prospects is the ability of AI to personalize development strategies. By understanding the unique requirements and challenges of different projects, AI-driven tools can tailor development processes, choose the most effective frameworks, and optimize resource allocation.

- **Predictive operations and maintenance**: Beyond development, AI plays a crucial role in the operational phase of microservices. It can predict system failures, analyze usage patterns to optimize resource allocation, and even suggest enhancements based on real-time data. This predictive maintenance capability ensures higher reliability and availability of services.

- **The future landscape**: Looking ahead, the possibilities with AI-driven operations in microservices are vast. We are moving towards a future where AI not only assists developers but also potentially takes on more creative aspects of software development. This could lead to faster development cycles, more innovative solutions, and systems that continuously evolve and improve over time.

The integration of AI into microservice development and operations represents a significant leap forward in software engineering. As we advance, this trend is set to redefine the paradigms of software development, deployment, and maintenance, heralding a new era of efficiency, scalability, and innovation in ML microservices.

Edge computing and ML microservices

Edge computing is a distributed computing paradigm that brings computation and data storage closer to the location where it is needed, to improve response times and save bandwidth. The core concept of edge computing is to process data and provide services as close as possible to the end-users or data sources, rather than relying on a central data-processing warehouse. This approach minimizes the latency and bandwidth use between clients and servers, enhances the performance of applications, and can also provide improved data privacy and security. Edge computing is particularly relevant in scenarios involving large amounts of data and the need for real-time processing, such as in **Internet of Things (IoT)** devices, autonomous vehicles, and smart city applications.

In recent years, there has been a noticeable shift towards edge computing in ML microservices. This transition marks a move from centralized, cloud-based computing towards processing data closer to where it is generated—at the *edge* of the network.

The following points make clear the key drivers behind this transformative move towards edge computing, underscoring its impact on reducing response times, minimizing reliance on centralized data processing, and ensuring data privacy and security:

- **Speed and latency reduction**: One of the critical advantages of edge computing is the significant reduction in latency. By processing data on local devices or nearby edge servers, response times are drastically decreased, which is crucial for applications requiring real-time analysis, such as autonomous vehicles or real-time health monitoring systems.

- **Bandwidth optimization**: With edge computing, large volumes of data are processed locally, reducing the need for data transmission over long distances. This not only conserves bandwidth but also minimizes data transfer costs and dependency on constant connectivity.

- **Enhanced privacy and security**: Local data processing means sensitive information does not have to traverse through the network to a centralized server. This proximity to the data source enhances privacy and adds a layer of security, as data exposure to external networks is minimized.

The impact of edge computing on ML microservices is as follows:

- **Real-time data processing**: ML microservices can leverage edge computing for immediate data processing, which is especially beneficial for time-sensitive applications.

- **Decentralized AI**: This trend leads to a more decentralized approach to AI, where ML models are deployed on edge devices, making AI ubiquitous and more accessible.

- **Customized local models**: Edge computing allows for the development of localized ML models that are tailored to specific regional or situational needs, enhancing the accuracy and relevance of predictions.

The challenges and considerations of edge computing are as follows:

- **Hardware limitations**: Deploying ML models at the edge often means working with constrained resources in terms of computing power and storage.

- **Model management**: The distribution of models across numerous edge devices raises challenges in model updating, version control, and consistency.

- **Data integration**: Integrating data from various edge sources into a coherent dataset for analysis can be complex.

Edge computing is redefining the ML microservices, pushing the boundaries of where and how AI can be implemented. As this trend continues to evolve, it promises to bring more responsive, private, and efficient ML solutions, tailored to the immediate needs of users and systems at the network's edge.

Quantum computing and ML microservices

Quantum computing is a rapidly evolving technological frontier which holds the promise of revolutionizing ML microservices. Unlike classical computing, which processes information in binary bits (0s and 1s), quantum computing uses quantum bits or qubits, which can represent multiple states simultaneously, offering unprecedented computational power.

- **Integration possibilities**
  - **Enhanced ML models**: Quantum computing can process complex datasets much faster than traditional computers, potentially leading to the development of more sophisticated and accurate ML models.

  - **Optimization problems**: Quantum algorithms excel in solving complex optimization problems, which are commonplace in ML. This can enhance neural network training, feature selection, and hyperparameter tuning.

  - **Data encryption and security**: Quantum computing can introduce new methods of data encryption, providing enhanced security for ML microservices. This is crucial, given the sensitive nature of the data often handled by these services.

  - **Quantum Machine Learning**: A new field that combines quantum computing with ML techniques, aiming to develop quantum algorithms that improve upon classical ML methods. **Quantum Machine Learning (QML)** can potentially solve certain types of problems much faster than classical algorithms.

- **Future scenarios and use cases**
  - o **Drug discovery**: Quantum computing could significantly speed up the process of identifying potential drug candidates, by rapidly analyzing complex molecular structures.
  - o **Financial modeling**: Quantum computers could handle the vast amount of data used in financial markets more efficiently, leading to better risk management and investment strategies.
  - o **Traffic optimization**: In smart cities, quantum computing could optimize traffic flow and public transport routes by processing vast amounts of data from various sensors and cameras in real-time.
  - o **Climate modeling**: Enhanced computational abilities could improve climate modeling, leading to more accurate predictions of weather patterns and climate change impacts.
  - o **Personalized medicine**: Quantum computing could enable the analysis of massive datasets of genetic information, leading to highly personalized healthcare treatments and interventions.

As we stand on the cusp of a quantum era, the integration of quantum computing with ML microservices is not just a possibility but an impending reality. It promises to not only enhance existing applications but also unlock new capabilities that were previously unattainable in ML and data processing.

Sustainable AI and green computing

The intersection of ML and environmental sustainability is increasingly gaining prominence, leading to a conscious shift towards *Green Computing* in ML microservices. This emerging trend is characterized by efforts to minimize the environmental impact of AI technologies while ensuring their scalability and efficiency.

Some environmentally sustainable AI practices are:

- **Energy-efficient algorithms**: Developers are focusing on creating ML algorithms that require less computational power, thereby reducing energy consumption. This involves optimizing existing models and inventing new models that are inherently more efficient.
- **Hardware optimization**: There is a growing emphasis on using energy-efficient hardware for training and deploying ML models. Innovations in this area include specialized processors and chips that are designed specifically for ML tasks and consume less energy.
- **Renewable energy sources**: More companies are turning to renewable energy sources like solar and wind power to run data centers that host ML microservices. This shift is crucial in reducing the carbon footprint associated with large-scale computational tasks.

- **Data center efficiency**: Improving the energy efficiency of data centers, which are the backbone of cloud-based ML microservices. This includes advanced cooling techniques, optimized server utilization, and the adoption of smart grid technologies.

Some innovations in green computing for ML workloads are as follows:

- **Cloud efficiency**: Cloud service providers are innovating ways to offer more energy-efficient cloud computing services, which include dynamically allocating resources based on demand and using AI to optimize energy usage.

- **Decentralized ML**: Edge computing and decentralized ML models reduce the need to transmit large amounts of data to centralized data centers, thereby saving energy and reducing latency.

- **Carbon footprint tracking**: New tools and metrics are being developed to accurately track and report the carbon footprint of ML operations, encouraging more environmentally responsible practices.

- **Life cycle assessment**: Emphasis on the full lifecycle assessment of AI models, including their development, deployment, and decommissioning phases, to ensure overall sustainability.

- **Green software engineering**: A growing field that focuses on designing software and algorithms in a way that considers their environmental impact, promoting more sustainable coding practices.

In conclusion, as we advance towards integrating AI more deeply into our daily lives, the need for sustainable AI and green computing becomes more critical. This trend represents a pivotal shift in the ML microservices domain, aligning technological advancement with environmental stewardship, and paving the way for an AI-driven future that is not only smart but also sustainable.

Generative AI in ML microservices

The Gen AI is transforming ML microservices by introducing capabilities that extend beyond traditional analytical tasks. This technology empowers machines to generate new, previously unseen data points, simulations, or content that can mimic real-world data, offering innovative solutions and enhancing the creative process within the AI domain.

Challenges addressed

Gen AI addresses several challenges in ML microservices, such as data scarcity, privacy concerns, and the need for personalized content. By generating synthetic data, Gen AI can overcome the hurdles of limited or biased datasets, ensuring robust model training without compromising sensitive information.

Integration with ML microservices

Incorporating Gen AI into ML microservices facilitates a range of functionalities, from creating realistic datasets for training purposes to generating real-time, dynamic responses in user interactions. This integration enhances the adaptability and efficiency of services, enabling them to deliver more personalized and contextually relevant outcomes.

Future implications

The future of Gen AI in ML microservices promises unprecedented levels of personalization, efficiency, and innovation. As the technology matures, it will enable more sophisticated simulations, advance privacy-preserving techniques, and foster creativity in AI-driven applications, significantly broadening the scope and capabilities of ML services.

Embracing Gen AI within the ecosystem of ML microservices not only resolves existing limitations but also unlocks new avenues for growth and innovation. By generating high-quality, diverse, and compliant data, Gen AI stands as a cornerstone technology that will shape the future of AI applications, making services more adaptable, personalized, and secure.

Conclusion

In this chapter, we have explored ML microservices, focusing on their core challenges and the transformative potential of emerging trends like generative AI. We discussed the intricacies of scalability, efficiency, interoperability, and security, and highlighted how advancements in technology provide innovative solutions. The integration of edge computing, quantum computing, and AI-driven approaches promises to revolutionize ML microservices, making them more adaptive, resilient, and capable of meeting the demands of future digital landscapes. As we look ahead, the continuous evolution in this field signals a future where ML microservices are pivotal in driving technological innovation, enabling businesses to harness the full potential of AI in a scalable and sustainable manner.

Points to remember

- **Core scalability and efficiency**: Understand the importance of efficiently managing growing demands and maintaining high performance in ML microservices.

- **Interoperability and integration**: Recognize the challenges and solutions in ensuring seamless communication and function among diverse microservices.

- **Security and privacy**: Acknowledge the critical need for robust security measures and privacy protocols in the deployment of ML microservices.

- **Generative AI**: Grasp how generative AI can revolutionize ML microservices by generating synthetic data and enabling advanced problem-solving capabilities.

- **Future trends**: Be aware of the evolving landscape, including the impact of edge computing, quantum computing, and AI advancements on the future of ML microservices.

Assignment

Objective: To apply the knowledge acquired from the entire chapters in a practical scenario, focusing on addressing challenges and leveraging emerging trends in ML microservices.

Tasks:

- **Develop design a mini ML microservice**
  - o Develop a small-scale ML microservice using a framework like Flask or FastAPI.
  - o The service should incorporate a basic ML model, such as a classifier or a recommender system, tailored to a dataset of your choice.

- **Incorporate key features**
  - o Implement features that address scalability and efficiency, utilizing concepts like containerization with Docker and orchestration with Kubernetes.
  - o Integrate security measures, such as authentication and data encryption, to safeguard the microservice.

- **Utilize Gen AI**
  - o Enhance your microservice by integrating a Gen AI component, such as a module to generate synthetic data or to provide AI-driven insights.

- **Simulate real-world load**
  - o Test the microservice under simulated real-world conditions to evaluate its scalability, resilience, and performance.
  - o Use tools like Apache JMeter or Locust to simulate traffic and data load.

- **Analyze and optimize**
  - o Monitor the performance of your microservice using monitoring tools like Prometheus and visualize the metrics using Grafana.
  - o Based on the observed performance, optimize the microservice for better efficiency and resource management.

Multiple choice questions

1. **What is a primary benefit of integrating Gen AI into ML microservices?**
   a. Reducing computational costs
   b. Generating synthetic data for training models
   c. Simplifying the user interface
   d. Decreasing network latency

2. **How does Edge Computing enhance the scalability of ML microservices?**

   a. By centralizing data processing

   b. By processing data closer to the data source

   c. By increasing data storage capacity

   d. By reducing the accuracy of computations

3. **Which technology is known for its potential to process complex computations much faster than classical computers, thereby benefiting ML microservices?**

   a. Blockchain

   b. Quantum computing

   c. Neuromorphic computing

   d. Cloud computing

4. **What challenge in ML microservices does quantum computing primarily address?**

   a. Data privacy

   b. Computational efficiency

   c. User authentication

   d. Network speed

5. **Generative AI can help overcome which common challenge in ML?**

   a. Overfitting due to limited data

   b. Excessive energy consumption

   c. Inadequate user interfaces

   d. Slow network connections

6. **Which aspect of ML microservices is crucial for maintaining system health and optimizing performance?**

   a. Continuous deployment

   b. Real-time data streaming

   c. Monitoring and maintenance

   d. Automated model training

7. **Blockchain technology enhances ML microservices by providing:**

   a. Faster data processing

   b. Improved model accuracy

   c. Enhanced security and transparency

   d. Reduction in computational resources

8. **What role does edge computing play in the context of ML microservices?**

    a. It eliminates the need for data encryption.

    b. It centralizes all computational tasks.

    c. It facilitates faster data processing and reduced latency.

    d. It increases the dependency on centralized data centers.

9. **In ML microservices, the term scalability refers to the system's ability to:**

    a. Maintain functionality with an increasing number of requests

    b. Reduce operational costs over time

    c. Operate independently of the network

    d. Ensure 100% uptime

10. **Which future trend in ML microservices focuses on creating systems capable of self-management and adaptive functioning?**

    a. Autonomic computing

    b. Distributed ledger technology

    c. Federated learning

    d. Ambient intelligence

Answer key

1	b
2	b
3	b
4	b
5	a
6	c
7	c
8	c
9	a
10	a

Index

A

A/B Testing
  about 300-302
  model, managing 301
  role, features 301
  strategies 300
Apache Paraquet
  about 182, 183
  advantages 182
  files, storing 183, 184
Apache Spark
  about 195
  advantages 196
  Apache Kafka 199, 200
  Batch Processes, using 197, 198
  hypothetical, scenario 200, 201
  key components 195
  Real-Time Processes, using 198, 199

API Contracts
  about 96
  application,
      recommending 97
  best practices 96
  components 96
  importance 96
API Gateway, benefits
  aggregating 110
  client, simplifying 110
  request number,
      reducing 110
API Gateway Pattern
  about 35
  benefits 35, 36
  considerations 36
  examples 36
  key concepts 35
  scenario 36

API Gateways
  about 105
  advantages 106
  applications, using 106
  considering 106
  key features 105
  solutions 105
API key authentication
  about 237
  best practices 238
  ML, relevance 238
  strengths, limitations 237
  working 237
asynchronous communication
  about 101
  advantages 101
  choice, considering 101
  disadvantages 101

B

Batch Processing
  about 194
  characteristics 194
  resources, deploying 195
bounded contexts
  about 87
  examples 87
  key, considering 88
  reasons 87

C

CD 25
CI 25
CI/CD, automation tools
  GitLab with Kubeflow,
    integrating 297, 298
  Jenkins 286
  Jenkins with Kuberflow,
    integrating 298-300
  Kuberflow 294-296

CI/CD, cloud services
  AWS CodeBuild 25
  AWS CodePipeline 25
  AWS ECS, EKS 26
CI/CD, deployment tools
  CircleCI 25
  GitLab 25
  Jenkins 25
  Travis 25
CI/CD pipelines, case study 304, 305
CI/CD pipelines, flow
  automate, testing 285
  deployment, staging 285
  feedback, monitoring 285
  model, code developing 285
  model, evaluating 285
  production, deploying 285
CI/CD pipelines, key components
  artifact, repository 285
  CI server 285
  frameworks, testing 285
  log tools, monitoring 285
  mechanisms, deployment 285
  Version Control System (VCS) 285
CI/CD, principles
  data, dependency 284
  experiment, versioning 284
  model drift, monitoring 285
  model, evaluating 284
  resource, intensiveness 284
Confusion Matrix
  about 69
  components 69
  importance 69, 70
Cross-validation
  about 73
  benefits 73
  considering 74
  process 73
  variants 74

D

Data Encoding, methods
  Label, encoding 62
  One-Hot, encoding 62
Data ingestion 174
Data ingestion, types
  Batch 174, 175
  Real-Time 176, 177
Data Pipelines
  about 97
  application, using 99
  best practices 99, 100
  importance 98
  key components 97, 98
  tools 98, 99
Data Pipeline, stages
  analytics, service 114
  Apache Spark 113
  data, ingest 113
  engine, recommending 114
  ML algorithms 113
  Model, deploying 113
  Real-time Queue 114
  stream, processing 114
Data resource, utilizing 173, 174
Data Sources, characteristics
  external APIs 173
  song metadata 173
  streaming 172
  user profiles 173
Data storage, types
  distributed file systems 178, 179
  NoSQL databases 178
  object storage 179
  relational databases 178
Data Transformation, types
  Normalization 61
  Standardization 61

Data versioning
  about 184
  Delta file, formatting 186
  Delta Lake, using 187-191
  Hadoop, Apache Spark 187
  Lineage Tracking 191
Data versioning, tools
  Amazon S3 185
  Data Version Control (DVC) 184
  Delta Lake 185
  Large File Storage (LFS) 185
  MLflow 185
decentralized governance
  about 27
  examples 27, 28
  services 27
decentralized data management,
      principle
  cloud services 22
  databases 21
  data, integrating 22
  event, sourcing 22
Deletion, techniques
  listwise deletion 58
  pairwise deletion 58
  variables, dropping 58
design patterns, types
  API Gateway Pattern 35, 36
  Publish-Subscribe
      Pattern 36
  Saga Pattern 39
  Sidecar Pattern 38
Domain-Driven Design (DDD)
  about 86
  aggregates 89
  bounded contexts 87
  domain, understanding 86, 87
  entities 89
  value objects 89, 90

E

event bus, key roles
  Apache Kafka 112
  data, pipeline 112
  event, publishing 112
  service, consuming 112
Event Streams
  about 103
  application, using 104
  key characteristics 103
  queues, comparing 104
  tools 103
  use case 103
  uses 104

F

Feature Extraction
  about 63
  advantages 63
  disadvantages 63
Feature Extraction,
    feature
  autoencoders 63
  Linear Discriminant Analysis
    (LDA) 63
  Principal Component Analysis
    (PCA) 63
  t-SNE 63
  wavelet, transforming 63
  word, embeddings 63
Feature Selection
  about 64
  advantages 64
  disadvantages 64
Feature Selection, methods
  embedded method 64
  filter method 64
  wrapper methods 64
Flask 127

G

Grafana
  about 263
  benefits 263
  key features 263

H

Hadoop
  about 180
  distributed file system,
    architecture 180, 181
  distributed file system,
    interacting 182
Hadoop, benefits
  Avro 181
  CSV 181
  file, sequence 181
  JSON 181
  Parquet, ORC 181
  Protobuf/Thrift 181
  text file 181
Hadoop, key reasons
  cost-effectiveness 180
  data locality 180
  fault, tolerance 180
  flexibility 180
  open source 180
  parallel, processing 180
  rich ecosystem 180
Handling missing data
  about 57
  Deletion 58
  Mean/median imputation 59
  Model-based imputation 60
Handling missing data, values
  Missing at Random (MAR) 57
  Missing Completely at Random
    (MCAR) 57
  Missing Not at Random 57

Horizontal Scaling
    about 209
    advantages 209
    challenges 209
    key characteristics 209
hybrid approach
    about 211
    advantages 211, 212
hybrid approach, aspects
    cost, optimizing 211
    flexibility 211
    service-specific,
        scaling 211

I

Inter-Service Communication
    about 111
    keys 111
Inter-Service Communication,
        paradigms
    event-driven system 148, 149
    HTTP/REST 147
    message brokers 148

J

Jenkins
    about 286
    GitLab CI/CD,
        integrating 288-291
    key concepts 288
    MLflow, tracking 291-293
    setting up 288

K

Kuberflow
    about 140
    deploy, steps 141, 142
    facilitates 140
    prerequisites 141

Kubernetes
    about 221
    auto-scaling, features 222, 223
    concepts 221
    ML, environment 223-225
    ML microservices,
        key features 222

L

Lineage Tracking
    about 191
    conceptual, flow 192
    implementing, steps 191
    prerequisites 192
Load balancing 217
Load balancing, applications
    AWS API Gateway 150, 151
    Kong 151
    Kubernetes 149, 150
    microservices 149
Load balancing, strategies
    Hash-based 149
    least, connecting 149
    resource-based 149
    round robin 149
Load balancing, techniques
    common, techniques 218, 219
    music recommend engine,
        implementing 219, 220

M

Machine Learning
    about 7
    algorithms, developing 48
    data-driven, revoluting 7
    data preprocessing 57
    feature engineering 57
    microservices, need 10
    Model Deployment 74

Machine Learning, applications
  agriculture 10
  autonomous vehicles 9
  energy, utilities 10
  entertainment, recommending 10
  finance 9
  healthcare, medicine 8
  image, video analysis 10
  manufacturing 9
  Natural Language Processing
    (NLP) 9
  retail, e-commerce 9
Machine Learning, benefits
  diversity, flexibility 11
  efficient resource, managing 11
  fault, resilience isolating 11
  models, scalability 11
  modular, extensibility 11
  rapid experiment, deploying 11
  real-time decision, making 11
  specialization, collaborating 11
Machine Learning, industries
    domains
  automation, efficiency 8
  challenges, ethical considering 8
  customer experience,
    personalizing 7
  data insights, harnessing 7
  decision, making 8
  healthcare, advancement 8
  predictive, analytics 8
Machine Learning, key components
  data, learning 48
  experience, improving 48
  generalizing 48
Machine Learning, key concepts
  data test, training 54, 55
  labels, features 52-54
  Loss functions 55-57

Machine Learning, libraries
  Docker 12
  FastAPI 12
  Kafka 12
  Kuberflow 12
  Kubernetes 12
  Pandas, NumPy 12
  Scikit-learn, TensorFlow 12
  Spark, Hadoop 12
  XGBoost 12
Machine Learning, privacy concerns
  data, masking 240
  differential, privacy 241
  information, exposing 239, 240
  pseudonymization 240
Machine Learning, types
  Reinforcement Learning (RL) 51, 52
  Supervised Learning 48
  Unsupervised Learning 50, 51
message queue
  about 102
  key characteristics 102
  tools 102
  use case 103
microservices architecture,
    evaluating 2
microservices API layers 116-119
microservices application,
    orchestrating
  AWS, setting up 160-165
  Docker 157, 158
  Kubernetes 159, 160
microservices architecture 5
microservices architecture,
    advantages
  agility, flexibility 6
  CI/CD 6
  decentralizing 6
  independent, deploying 6
  loose, coupling 6

modularity 6
polyglot, programming 6
resilience 6
scalability 6
single responsibility 6
microservices architecture,
    best practices
  API Gateway, using 41
  centralize log, monitoring 42
  CI/CD, embracing 42
  data consistency, ensuring 43
  Decentralizing 41
  design, failure 42
  prioritize security 42
  service boundary, defining 41
  service discovery,
    implementing 42
microservices architecture,
    disadvantages
  challenges, testing 7
  communication, complexity 6
  complexity, deploying 7
  data, consistency 6
  initial effort, developing 7
  latency 6
  operational, complexity 6
  overhead 7
microservices architecture, types
  Event-Driven Architecture
    (EDA) 31, 32
  Gateway Aggregation 28-31
  Service Mesh 33-35
microservices, boundaries
  API Contracts 96
  Cohesion 94
  Coupling 94, 95
  data, functionality 90-92
  Single Responsibility Principle
    (SRP) 92

microservices, challenges
  agile security, updating 3
  attack surface, reducing 3
  security layers, independency 3
microservices, key aspects
  API Gateways 105
  asynchronous communication 101
  Data Pipelines 97
  Event Streams 103
  message queue 102
  synchronous communication 100
microservices, principles
  CI/CD 25
  decentralized governance 26
  decentralized data management 21
  resilient communication 23
  service independence 19, 20
  Single Responsibility
    Principle (SRP) 18
microservices scalability, modularity
  architecture style 28
  design patterns 35
microservices, tools
  Microservices architecture 5
  Monolithic architecture 3
ML, applications
  Apache Spark 195
  Batch Processing 194
ML data models, value
  data, sensitivity 234
  data value, intrinsic 234
  model, integrity 235
  regulatory, compliance 235
  value, competitive 235
ML microservices
  A/B Testing 300-302
  algorithm, processing 115
  API Gateway 110
  Data Access Object (DAO) 127
  Data Ingestion 114

Data Pipeline 113
Data Processing 114
data, serving 115, 116
designing 108
event bus 111
Flask 127
industries, implementing 312, 313
Inter-Service Communication 111
ML microservices, agriculture services
  accurate yield, forecasting 331
  crop yield, predicting 331
  impact ,results 332, 333
  ML, integrating 332
ML microservices, best practices
  API key authentication 237, 238
  OAuth 2.0 238
  SSL, TLS 236, 237
ML microservices, components
  analytics service 109
  API Gateway 109
  database 109
  data pipeline 109
  engine, recommending 109
  frontend 109
  kuberflow 109
  playback service 109
ML microservices, core challenges
  data quality, managing 347, 348
  efficiency, scalability 344, 345
  interoperability,
      integrating 345, 346
  maintenance, monitoring 349
  security, concern 346, 347
  service orchestration 348
ML microservices DAO, service
  analytics service 135
  catalog service 129
  playback service 130
  recommendation service 131-134

user service 127
ML microservices, energy services
  energy prediction, consuming 334
  energy prediction, solutions 334
  ML driven, case study 335-337
  real-world, impacting 335
ML microservices entertainment,
      enhancing
  challenges, considering 317
  media, personalizing 314, 315
  moderation, methods 315, 316
  moderation services,
      workflow 316, 317
  service architecture,
      personalizing 315
ML microservices FastAPI, service
  analytic service 139, 140
  catalog service 136, 137
  playback service 138
  recommendation service 139
  user service 137
ML microservices, financial services
  architecture fraud,
      detecting 320-322
  banking fraud detection
      systems 318, 319
  challenges, best practices 322, 323
  real-time transaction,
      analysis 319, 320
ML microservices, healthcare
      services
  future, challenges 326, 327
  ML architecture,
      analyzing 325, 326
  patient data, analytics 324, 325
  Predictive diagnostics 323, 324
ML microservices, reasons
  deployment, integrating 126
  resilience 126
  resource, optimizing 127
  scalability 126

technology, flexibility 126
ML microservices securing, importance
  ML contexts, monitoring 260, 261
  ML service, consequences 235, 236
  proactive error resolution,
    optimizing 261, 262
  sensitivity, value 234
ML microservices, smart cities
  case, studies 328
  future, peering 330
  future prospects, challenges 329
  ML-driven, insights 328
  ML insights, preventing 329
  predictive, modeling 328
  predictive, policing 328
  public surveillance, integrating 329
  real-time traffic, analyzing 328
  response, optimizing 329
  urban, managing 327
  urban traffic, teckling 327
ML microservices, spotlight tool
  Grafana 263
  Prometheus 262
ML microservices, storage handling
  Apache Paraquet 182
  Data ingestion 174
  Data Sources 172
  Data storage 177
  Hadoop 180
ML microservices, trends emerging
  AI driven, developing 350, 351
  Edge, computing 351-353
  Gen AI, transforming 354, 355
  Quantum, computing 352
  sustainability, gaining 353, 354
ML microservices, troubleshooting
  effective, debugging 272, 273
  Jaeger 274
  Pdb, interactive 273

pitfalls, affecting 269-271
resolve, approaching 271, 272
ML Model, ensuring
  Access, controlling 243
  Model, encrypting 242, 243
  secure containers 242
ML, model evaluating
  AUC-ROC 71
  Confusion Matrix 69
  Cross-validation 73
  Normalized Discounted
    Cumulative Gain (NDCG) 72
  Root Mean Squared Error
    (RMSE) 71
ML models, rollback
    capabilities 303, 304
ML, Model training
  bias, variance 67, 68
  models, fitting 65, 66
  underfitting, overfitting 66
ML Model, training steps
  error, minimizing 65
  initializing 65
  interating 65
  process, learning 65
ML pipelines
  Caching 155
  HDFS and Spark, Batch
    processing 153, 155
  Inter-Service
    Communication 147
  Load balancing 149
  real-time, processing 152, 153
  scalability 140
ML pipelines, caching methods
  cache invalidation 157
  Redis 155, 157
ML pipelines scalable,
    complexity
  AWS features, adding 142

data outline, handling 142-146
Kuberflow 140
ML project, features
Data Encoding 62
Data Transformation 61
Feature Extraction 63
Feature Selection 64
Handling missing data 57
ML services, implementing
ELK stack, centralizing 266, 267
key metrics 263-265
logging, strategies 265, 266
TensorBoard, visualizing 268, 269
Model-based imputation60
Model-based imputation, approach
decision tree 60
K-NN imputation 60
linear regression imputation 60
neural network, learning 60
Monolithic architecture 3
Monolithic architecture,
        advantages
deploying 4
ease, developing 4
performance 4
resources, sharing 4
simplicity 4
Monolithic architecture,
        disadvantages
bottlenecks, developing 5
flexibility 4
maintenance 5
resource, utilizing 5
scalability 4
technology diversity 5
Music Recommendation Engine
data privacy, ensuring 249-252
grant types, handling 246-248
legal, repercussions 253

OAuth 2.0,
        authorizing 244-246

O

OAuth 2.0
about 238
challenges 239
components 238
ML, relevance 239
process 238
strengths 239
token, types 238

P

Prometheus
about 262
benefits 262
key, features 262
Publish-Subscribe Pattern
about 36
benefits 37
considerations 38
examples 37
key concepts 37

R

Reinforcement Learning (RL) 51, 52
resilient communication,
        strategies
API, gateway 23
client-side, libraries 23
cloud service 24
mesh service 23

S

Saga Pattern
about 39
benefits 40
considerations 40
examples 40

ways 40
Scaling
 about 208
 challenges 225, 226
 cost 226
 ML consistency, ensuring 226
 MRE, addressing 226-228
Scaling, strategies
 factors, deciding 210, 211
 Horizontal Scaling 209
 hybrid approach 211
 Vertical Scaling 209
Scaling, use case
 alerts, monitoring 212
 database, replicating 212
 load, balancing 212
 mechanisms, caching 212
 post-even, scaling 213
 service, authenticating 212
 service, recommending 212
service independence, examples
 E-commerce application 21
 music application, streaming 20
service independence, feature
 API, gateways 20
 cloud services 20
 containerization 20
 mesh service 20
 orchestration, scheduling 20
Sidecar Pattern
 about 38
 benefits 38
 considerations 39
 examples 39
 key concepts 38
Single Responsibility Principle,
  functionalities
 cloud services 19
 languages 18
 proxy, mesh service 18

Single Responsibility Principle
  (SRP)
 about 92
 application, service 92, 93
 best practices 93
 importance 92
software architecture 3
software architecture, key
 advance, technology 3
 agility, demanding 3
 complexity, growing 3
software architecture, milestones
 client-server 2
 microservices 2, 3
 monolithic 2
 Service-Oriented Architecture
   (SOA) 2
 three-tier 2
Supervised Learning 48, 49
Supervised Learning, category
 Classification 49
 Regression 49, 50
synchronous communication
 about 100
 advantage 100
 disadvantage 100
 use case 101

U

Unsupervised Learning 50, 51

V

Vertical Scaling
 about 209
 advantages 210
 challenges 210
 key characteristics 210

Printed in Dunstable, United Kingdom

71557437R10221